ONLY PARALYZED
FROM THE NECK DOWN

THE LIFE AND MINISTRY
OF TOM BREWSTER

DAN BREWSTER

William Carey Library

P.O. BOX 40129
PASADENA, CALIFORNIA 91114

Published by
William Carey Library
P.O. Box 40129
Pasadena, California 91114
(626)798-0819

ISBN 0-87808-275-1

PRINTED IN THE UNITED STATES OF AMERICA

**TO
BETTY SUE**

TABLE OF CONTENTS

LIST OF ABBREVIATIONS

AIM	Africa Inland Mission
CCC	Campus Crusade for Christ
CHP	Center for Human Potential
EFMA	Evangelical Fellowship of Mission Agencies
ELIM	Evangelical Language Institutes for Missionaries
IFMA	International Foreign Mission Association
IICC	International Institute of Christian Communications
IRM	International Review of Missions
LAMP	Language Acquisition Made Practical
LBI	Living Bibles International
LEARN!	Language Exploration and Resource Notebook
LEAP	Language Exploration and Acquisition Project
SIL	Summer Institute of Linguistics
SWM	School of World Mission
TIL	Toronto Institute of Linguistics

FOREWORD

It was the afternoon of December 12, 1985. We were sitting on the newly cleaned rug in our living room, before we moved the furniture back in. We were chatting, but with our minds partly on the operation going on at UCLA Medical Center and the prayers in our hearts for our brother Tom. Things had not been going well for him physically and it was the best judgment of the doctors that he undergo an operation to repair some blockage in his bladder.

During recent weeks Tom had stopped by my office several times for prayer to return his system to normal. And his body had responded well to our prayers each time. So, even though such an operation for a quadriplegic is always risky, our expectation was that this fairly small repair would make life quite a bit easier for him. We were, therefore, surprised and shocked when the telephone rang and Dan's first words were, "I think we've lost him!"

Knowing the power of prayer, then, Dan and I decided I should call John Wimber, a friend of Tom's and mine whom God has used powerfully in healing, to see if he'll agree to pray that God will bring him back. I made a couple of calls but could not locate John. So Dan and I reluctantly decided to agree with what seemed to be God's will that it was time for Tom to be promoted to hea~

Actually, the operation was a success. But there on the op~ table, Tom's heart stopped and would not start again. A colleague, a good friend, in some respects a protégé felt so hurt.

I first met Tom and Betty Sue in the ear~ Kenya, at Daystar Communications wher~ producing materials designed to assist ~ African languages under the auspices ~ tional. I met them again a few years later ~ for Campus Crusade for Christ, overseeing adaptation of the Four Spiritual Laws into several different languages. And whenever I wasn't meeting them in my travels, I was hearing of their work in language learning and Bible translation.

Then one evening in 1974 we invited them to our home for supper and friendly conversation. We were amazed at how much we had in common. Some time late in the evening I shared with them my vision of a Bible translation program at Fuller. "Would they be interested in heading up such a program?," I asked. "Of course, we have no salary to offer . . . And I have no official permission to offer you a job . . . But perhaps Fuller would be just as good a base for you as any other place." Miraculously, within a few months the Fuller administration had both bought the idea and worked it out for the Brewsters to join the faculty of the School of World Mission. And we got to be colleagues for the next ten years.

But my dream of the Brewsters heading up a Bible translation program was not to be. Instead, they returned to their first love and gifting—teaching people how to learn a language—and added that very important component to our offerings. And without requiring a salary! I didn't complain that my plan wasn't the one they followed. By that time I had learned that God does things His way and His way is full of surprises. We had the Brewsters on our team and we and our students were all enriched by their presence. And my dream of a Bible translation program did eventually come into being, but under someone else.

Tom Brewster was an amazing man by any standard. Though "challenged" (to use today's politically correct term) by a body that did not permit the normal support for his very creative mind, he (with lots of very capable help from Betty Sue) set a pace that few of us could keep up with. Our eyes told us he was disabled from the neck down. But his mental alertness, his brilliance, his creativity, his wisdom, and above all his commitment to Jesus Christ and to helping Christian witnesses to communicate Jesus' love effectively—these characteristics of Tom kept us continually aware of the fact that what God had given him from the neck up was functional well and made him a valued member of our team.

Only Paralyzed from the Neck Down is the story of a life lived all out for God in spite of the challenge of quadriplegia. No one would have faulted Tom if he had attempted no more than his body allowed. But that was not Tom. He who, when his body was at full strength, regularly challenged Pike's Peak, was not about to let the limitations imposed on his body cripple him. He went to school to prepare for a future the doctors refused to predict for him. He married. He eventually earned a Ph.D. So did Betty Sue. They traveled and traveled and traveled. They have a son. They taught effectively. They wrote books. And they have inspired many and changed many lives.

Tom did not live long. (Neither did Jesus.) But he touched many and his memory is precious to all of us, especially to younger brother Dan for whom this book is a labor of love. Many of us have big brothers to look up to. But few have a big brother like Tom. And Dan wasn't sure he could do Tom's memory justice. But with several years of prodding, lots of solid research, a heart full of both love and loss and an admirable skill in writing, Dan has both recorded a remarkable story and honored a remarkable big brother.

You are not likely to get through this book dry eyed. I couldn't, even when an earlier version of it came to me as a doctoral dissertation.

Charles H. Kraft
September 1997

PREFACE AND ACKNOWLEDGMENTS

On December 12, 1985, a remarkable man went to be with the Lord. Almost totally paralyzed for the last twenty-seven years of his life, he nevertheless ministered to thousands of students, missionaries and national Christians all over the world. This is the story of his courage, commitment to Christ, and very special humility and vulnerability that drew others to himself.

Certainly Tom's story is inspirational, and I trust that many readers will be inspired by his courage and commitment. Rarely have handicapped persons been so genuinely grateful for their condition, secure in the knowledge that even a serious, crippling injury is within the plan of God. But this is more than a story of inspirational courage. Tom also made some very significant contributions to mission strategy—the task of fulfilling the Great Commission. Many missionaries and others involved in sharing Christ with the Nations have been able to do so more effectively, more rewardingly, and with more credibility because of his teaching and his example.

But there is yet more to the story. It is also a tribute to a remarkable woman, Tom's wife, Betty Sue. There are many people who, like Tom, have serious handicaps which render them unable to care for themselves. Many of these, with similar unshakable courage, live productive lives without bitterness, while confined to their wheelchairs or even to their beds, never leaving their homes. That could have been the case for Tom as well. That Tom was able to travel frequently to every corner of the globe, to more than eighty countries, in every form of conveyance is a tribute not just to his own courage and stamina, but to the incredible unselfishness and energy of Betty Sue.

Betty Sue gave her life for Tom. She was Tom's legs and arms. For nearly nineteen years she was almost never away from his side. Tom could not dress himself. He could not get into and out of a chair or his bed or a car—not to mention airplanes, boats, trains and other modes of transportation that he used. Nearly every hour of those nineteen years they were married, Betty Sue was by his side. For her, servanthood was not just a concept—not just an occasional act of kindness. Rather, it was a day in and day out vocation. In nineteen years she never got to stay in bed later than Tom, for she always had to get him up. She never had someone else to do the chores around the house or garden or to clean up the garage.

Yet in all those years, Betty Sue never said "no." She never said, "Enough is enough." If she was ever frustrated with the task, she never showed it, never raised her voice in protest, and never once complained. No matter what she was doing, she was always there with a "Yes, Love" when he called.

I started out to write a book about Tom, thinking that I would acknowledge Betty Sue whenever it seemed appropriate. I found though, that from the time of their marriage, I could not write about just Tom. It is not uncommon for a great man or woman to have a very helpful and supportive spouse. But even greater was Betty Sue's contribution to Tom's life and ministry. Virtually everything Tom did, he did with Betty Sue. From the mundane of everyday personal hygiene, to the conceptual work of *LAMP* and the challenging of missionaries to look to Christ's incarnation as the model for missions, Betty Sue was literally always there. There was nothing that Tom ever did while they were married, almost nowhere that Tom ever went, no course that he ever taught that she was not there beside him or in the background, ready to lend a hand. Any book about Tom, then, is also about her and her devotion. Wherever she is not included, it is an oversight on my part.

I am deeply indebted to Dr. Charles Kraft for his encouragement and facilitation in writing this biography. His love and appreciation for Tom has always been evident. Chuck believed in Tom and he believed in me. Chuck felt I was the one to write Tom's biography, and he "hounded" me to do it. Without him, this labor of love would not have been completed.

I am also deeply indebted to Betty Sue Brewster, Tom's wife and my sister-in-law. The biography clearly shows not only that she was the arms and legs for Tom's mighty vision and ambition, but that she also contributed very significantly to Tom's creativity and intellectual innovation. But what stands out in a most heroic way is her servant's heart, giving totally of herself for almost nineteen years to Tom's care. Thank you, Betty, for that commitment and sacrifice. It was also Betty who was most familiar with Tom's travels, intellectual and spiritual journeys, trials and triumphs, for she was with him virtually every minute of all of them. Her notes and recollections at every point were invaluable.

A big thank you also to many others who knew Tom and who wrote letters and testimonials or otherwise provided valuable insights and background to the importance of Tom's life and ministry.

I want also to extend my appreciation to the late Dr. Don Miller, Dr. Wess Stafford, and Mark Yeadon, my colleagues at Compassion International for their encouragement to undertake the project and for being forgiving when my thoughts and energies were directed to this task rather than others which I was paid to do. My assistant at Compassion, Janice Campbell, was also extremely helpful in typing, correcting, advising, and generally keeping my various commitments on track during this process, for which I am most grateful.

Finally, like all writers who are also committed to their families, I am indebted to mine. My sister Mona provided much encouragement and insight, as well as much "passion" for the work. My other sisters contributed as well. My wife, Alice, spent many hours transcribing taped interviews. To Alice, and to my children Brian, Julisa, and Kara, I appreciate your patience and willingness to give up hubby and Dad's time more than I can say.

INTRODUCTION

In many ways this accident has been a great blessing in my life. In fact, apart from the privilege of knowing Christ as Lord and Savior and the wonderful family that He has given me, this injury and the paralysis over these years have been the biggest blessing in my life. That may sound a bit strange, and I'm sure that it's nothing that any of us would ever wish for, but God has used this in a way in my life to give me a sense of His leading and of His power. Sometimes when we have things happen to us that are out of our control, our attitude is one of bitterness and anger against God. I'm thankful that He spared me all of that. I wasn't supposed to live. But I realize through this injury that God is the giver of life, and that He chose to give my life back again for the second time. So my attitude has not been one of questioning God as to why it happened, but rather I've asked God why He gave me my life back again. What purpose did He have for me? What was His plan for my life? That has resulted in an entirely different kind of availability to the Lord than I ever had before (T. Brewster 1983:13, 14).

PART I
RUGGED ROOTS

1
EARLY LIFE

"Once a job is first begun,
Never leave it 'til it's done.
Be the labor great or small,
Do it well or not at all.
(author unknown)

August 1939 was hot and dusty in the high plains town of Gunnison, Colorado. The sun beat down from the clear blue skies and the hot wind whipped around the motley collection of shacks and shops in this small college town. Young Roy Brewster carried his day old son Tom in his arms around to the back of the log cabin home that he and his twenty-one year old student bride shared. Roy was a fiery Christian and as he walked, he prayed that someday his son would be a missionary in some foreign land. His fondest wish was that the two of them might one day be able to be involved in furthering God's Kingdom together. If Roy himself would not be able to go, he prayed that this precious newborn son would be able to carry out the vision on his own.

Roy was in his second year at Western State College in Gunnison and had already shown his professors and colleagues the stuff he was made of. The editor of the Montrose newspaper, near Gunnison, was impressed with the way he was working his way through college. "Roy is a bright looking young man," the editor wrote, "imbued with an ambition to succeed. His education is coming by hard knocks—when he gets through he will know that he has paid something for it. Keep an eye on a young man with the vision and intestinal fortitude Roy Brewster has. I am confident he will be going places one of these days" (Montrose 1938).

That intestinal fortitude was a characteristic of the Brewster family. His father, Thomas C. Brewster, born in Washington, Indiana on September 27, 1873, came from people who for generations

3

had pushed the frontiers of farming across the continent. For the most part, these farms were small—sometimes rented and always worked with horses rather than tractors. By modern standards the Brewster family had little and what they had came hard. Roy was born in Jay, Oklahoma in the winter of 1916. Soon thereafter, his family moved by covered wagon to Utah where his father rented a farm. In 1919, the family moved back from Utah, again by covered wagon, to Lakin, Kansas where they stayed for a year before moving back to Oklahoma. Roy was the youngest of six brothers, John, Jim, Joe, Clark, "Toots," (Bill), and "Babe," (Roy). All of them learned discipline through hard work and hard times. All worked their way through college. Roy's oldest brother John was a national debating champion, took his Ph.D. from Colombia University under George Herbert Mead and John Dewey, and worked for nearly thirty years in the Department of Agriculture in Washington, DC. Another brother, Jim, became a state senator in New Mexico, and Joe founded one of the largest ship repair businesses in San Francisco.

Roy's marriage in his junior year at Western State to pretty, young Elnora Cochran of Penrose, Colorado was a surprise to a lot of people, not the least of whom were the bride's and groom's four parents. In the wedding announcement in the Penrose Press on January 20, 1939, the social editor could not resist sharing that the bride had failed to reveal their December 2 wedding when she had gone home to Penrose for the Christmas holidays. But he went on very charitably saying that "she is a dignified young lady with a decided Christian poise of character, which has endeared her so much to true friends." The article concluded that the newly-weds would continue their college work, supporting themselves through their outside jobs.

For Roy, the outside job meant "workin" on the railroad. He had gotten acquainted with the railroad men by visiting the shops in the local rail yard, and done little errands for them when the opportunity was presented. Finally he was given something to do and before long was a regular, firing a railroad engine on nightly runs up and down the Arkansas River Valley. But what he really wanted to do was to be a missionary. Roy was the only one of the Brewster brothers to give his life to Christ, and though he toiled all his life in high school teaching or manual labor jobs, he took with him to his grave a burden to travel to the Holy Land, and to share the Gospel with those who had never heard.

Hard Times on the Prairies
. . . and New Mouths to Feed

The arrival of little Tom must have complicated life for the young couple, but Roy, (my dad), went on to finish school, receiving a degree in chemistry. His first job out of college may have been with the Bureau of Land Management in Gallup, New Mexico as a soil conservation chemist. The details are murky, but there are hoary stories of our family living in a Navajo hogan in Gallup while Dad moved about in the conservation job.

Tom's independence and wanderlust were apparent even from those early years, as his mother had more than the typical mother's job of keeping track of him. Many times he would wander off in his night clothes down the dusty streets of Gallup when he was only barely able to walk. His wanderings became so common-place that the neighbor did not even need to discuss it with Mom when she noticed he was missing and came charging out of the house looking for him. He would simply look up and point with his lower lip the direction which the little traveler, often naked or with his bathrobe flying open, had wandered. Usually she found him on the playground at the nearby school or riding on a merry-go-round.

In 1940 Dad moved the family to Pueblo, Colorado, and lived in a tiny, 8' by 10' travel trailer with no running water or bathroom. He had no job and the family had no place to live. A gas station owner took compassion on and Dad and let them park the trailer behind his shop. Dad finally got a job in the busy steel factory there as the country geared up for war. It was there in March of 1941 that Tom's twin sisters Mary Lela and Martha Lila were born. Those "good ol' days" for Mom meant washing the diapers of three toddlers in the bathroom of the filling station, and hanging them to dry on the bushes in the back.

The financial burden of caring for the young family pretty much put a damper on the possibility of Roy being a missionary any time soon, but the dream lived on.

After two years in Pueblo, Dad moved the family to the tiny but optimistically named town of Buelah, Colorado. Whatever he attempted there did not work out either, but he finally got a teaching and coaching job in La Junta, a small farming town on the Arkansas river. But still it was a struggle. Dad bought a tiny house (actually nothing more than a shack) a few miles up the road at Swink with some acreage for farming, and supplemented his teaching income with what he could grow. Next to that shack he moved a small wooden boxcar, with no insulation and no heat, to increase the space for his wife and three little children. One end of that boxcar was Tom's bedroom for two or three years when he was a child.

It was there, in October, 1947 that Tom's other twin siblings, myself and my "wombmate" Doris, were born. Dad sold that little house a couple years later when our family moved to Colorado Springs. Our family was excited to discover that it still stands, still owned by the man who bought it from Dad, but long since abandoned. When Tom made a "pilgrimage" back to Swink in 1970, he wrote of that house in a "Round Robin" letter to the family on September 10, 1970:

> I have many memories of that farm—weeds in the corn field, cows in the grain, the cow that stepped on me, Mary, Martha and I jumping from the roof into the snow drift. That was where I once determined to ride my bike down the hill and turn in the driveway without using any brakes—I landed in a heap below the embankment. That was the bike I traded a pig for!

Principles

Dad refused to leave his Christianity at home when he got his teaching jobs. Eventually his outspokenness and "fanaticism" caused him to be asked to leave the La Junta school system. He got another teaching job in the tiny farming town of Campo in the southeast corner of Colorado. The job also included coaching the basketball team for the Springfield High School, forty or so miles up the road, but again he had to move on after only two years.

Looking for places with greater opportunities for teaching and ministry, he packed his young family again and moved to the growing city of Colorado Springs. He was disappointed in not being able to secure another teaching job so began to work as a carpenter when work was available. When he could not get a steady carpentry job, he went door to door doing tree trimming and odd jobs, and eventually took work as a truck driver. Everywhere he went, and with every one he met, he never failed to find a way to ask his standard door opener for constant witnessing—"Where are you going when you die?"

The last member of the Brewster family, Ramona, (always just "Mona " to us), came along in Colorado Springs in 1953—an afterthought for her parents, but an important piece of God's plan for the Brewster mosaic. She was fourteen years younger than Tom and, along with him, the only non-twins of the Brewster siblings, so they referred to themselves as twins as well. Indeed, they became true soul-mates later in life.

Early on, Tom had a full load of chores. He learned about morning milking and caring for other livestock. Dad had high expectations of Tom and his other children. He expected Tom to be the best, and he opened the door for Tom to be independent. One of the early neighbors, Carla Cocking, later a missionary to Guatemala, remembers that Tom was conscientious even as a young lad: "When we'd go to get our horses at your place, we'd always find Tom very much in control of the situation. He used to keep everything very much in good order, I remember" (n.d.).

There were other powerful values and character traits being shaped at that early age. Dad was never one to let an issue that violated his values or Christian principles go unchallenged, a trait that characterized Tom's life in later years.

Dad frequently wrote letters to the editor expressing his concern for the growing secularism he saw around him. He saw early on the coming trend to put the Bible out of the public schools. His solution to getting rid of the "Communist influence" in the schools was to "turn on the light of the Scriptures in the classroom." He wrote:

> The Bible is practically a forbidden Book, and the teacher that uses it is counted as a trouble maker. The Christian teacher is told not to bring religion into the classroom. (Every teacher either brings a worship of Christ or Satan into the classroom.) The Word of God which was given to be a "Lamp unto my feet and a light unto my pathway," is put out. God's Light has been turned out (R. Brewster 1953a).

(Imagine his dismay if he had lived to see the extent to which the Bible and religion are not only left out in education today, but thoroughly ridiculed by most of the education establishment.)

Everything about Dad taught integrity, honesty, discipline, self sufficiency, and courage. He would have been insulted by any notion of charity as a handout—even when he literally did not know where the next meal for his family would come from. He never failed to stand up for what he believed. Some of what he said and did caused conflict, but everything planted seeds that sprouted into unshakable values in each of his children.

Eventually he took work as a route driver for a trucking firm. Given responsibility for expanding the route, he began contacting all the Jewish businessmen he could find and created his own informal "mission to the Jews" in the city of Colorado Springs. He made up a calling card that described his views of the dispensations of the Bible, and for eleven years regularly attended the Orthodox Jewish synagogue every Friday night.

Dad tirelessly studied the Scriptures and understood well how the New Testament is a fulfillment of the Old. He pored over maps of Palestine and knew the Jewish laws and lifestyle intimately. He longed to visit the Holy Land and walk those dusty paths where Jesus walked and where his beloved prophets had decried idolatry and foretold the coming of the Jews' Messiah

He was a true friend of the Jews. The Rabbi complimented Dad saying that he was more regular at the synagogue than were the Jewish faithful. He wore a yarmulke (Jewish headcovering) to the synagogue, studied Hebrew with the Rabbi, and was the only Gen-

tile allowed by the Rabbi to teach a Bible study at the synagogue—
as long as he did not teach from the New Testament. He was convinced that not only the local Rabbi, but the Rabbi's father, who
was the president of a Jewish seminary in New York, were almost
ready to accept Christ as their Messiah. It has been suggested that
if the Messianic synagogue mentality had been around in the '50s,
the orthodox synagogue of Colorado Springs would have become in
its entirety a Messianic Synagogue. Unfortunately, Dad did not
live to see that "people movement" to Christ.

Always and in everything, Dad was a passionate man, whether
it was winning the Jews to Christ or monitoring and decrying the
decline of the school systems in which his children were enrolled.
One recurring issue in the schools was the new idea of conducting
raffles and bingo lotteries to raise money. Dad saw it as out and
out gambling and covetousness and viewed it as the first step
toward corruption, prostitution and other vices in the neighborhood. He threatened a law suit if the PTA went ahead with plans
to hold a planned raffle in the grade school where Tom, Mary and
Martha were enrolled.

> No person gambles at race tracks for 5 or 10 dollars without first
> having gambled at a "good clean" gambling joint for 5 or 10 cents.
> The 18 or 21 year old, gambling at the race track has already gam-
> bled as a 6 or 10 year old at some "good clean joint" sponsored by
> the PTA or by some other supposedly "worthy organization."
>
> Of course the "worthy organization" uses the excuse, "We use the
> money for the good of the community." This is like tying a pretty
> red ribbon on a skunk and saying, "He shore smells sweet." Those
> who make excuse for gambling and desire to have it in "worthy
> organizations" should read John 12, verse 6: "This he (Judas) said,
> not that he cared for the poor; but because he was a thief, and had
> the bag, and bare (took away) what was put therein" (n.d.).

To the superintendent of the Littleton, Colorado Public Schools,
whose teacher, Mrs. Chandler, also resigned over the same issue,
Dad wrote:

> I am certainly glad to see some exhibit (sic) of courage to stand
> against that which is SIN. Don't you feel pretty small to let a

woman have more courage than you? . . . I was a teacher for six years in our public schools. I know the price to be paid for such a stand. The price is often what Mrs. Chandler paid. But Mrs. Chandler has HONOR. What do you have more than pottage (1953b)?

It was a lonely battle though, and he stood virtually alone against the crowd. "If it is only for a penny," he argued, "it is still gambling, and how could the school promote the spiritual welfare of the children if the school officials refused to abide by the regulations?" The next Letters to the Editor page was filled with reaction, both positive and negative to the lonely dissenter. One sympathetic supporter wrote of his dismay in seeing the presence of many children in the meeting. "To see bright-eyed girls and boys casting dour looks at the lone champion of the right, and joining with their elders in applause at every dirty crack aimed his way, was not a pleasant picture" (Leigh n.d.).

Naturally, the Brewster family never missed church. For many years we regularly attended the Southside Bible Chapel in South Colorado Springs. Dr. Waldron Scott, now of Holistic Ministries International, also attended Southside at that time and for a while was Tom's Sunday school teacher. Later when Tom and Waldron were both respected mission leaders, Tom told Waldron that it was in that Sunday school class that Tom first thought seriously of missions and told God that he wanted to be a missionary (1986).

Mastering Math . . . and Life

Another of Dad's passions which had a profound influence on Tom was teaching his children math.

Dad installed a black board right by the kitchen table and throughout my youth I remember night after night math lessons often lasting long into the night. Tom's time came first, ours in later years. Dad's particular interest was algebra and equations. Solve for "X" he would say. What you do to one side of the equation you must always do to the other side, often illustrating this point with a slap, first to one side of our face and then to the other. If the answer was too slow, he would shout, "Look at the board, the answer is not in my face!" The sessions would often go on and on, sometimes ending tearfully long after we had become too fatigued and too intimidated to think clearly.

(Interestingly, he apparently also used a variation of this method in his classrooms. Many years later, trying to learn more about my heritage, I stopped over in the tiny town of Campo, Colorado and asked some old timers if they remembered a Roy Brewster who used to teach school there. "Hell, yes," one of them remarked. "He's the one who used to yank on one ear and then on the other to help us learn equations!")

For myself, the fun of any outing with Dad was tainted with the fear that the conversation would turn to math and I would have to respond verbally to questions from his homemade lessons, or worse, even have to take out pencil and paper to work through a few problems. On the one long family vacation we took, a drive to California, I remember more than one session. In Dad's last year or so of life, he drove a big delivery truck which should have been great fun for a young lad like myself to ride with him on his routes, but the same dread of providing him an opportunity to give me a math lesson removed any desire to do so, and any joy if asked.

It is possible that Mom would have liked to have him let up on us, but she knew better than to interfere. She was intimidated by my dad, and always retreated to her bedroom or remained silent when the math lessons started. She worked very hard, but was often sickly, and had very little role in the upbringing of her children. She is, in fact, almost a "non-person" in my own memory until I was in college, long after Dad died. My sisters say that the same was true for them.

My recollection is that the home math lessons were almost a nightly affair. Perhaps it was not quite that frequent. I do know it was something that hung over us. My own best night of the week was Friday nights, when I knew Dad would be going to the synagogue. If we could avoid him till he left, he might not be able to give us problems to do and we would not have to stand at that dreaded blackboard.

Predictably, math became a stumbling block for me and my sisters. I have often looked back to try to see why it could have been so important to him that his children understood math at a level far above their grade in school. I believe though, that it was his way of communicating a discipline and toughness to his children. Yes, he hammered away at it with a fervor that would be considered excessive today, and he never let us quit. But that is the point. He never let us quit. The one thing Dad did not do was quit. And he was not about to let his children be quitters either.

Dad was a "loser," I guess, in the economics of life, but he was not a quitter. He was a flawed vessel, but his motives were good. He expected a lot of his children. He had high standards and high expectations. He knew the value of math in a person's life, but at a deeper level he knew the value of teaching his children to use their heads to find the right solution to problems, to discipline themselves to accomplish a task and to stick with it even when the going was tough.

Dad's methods for teaching math would be considered suspect today, but he communicated to his children that you do not quit, you do not expect someone else to bail you out. If you do not get it right, you keep trying, you never give up. Those hours at the math board built much in Tom and the rest of the family.

Tom's temperament was different than that of the rest of the children, for he never spoke bitterly about the math lessons as the rest of us did. Tom down-played considerably any resentment for it and saw its long term value. Certainly he learned discipline and the ability to solve problems, both mathematical and other kinds he would face in life. Tom remembered far more Dad's zeal for souls than his zeal to teach his children math. And it seems too that Tom responded better to the pressure of the math lessons than the rest of us did—he did not retreat into a shell of fear and avoidance. In fact, the math lessons for Tom were a strong positive factor in Tom's formative years. And it must be said that all of Dad's six children followed in his Christian footsteps, and not one has turned away from the faith.

Dad loved Tom, and, being a teacher, desired to teach him in all areas of life. Dad bought cows and pigs to raise on our property at the edge of town. Tom milked cows early in the mornings, chased the pigs down when they managed to get away, and learned about life and death when the cows were calving—and when they died.

Hunting trips in the Colorado mountains were another treasured time together in the fall of each year—and not just for the sport. Dad always struggled financially, and the meat that Dad and Tom butchered together in our basement was an important part of our diet for the winter months.

Our financial difficulties were no laughing matter, as Tom found out one April Fools' day. Tom decided to pull an April Fools' joke on the family. He switched the sugar and the salt. When the oatmeal (of course it was oatmeal—Tom was nearly an adult before he knew there was anything else for breakfast!) was served, everyone put "sugar" (really salt) on it, and it tasted horrible! So Mom quickly threw out the rest of the oatmeal and made another batch thinking she had done something wrong. When the truth came out, Tom was disciplined, for wasting the family's valuable resources.

Dad had lots of schemes though, to help make ends meet. One was to package mistletoe during the Christmas holiday seasons. I remember several Christmas seasons spent in our basement around large tables piled high with mistletoe. Dad organized us into quite an assembly line; Mom and Dad and the older twins would package the mistletoe into plastic bags while Doris and I stapled on bag tops and labels which we had carefully folded. Tom would keep the table supplied and pack the filled bags into crates for shipping. It was just one of many ways that Dad devised to help keep food on the table during long periods of unemployment.

Tom also found ways to get involved in outside activities like part-time jobs and sports. Perhaps my earliest recollection of Tom was on a rare morning when I happened to awake early and came down and watched him fold newspapers and put rubber bands on them before loading them on his bicycle in the early morning darkness and heading off down the street. I was maybe four years old, and he would have been twelve.

Tom did so well at the paper route that he eventually won a new bike in a paper boy contest. On his first ride down the steep gravel road in front of our house, it seemed the front wheel was loose.

Rather than stopping to investigate, he jerked up on the handle bars. He was right! The wheel was loose and went on down the hill, while Tom and the rest of the bike wound up in a heap.

Tom's bicycle was more than just something to ride; it was something that liberated him. He used it to get to school as well as for his work. But he also used it to get away. He often took long rides just to be out of the house. He sometimes rode to his grandmother's house in Florence over thirty miles away and had Dad bring him and the bike back in the car. (His grandmother had told him it was downhill all the way. He told her, "You'd be surprised how many uphills there are on the way to Grandma's house!")

God Was Bothering Me!

Tom's bike riding also got him a job as a Western Union telegram delivery boy. Often his deliveries would take him long distances across the city and require him to be out long after dark and in all kinds of weather. That was the case one stormy evening when a fierce "Chinook" wind blew in, threatening trees and roofs and other property all over town. Our old two-story house shook and shuddered with the ferocious blasts, and Dad ordered us all downstairs to the basement lest the big old house be blown apart with us inside.

But Tom was out somewhere in the storm. Somewhere he was finishing up the last of his deliveries and struggling to get home. Dad went out to search for him in our old Ford, and found him struggling against the impossible wind about a mile from home.

In the summer of 1952, when he was thirteen, Tom rode some 140 miles to the Covenant Heights youth camp in Estes Park in the Colorado Rockies. On his way, near Denver, the police stopped him—figuring he was running away since he had his bed roll and clothes strapped to the bike. After calling his home and being assured by his father that he had permission, Tom was allowed to continue. It was at that camp that Tom first gave his life to the Lord. Tom talked about having been "bothered" by God over the previous year—like when he came home and found the house unexpectedly empty and had a sinking fear that the rapture had taken place without him. In an early description of his conversion experience he wrote:

> One night, as I imagine in my mind's eye . . . I heard as though it were an angelic host singing to me specifically, over and over and over again the words of a chorus, "Come home! Come home! Ye who are weary come home!" . . . And yet I rejected Christ at that time, and did not receive Him as my personal Savior, and I lived a year of real terror after that. In our Christian circles, we call it "conviction of God." I like to think of it as "God bothering you." God was bothering me that year. . . . A year later at that same camp, I did receive the Lord Jesus Christ as my own personal Savior. Immediately the fears, which I had experienced for the previous year, were taken away (n.d.).

The Pikes Peak Marathon

Along with the part-time jobs Tom also found time to get involved in school athletic activities. For a time he was the radio broadcaster for some of the "Terror" team games. He also participated in cross-country running and track at the Colorado Springs High School. Tom's personal discipline manifested itself early in his running. He developed his own training regime and followed it rigorously. Part of it involved very early morning runs along the Old Gold Camp Road, the former railroad bed for the gold trains from Cripple Creek, which ended not far from our old house. For two years he was captain of the cross-country team, and also ran a very respectable under-five-minute mile. Running was a joy to him, and he drove himself for better times. In an era before physical fitness really became a household activity, he got involved with a Colorado Springs physical fitness buff named Monty Wolford.

Together they trained for a new challenge thrown out by a fifty-six year old Finnish doctor who was a former marathon runner, Arne Suomineu. A non-smoker, the doctor had announced that he would beat any smoker of any age in a foot race up Pikes Peak. The race would be a grueling twelve-mile trip up the rock strewn Barr trail on the face of the famous mountain. The distance and the terrain, not to mention the 7,500 feet altitude change from bottom to top, would test the mettle of the best lungs. Tom finished second in a time of three hours, twenty-three minutes, and was just a tenth of a second behind his friend Monty Wolford. No smoker finished the race that year.

Later that same year, the race was extended to full marathon length—twenty-six miles up and down the rugged Barr trail. Again Tom finished second behind Monty. Tom ran that race a third time, his last, the summer of 1957 as a seventeen-year old—again finishing second, again behind the powerful Monty Wolford.

On His Own

There is no doubt that Tom had a natural wanderlust. There is also no doubt that Tom was a bit rebellious during his last years in high school. I and my sisters remember a lot of conflict in our home, and a lot of avoidance and tolerance of Dad. But whether it was wanderlust or a desire to get out from under the roof with our math teaching father, he left home virtually the day he graduated from high school. Somehow he wound up in Houston where, picking up a Sunday paper, he saw page after page of "Help Wanted" ads. If he could not get a job here, he reasoned, he probably could not get one anywhere.

What he took was uninspiring work as an encyclopedia salesman. He never had much success, perhaps because he never really applied himself. There were lots of distractions—like diving off oil installations in the Gulf of Mexico—that kept him occupied. (A serious attack by a Portuguese Man-o-War eventually put a damper on that activity.) The fact that our own austere home was soon graced by a complete set of Collier's Encyclopedias is evidence, however, of considerable persuasiveness on his part, even as a youngster. Apparently his life was a feast or famine kind of existence at this time—a binge of sorts when he would make a sale, followed by several days or even weeks living mostly on cottage cheese and cheap, dry cereals.

Tom was on his own, finding himself. Mostly he was goofing off, being independent. He was sowing his wild oats and looking for the next adventure.

2
THE ACCIDENT

Modern medicine and equipment should enable him to have a near normal life expectancy, but what he does with his life will depend on the effectiveness of his adjustment to his disability and his acceptance of his new self (T. Brewster 1968).

Tom stayed in Texas throughout the winter of his eighteenth year, and the next summer found him up in Michigan. There he found the kind of summer work he could really put himself into, as a counselor at a YMCA camp on Twin Lakes, Michigan, just north of Muskegon. One wonders what counseling qualifications he had at that point, but he certainly was qualified and excited about his main job—teaching his young charges swimming, water-skiing and other sporting activities.

Now Tom was in his element. What more could he ask for than to be paid $240 for a summer of doing what he liked to do best!

July 24, 1958 was an exciting day at the camp. The equipment at the camp was adequate, but it improved a lot the day the water slide, finally arrived. It was a tall, playground slide, and the boys and Tom spent the morning putting it together and positioning it in the shallow water at the edge of the lake. Finally, by mid-afternoon all was ready. Tom was the first one to use it.

As many other youngsters have done before and since, Tom bounded up the steps and started down headfirst, his hands to the sides rather than out in front to break the water. The slide was tall and steep. Tom knew he was going too fast. He gripped the rails and pressed his forehead to the slide. That was the last voluntary movement most of the muscles in his lower body ever made for Tom.

As his head hit the water, it was forced down on to his chest. One vertebrae rode up over another, instantly severing the nerves to his lower body.

Meanwhile, the watching young campers waited for Tom to jump up so they could have their turn. But he stayed in the water, and they thought he must be prolonging the sensation of the thrill from the slide. And still they waited. Finally some got concerned and caught him, pulling his head out of the water. "Help me out!" Tom gasped, finally able to take a breath. The young campers dragged Tom out onto the sand and laid him there while some others went for help. (The sand he got in his hair as they pulled him out wound up being with him for weeks in his hospital room before he was able to get it washed properly.) Initially, Tom felt little pain and did not understand enough of what had happened to be afraid. They'll just un-pinch that nerve, he thought, and I'll be right back out here. Tom was concerned, but not frightened, though it felt odd not being able to feel anything below the shoulders when they slid him into the car. The pain became serious as he rode to the hospital. Incredible by today's cautious and more enlightened standards, his hospital ride was in the back of a station wagon with his head on someone's lap, no effort made to stabilize his neck or his head.

For the emergency staff at Hackley Hospital in Muskegon, there was no question of just how serious the injury was. Life saving procedures began immediately. Most important was to prevent further injury to the spinal cord. To do so, weights were suspended through pulleys which were attached to his head with "Crutchfield tongs" by drilling small holes into his skull just above his ears. Awake and still under the initial shock during this crucial procedure, Tom asked how far the tongs were from his brain. He was not sure that he really wanted to know.

A tube was placed in his nose to his stomach, and a urinary catheter inserted. Another suction device was added for the mucous he was unable to swallow or spit out. Then he was placed in a special bed called a "Stryker frame"—a kind of sandwich-like affair that permitted the staff to flip him over like a pancake every couple of hours to prevent pressure sores. A neurosurgeon in Grand Rapids was called, but on hearing of Tom's condition he said, "That young man won't survive 48 hours. If by some miracle he does live beyond that, call me and I'll come over to see him."

Will the Circle Be Unbroken?

Back in Colorado on that hot Thursday afternoon, Mom and Dad got the grim message, "Your son has been seriously injured and is not expected to live. Better get out here in a hurry if you want to see him alive." I recall coming down the stairs in our big old house and being astounded to see Mom and Dad both sitting on the couch weeping. I had never before seen either of them cry. They hurriedly began to make preparations to fly immediately to Michigan. They had no money for the trip, so they "borrowed" all of Martha's savings from her restaurant waitress job. Dad of course intended to repay her, as it was her savings for college, but he was never able to get any extra money together. The flight to Michigan was the first airplane flight that either had ever taken, and their first time east of the Mississippi.

What a shock! Dad's first-born son, the one he prayed over on the first day of his life—his hopes and dreams that he and Tom would someday be missionaries together, in a moment smashed into pieces. But God's plans are not fulfilled our way. God fulfills His plans out of brokenness, in His own way.

Tom still did not realize how serious his condition was until late that night, about twelve hours after the accident when he was shocked to see his parents walk into the hospital room. For them to come so far—and so fast—brought the first real awareness and fear to Tom about what had happened. "What have they told you?" he whispered. Dad broke the news. "You are not expected to live. You might die any time in the next five days."

The visit was short. The doctors wanted Tom to rest. For Dad though, there was one issue that could not be postponed, could not be left unsaid even until morning. Drawing himself close to Tom and with tears streaming down his face, he said to Tom, "If this is your time to go, will the family circle be unbroken in heaven?"

Up until a few hours before, Tom had been a very healthy, active young man with a lot of "here and now" activities. It is probable that he had not thought a lot about the wholeness of the family circle in heaven in recent months or even years. At that moment, Tom gave his heart back to the Lord.

This was bedrock for Dad. This was who he was in every fiber of his being. Nothing else really mattered to him, and certainly it was his sincerest prayer for Tom now. Tom assured Dad that though he had strayed a bit, he had given his life to Jesus, and if he did die, he knew where he would spend eternity.

Over the next few weeks lying there in the frame, and later in a full body cast, Tom had many hours to think. He examined his life a great deal in those months. He might have wondered what good life was for a young man whose very existence revolved around activities and sports, when now he could not so much as lift his hand. He could have thought a person like him would be better off if he did not make it.

But that was not what he thought about. Dad's prayers and the conviction instilled in his younger days that God had control of everything began to take on meaning. He was thankful to be alive.

A Supernatural Visit?

Naturally, there were times when the sheer profoundness of what had happened to him was overwhelming. But God ministered to him in very special ways throughout. On one occasion when he was feeling low a nurse came in, had a pleasant talk and left him with a poem that he carried with him for the rest of his life. It was "In Acceptance Lieth Peace," by Hannah Hurnard:

> In acceptance lieth peace, oh my heart be still;
> Let thy restless worries cease and accept His will.
> Though this test be not thy choice,
> It is His—therefore rejoice.

> In His plan there cannot be, ought to make thee sad;
> If this is His choice for thee, take it and be glad.
> Make from it some lovely thing,
> To the glory of the King.

> Cease from sighs and murmuring,
> Sing His wondrous grace.
> This thing means thy furthering to a wealthy place.
> From thy fears He'll give release,
> In acceptance lieth peace (n.d.:50).

According to our sister, Mona, Tom had never seen that nurse before, and never saw her again afterwards. Nor were there any records of that particular person being on staff. Supernaturally provided or not, the poem was one which helped to shape his own attitude and one with which he blessed the lives of many others all of his life.

"I decided that God must have had a reason for so nearly taking my life," he said. "I realized that God doesn't give someone his life the first time without a reason, and He sure wouldn't give my life back again without a purpose."

So from that first night in the hospital room Tom began to resolve that if God did indeed spare his life, he would dedicate himself to discover what it was that God had planned for him. His question was not then nor ever, "Why me?" Rather, he asked "Why am I still alive?" Tom later confided in Mona, "I had some kind of gift of grace so that I never despaired."

When Tom survived the first critical days in the hospital, his life was temporarily out of danger. Still, the prognosis was not good. An Aetna Insurance Case Study report described the injury and the outlook in clinical and pessimistic terms:

> X-rays eventually disclosed fractures and dislocations of the cervical spine at the c-4 and c-5 level. Claimant has feeling and motion in his left shoulder but none in the right. Reports from the neurosurgeon and attending doctors indicate that there is no chance for rehabilitation to even a remote self-care existence, and he is ruled a complete quadriplegic (n.d.).

However, after further review, the insurance carrier's surgical advisor more hopefully noted in the same report:

> This may be the true state of affairs, but we have no way of proving this except by a concerted attempt to disprove that gloomy prediction. Experience has shown that in modern rehabilitation centers seeming miracles can be obtained, and . . . with an intelligent and cooperative young man, he can become a productive member of society.

Amazingly, Tom was never aware of going through a major adjustment period as a result of this transformation from complete independence to total dependence. His immediate physical needs were being taken care of by others, and it was more than obvious to him that this was necessary. But right from the start an unusual thing began to happen.

Tom never could explain why it was that other young people discovered him and made him their own. It started with one of the student nurses who found out he was a Christian and started telling the other student nurses about him. The nurses from the Student Nurse Fellowship started spending time with Tom. Then one of the nurses told a friend who was in high school about Tom and the friend came to visit.

The Resident "Dear Abby"

Suddenly it began to catch on. Before long, youth groups and clubs began to come over for a little after meeting fellowship. Then the football team and even some professional athletes took a personal interest in him. Tom's room became the regular meeting place for kids from all over the city. He had known no one in the city before his injury. But now, out of the blue, dozens—then scores—then hundreds of young people became his friends. Couples on dates would stop in after a show. Singles would come in for "Dear Abby" advice. Kids would bring by their dates and then sneak in afterwards to ask Tom what he thought of them. Some would even play hooky from school so that they could come and spend time with Tom when no one else was there. He would be the first to know of a party, an initiation trick, or a personal problem. He was even "Cupid" for some couples.

The kids came in droves, but not because they had to. As one of his visitors put it, "We didn't do things for Tom to cheer him up, we did them to be cheered up." Together, Tom and his friends turned what could have been a bleak hospital room into one filled with the laughter and enthusiasm of effervescent teens.

How was it that the hospital put up with all of this? Tom had a private room, so perhaps they decided to loosen the visiting hour rules a bit. Perhaps they were surprised and overwhelmed by something so spontaneous and refreshing. Or maybe they saw from the start the therapeutic value of what was going on and could find no reason to limit it.

The Muskegon Chronicle newspaper described the scene:

> Who knows where they all came from. All that matters is that they were there, and have been almost from the day Tom Brewster was carried into Hackley Hospital. The schools, the "Y," the college . . . the teenage grapevine is fast; and accurate. One of their number was in trouble and you take care of your own.
>
> That's the way it started. A handful of the gang for a pizza party, a couple stopping in after a date, a student nurse going off duty: Here was the kids' own therapy.
>
> Halloween and Tom's first day in a wheelchair so you "trick or treat" your way around the corridors. Take out orders of pizza, a birthday party in August; never a day, rarely a moment when one or two or a gang wasn't there (1958).

Perhaps Tom was realizing too what was important. Not walking, dressing or *doing* things, but being involved in relationships with people. He did not have anything else, so even then he began to pour himself into others. *For when I am weak, then I am strong.* Do what you can do—do not worry about what you cannot do.

God's providence could be seen in that Tom also had a good insurance policy at the time of his injury that covered well the costs of his care and rehabilitation, as well as a small permanent disability stipend that helped meet some financial needs for the rest of his life. His insurance company (Aetna) also recognized the value of Tom's positive attitude and its importance in mitigating the costs of long-term care. The Aetna case study review noted that

> he was an extremely intelligent young man, with a good family and educational background, a strong religious faith, and was very well motivated. There was no evidence of severe depression because of his injury. He became extremely popular with the hospital personnel, and was visited by literally hundreds of young people from various youth organizations in the city where he was hospitalized (n.d.).

This was Tom's environment for the first four months after his injury. Tom had begun his own rehabilitation therapy. He refused to be discouraged or bitter. He accepted his total dependence and vulnerability, and allowed others to minister to him. (About a year later another young man broke his neck and was rushed to Hackley Hospital. The word spread quickly among the young people that someone else had been hurt like Tom. He was soon engulfed by a crowd of teenagers who were anxious to stand by him. Unfortunately, he was moody and bitter and refused to let them be his friends. Needless to say, they got the message and after a few times did not bother to return.)

At the end of September, the traction pulleys were removed after surgery to fuse the bones of the injured vertebrae together. Then he was placed in a body cast that started with a "halo" around his forehead and extended down his neck and on to his waist. He was able to "shrug" his shoulders, but he avoided doing that since he would then have to ask someone to pull them down for him if he was not sitting up. He also had slight movement of the fingers in one hand.

A Recovery Diary

An old address book (Tom had a typical way of tracking all manner of mini-anniversaries) included the following chronology of his stay in Hackley Hospital, written in the neat handwriting of a nurse or visitor:

July 24— Day of the accident (Thursday)
July 29th— Day of near departure
August 20— Birthday (19 years old)
August 24— Anniversary of one month
August 27— Day of heart attack (just a little upset)
Sept. 9— A thrilling moment, 2:50 p.m. first movement of left arm. Hooray, all nerves and muscles aren't dead anyhow!
Sept. 12— 50th day
Sept. 30— Now I've had it (day of operation to fuse the vertebrae around the break)
Oct. 5— First movement of thumb on right hand
Oct. 7— 1st week anniversary of operation, 75th day since accident

Oct. 12—	All but three of 25 stitches removed
Oct. 25—	Frame thrown out, cast thrown on. 93 days spent on Stryker frame.
Oct. 31—	99th day, 1st day in wheelchair
Nov. 1—	100th day since accident
Nov. 2—	First movements of left hand middle finger
Nov. 20—	Ate at Bill Monroe's Steakhouse. Wonderful time. (Probably first time out of hospital after the accident)
Nov. 21—	Farewell party—200 present (all of whom he had met in his hospital room)
Nov. 22—	Awakened by J. Wierengo, given farewell kiss by J. Wierengo [Probably a nurse]
	Lacking 2 days of 4 months
	121 glorious days [!]
	Signed off with love by Joan Wierengo

Back Home to Colorado

On the day Tom left Hackley Hospital, the hospital allowed a big going away party for Tom. The paper called it the "best party in town" as over 200 people showed up to see him off. Tom meant it when he said that Michigan was home, and that was the first place to which he would come back if he ever was ever able to do so. It was a promise he kept.

After being driven around Muskegon by the ambulance driver in a makeshift "parade," Tom was flown by ambulance plane to Craig Rehabilitation Center in Denver on November 22, 1958, after almost four months in the hospital in Michigan.

The homecoming to his family in Colorado was an emotional one. I remember approaching his bed in the rehab center with a combination of fear and surprise. I had not seen Tom in well over a year. Seeing him immobilized with a huge cast, flipped onto his stomach by his rotating bed so he could see us, was pretty unnerving for a boy of eleven.

For my father, it was a time of hope and a time of agony. He was constantly praying that his boy would walk again and eventually fulfill that vision he had prayed about on the first day of Tom's life—that he would someday yet be able to go to the mission field.

He even had a dream that Tom would fully recover, and that they would be able to minister together. Over the next few months, he took every small recovery of muscle movement or even perceived movement as a sign that such a healing might occur. With every report of some controlled muscle movement, excitement and hope rose in Dad's heart. One day Tom found that he was able to make one of his big toes wiggle a tiny bit. That flicker was cause for Dad to be overcome with joyous weeping.

3
LEARNING TO COPE

It is better to be crippled in body than to be crippled in mind.
Because of the Resources of God I refuse to accept my limitations.

(Written in Tom's Bibles)

He who has a why to live for can bear with almost any how.

Nietzsche

It was in the days just after the transfer to Craig that Tom had the first letdown as a result of the injury. Away from all his marvelous new friends, just nineteen years old, and alone for almost the first waking time since the injury, he began to feel a loneliness. Placed in a room by himself at the end of a long hall, with no one to talk to for long hours, and unable even to reach the call button or to push it if he could have, the reality, at long last, began to dawn. As though he had had some choice in the matter, he recalled asking himself over and over those first few days, "What have you gotten yourself into now, Tom?" But God was ministering to Tom during the long hours, days, weeks, and months of rehabilitation. "When you spend a year in hospitals," he said later, "you evaluate and re-evaluate your life" (T. Brewster 1963:16).

Tom's family was glad to have him closer to home, but all were aware of the debt of gratitude owed to the hospital and friends who had supported Tom in Michigan. In a letter to the hospital and town of Muskegon printed in the *Muskegon Chronicle*, Dad wrote,

> We have much to be thankful for. Would you help us thank the people of Muskegon for the love and consideration shown Tommy and all of us while he was in Hackley Hospital.
>
> Last July 24 was a day of sorrow for us, for our son received a broken neck at Camp Douglas while working as a counselor. But many kindnesses and expressions of sympathy have caused much thanksgiving in our hearts. We are surely thankful to the Lord for

the thoughtfulness and consideration of the personnel of Hackley Hospital. Every effort has been made to show kindness and love to us and Tommy, beyond that which we might have expected. We have much cause to give thanks too, for the doctors and nurses for their efforts to help Tommy. We wouldn't know where to go to have found better ones (1958).

Referring to his prayer on the day Tom was born that he would someday be a missionary, he continued,

Our hearts would know no bounds of joy if the Lord would raise him up for such work. Our hearts are indeed full of thanksgiving to the Christians who have been burdened to pray for Tommy. I am sure much of his recovery is in answer to the prayers of the Lord's people.

The New Reality

Tom eventually got a roommate at Craig—a young woman named Irene Armitstead with an injury similar to Tom's. (There was not a whole lot these two quadriplegics could do to get into trouble!) Sharing that room together was the beginning of a long friendship, and Tom's optimism and ambition were soon sufficient to get his mind off himself and on to more constructive things.

However, bearing the weight of Dad's grief was another matter. Tom's injury affected our father in a profound and devastating way. In his complex personality, he could not keep from unreasonably, but quite seriously, blaming himself for Tom's injury. He felt he had not given enough of himself to Tom to provide direction in his life, and that through Tom's injury God was somehow punishing his own sinfulness. He could not stop thinking it was all his fault, that he had been too hard on Tom, that he had not spent enough time with him, and that he had failed him in a thousand other ways.

In a sense, Tom's accident was, for Dad, the death of a vision. Dad had kept alive his dream of going to Israel or the mission field with Tom. Dad's dream lived vicariously in Tom and now his son, his strength, his future ministry, lay there helplessly in bed, never to walk again.

During all his stay at Hackley Hospital in Michigan, Tom had been around cheerful people who were vibrant, joyful, exuberant and alive. Now his frequent bedside companion was his own father who had become morose, dejected and tearful. Dad's grief was overwhelming and debilitating. He was in deep depression much of the time.

Tom found himself struggling—not so much to deal with any sorrow and bitterness of his own, but rather with an incredible weight from his father's grief. His own morale largely remained good and his outlook very positive, but bearing his father's grief and assumed guilt was almost enough to get him down. Tom wanted and needed to get out from under it. He resolved he would waste not a moment of the rehabilitation therapy and get off on his own again—somehow, someway.

Tom was not too proud to be dependent on others, but then again, he was not going to be any more dependent than he had to be. At Craig, Tom met Dr. John Young, whom Tom was later to call "a colossus in my life." He had a very positive attitude about what people in Tom's condition could do, and always encouraged Tom to try anything that occurred to him. From the start, Tom was rehabilitating his mind and attitude as well as his body. And from the beginning his focus was on the possible, not the impossible.

At the rehab center he was provided with necessary equipment which included an undulating mattress, and an air filled seat cushion for his wheelchair, both of which helped prevent pressure sores from sitting or lying in the same position for long periods without being able to shift his weight. Because of his positive attitude and cooperative spirit, doctors and rehabilitation experts felt free to experiment with him and try all kinds of new and novel treatments, procedures, and experimental assistance devices. They tried several different braces and artificial muscles on him. With one, powered by carbon dioxide, he achieved some promising dexterity and while it did not prove practical for Tom in the long run, the information gained was valuable for future patients.

The relearning, though, did not come easily. Very simple tasks like gripping a glass of water took agonizing repetitions. His younger sister Mona remembers Tom at home one weekend, sitting at the table with plastic draped all over him, trying to get a cup of water to his mouth. He would concentrate intensely, but failed over and over again. Spill, mop, refill; spill, mop, refill. Tom cried. Mona cried. Mom cried. Spill, mop, refill.

But he did not give up. Dad had given him too much "never give up" for that. The principle he later urged so often later to language learners—learn a little, use it a lot—was how Tom had to re-learn every basic skill.

Over the period of rehabilitation, he regained a significant grip, but no dexterity, in the fingers of his right hand and some biceps use in both arms, allowing him to move his arms up. Gravity pulled them down. He also learned to balance himself in his wheel chair, such that, unless thrown about too violently, he could sit upright for many hours at a time. Leaning forward and from side to side was done by using balance and gravity. He was never without an air-filled cushion, though, to even out the pressure on his back side since he could not lift himself even a fraction of an inch out of his chair. It took long agonizing hours of practice to relearn the simple task of feeding himself. Many more hours were spent training his fingers again to hold and use a pen, and his hands to move his wheelchair a little.

That flicker of movement in his big toe that gave Dad so much hope turned out to be a tease. That was all the voluntary muscle control in his lower body he would ever again experience. His eventual travel around the world and almost detached lack of concern for his handicap throughout his life suggested to many that he had much more movement than he did. But the fact is, he had no lower body muscle control for the next twenty-seven years.

Mostly though, he just exercised constantly what slight muscle recovery he did have. Right from the start he wanted to use what little muscle he had—and every opportunity he had.

He also started dating. Naturally, he either had to go with a "chaperone" who could "throw him in and out of cars and such," or else make some unusual requests of his date. But it never slowed him down. He lacked balance, and had to carefully instruct his date not to upset him or overbalance him lest he find himself sprawled on the ground and the frantic date in a panic of fear. It was on such early dates that the true measure of his self accep- tance was apparent. He had not yet learned to fully sense his body signals (something he learned to a remarkable degree in later years), and lacking bowel control, he more than once had "blast- offs" that would have been crushing embarrassments to persons with less self esteem.

In June of 1959, eleven months after his injury, Tom had a short leave from the Craig Rehab Center to go to a family reunion in California. Tom flew out unaccompanied, while the rest of us went by car. We vacationed together for a few days in California, but it was stressful and awkward for all. We still were not really cognizant of Tom's needs nor how to meet them. Dad tried hard in his way, but Tom was used to professional care, and their strong wills got in the way of good intentions. Psychologically the exper- ience did not provide the right incentives toward Tom's further rehabilitation. So he returned to Craig and continued as well with his studies at the Denver campus of the University of Colorado.

That winter, Tom made another journey, a sentimental one back to Michigan, fulfilling the promise to come back to Muskegon. Once again, he made the trip by himself. He was greeted warmly by the city and friends he had come to love. The Muskegon Chroni- cle once again picked up the story and under the heading, "'Mr. Courage' Says Good-by," writer Bruce McCrea paid tribute to a young man who had won their hearts,

> Tom Brewster, a living example of youthful courage, said "good-by" today. His plane left County Airport at 2 p.m., winging its way to Denver. . . .
>
> His long hospitalization here saw him accumulate a host of new friends; youngsters who heard of his injury and came to the hospital to shorten the hours. But when he left, last Nov. 22, there was still only vague movement of the fingers of his right hand. And the doc- tors saw little chance of major improvement.
>
> But Tom has been busy since . . . and the doctors reckoned with- out the determination of a boy named Brewster. . . .

So rapid has been the advance he traveled extensively for the Colorado United Fund appeal, demonstrating the worth of fund-supported agencies which work with the handicapped. . . . And he is planning to come back.

"You don't find friends like this everywhere in the world," says the youngster who refused to quit. "Muskegon is my second home."

It's needless to point out Tom will be welcome (1959).

On the Road Again

On his return, Tom began to think again about improving the part of him that was not paralyzed—from his neck up. He took vocational tests and decided that he wanted to enroll in a liberal arts program at the University of Colorado Extension Center in Denver. To do so, he rented a room in the home of a couple who provided care for handicapped people. He thought about careers that he could pursue while sitting in a chair the rest of his life. Biology—looking in a microscope? Anatomy? (Nah, not that—could not turn the cadavers!) Pre-med., math or physics? Teaching? He could not really decide, so settled initially for one promising possibility, a speech major.

At the same time, he began to learn a new skill which, as far as he was concerned, was the most important thing in that phase of recovery. He learned to drive a car. He bought a used car and some rehabilitation assistants fitted it with a simple, effective hand control. It consisted of a steel horizontal bar just below the steering wheel attached to bars going to the brake and accelerator pedals. Also on the horizontal bar was a switch for dimming the lights. The accelerator was depressed by force downward (towards his lap) on the horizontal bar, and the brakes operated by downward force towards the brake pedal. It took some practice to learn, especially since Tom did not have the triceps muscles to extend his arms. He learned to use the brakes by locking his left arm and leaning forward with his body and shoulder. Tom was apparently the first quadriplegic in Colorado to get a driver's license.

His car was pretty special—a 1957 Cadillac chosen because of the comfort and safety and the latest feature, indispensable to him, a six-way power seat. He became quite a good driver, and again, because of his positive attitude, his rehab doctors had him demonstrating it to other patients who were less sure of their abilities or potential.

Getting a car at that point in his life had the same effect as getting the bicycle had in his childhood days. It gave him the independence he needed to find his own way in life. It is one of the most remarkable characteristics of Tom's life that even after his broken neck, the wandering spirit and exploring mentality never let up. Tom was not one to let a little thing like a broken neck keep him from enjoying anything he set his mind to.

Soon, the wanderlust returned and he began to make plans to travel around the country to demonstrate the hand controls and other devices of which he was making use. He felt these would be of value to many others who, while perhaps less handicapped than himself, were spending most of their time in bed. These plans also provided a great opportunity for me, his little brother, to get to know him in a very special way. He asked me to go along on the first leg of the trip to Texas and Mexico. I got to be the one to "toss him in and out" of his car and generally look after his personal needs.

Before that first trip, in the summer of 1960, the *Denver Post* wrote about Tom and his ideas about helping other persons with similar disabilities:

"Tourist" to Compile Rehabilitation Study

. . . Now he wants to see what's being done to help others like him. This summer he plans a tour of about 30 rehabilitation centers like Craig in the southern and northeastern states.

He will also visit Mexico to see what winter resorts are available for people in wheelchairs.

But his main interest is rehabilitation of people like himself.

"There are more than 1,000 persons in the United States less handicapped than I am with more potential than I have, who spend most of their time in bed.

"Welfare agencies spend a lot of money caring for these people. If some of that money were spent on rehabilitation, along with care, it would do more for the person at less total cost to the agency," he said . . . Tom will report on what he finds across the nation in a series of articles for the *Denver Post*.

Tom got his buddy from Muskegon, Phil Hollar, to join us as well, and off we went in Tom's Cadillac with Tom at the wheel heading first down to the familiar territory (to Tom) of Houston. While there, we visited a veteran's facility to demonstrate some of his equipment. That was, after all, why he was traveling. Sort of. I am sure that for a good part of the time there was no other motive for him than just being on his own, seeing what was out there. There is no record of him ever doing the articles he promised for the *Denver Post*.

Leaving Houston, we went on to Guadalajara (which was to be a significant place in both of our lives in the future), on to Mexico City, and then back up the east coast to Texas. I left them there, taking the train home, but there would be many other such trips for me long before I learned to drive, where he took me along to dress him in the morning, "throw him" into and out of the car, and "toss him" back into bed at night.

The Mexico leg of the trip was outwardly to see what resort facilities were available to handicapped people there. The demonstration objective was a real and worthy one, but there was something more to it. Tom's venturesome spirit was wanting to do something totally different and unexpected. What really could he do? Just how independent could he be? How much did he have to rely on other people? A lot, obviously, to meet his physical needs. But how about to make decisions for him? To tell him what he could do or what he should do? This was a test. Could he get out on his own? Could he begin again to shape his own destiny, to follow his own spirit, or would others have to both beat his drum and march to it for him as well?

Many things are memorable about those trips. There was the time he nearly lost the car when he hit the gas too hard. The car swerved sharply, causing him to lose his balance and throwing him into my lap. Somehow I was able to help him up and get him back in control, miraculously without disaster for us or for anyone else.

But there was a lesson there—about his own limitations, and about the potential danger of his powerful car.

Sometimes on our many long trips together we were accompanied by one of his "able bodied" friends, like Phil Hollar, and sometimes by another quadriplegic, an American Indian named "Morning Star." We rigged up a large cooler of warm tea (ice tea chilled him too much), and as we drove we sipped from long urinary tubes—unused of course!—that I rigged up for that purpose. We could go for hours on end without stops for any thing—except when I had to "go."

That was one human weakness though, that did not trouble Tom. With a catheter attached to a urinary leg bag, he could wait until the bag filled up, which was fairly frequent with the volume of tea that he drank to keep his kidneys flushed out and flowing smoothly. When the leg bag was full he would request that I "drain the main vein." I would simply drain the contents of the bag into a bottle, pan or other container and toss it out the window! The first time that someone else did it when I was in the back-seat with my window open, I insisted that I be forewarned next time to make sure I was not caught in the spray again!

(Experience though, was the mother of invention. After this we rigged a tube through the floorboard of the car, so that the leg bag could simply be connected to the tube and release the contents without stopping the car. Tom would often brag quite honestly that he could "pee for miles.")

On another trip, Tom and I traversed the southern states all the way down to Miami where we visited Tom's friend from college, Mike Eaton. Then we headed north and wound up in the Big Apple—New York City—where we stayed in the YMCA. What did people do in the Big Apple back then? Why, visit the Empire State Building, of course. Tom never did really get over his disappointment that a wheelchair bound person ca not see over the edge from the observation deck at the 102nd floor.

Tom and Phil carried on from New York up the east coast to Hartford, Connecticut where he visited the offices of the Aetna insurance company who were taking a special interest and pride in him and doing all they could to facilitate his progress—to thank them and to show off his skills with the hand control. On August 7, 1960, *The Hartford Courant*, the local newspaper, reported the visit, concluding with a quote from H. A Stoppels, superintendent of the rehabilitation department: "Aetna Casualty so far has spent about $30,000 on the Brewster case. In Tom's case, in particular, we feel that it has been well spent."

Tom's car was the symbol of the era for him. Tom and I, and a few friends toured the Southern states, crisscrossed the Appalachians, and "crossed the wide prairies."

I do not recall just how many trips I took with Tom. I do remember though that after returning from one, I was proudly able to count up forty-four states that I had been in during those three years of summer cruising, all before I was sixteen, either alone with Tom or as a passenger with Tom and one of his friends.

The adventurer—the explorer—the dreamer in Tom was never paralyzed.

Tom profited much about this time from the writings of Victor Frankl. He agreed with Frankl that ". . . everything can be taken from a man but one thing: the last of the human freedoms—to choose one's attitude in any given set of circumstances" (Frankl 1939:104). Tom recognized that while his physical ability (and thus choices) were limited, he still had a choice about attitude and what to make of the rest of his life He could still choose to live in bitterness and self-pity, blame God and curse God; or he could accept God's sovereignty and do the best he could with the rest of his life. Yes, there was pain, but he did not submit to it. Yes, there were things that he could not do, but what *could* he do? Yes, there was discouragement, but there was also hope.

Good-Bye to Dad

Unfortunately, Dad never was able to come to grips with Tom's injury or to stop blaming himself. He was under great financial pressure at the time, and involved in a stressful church dispute as well. In a very painful episode, he was thrown out of the Assemblies church he had attended for many years for "railing" against the Brethren. Perhaps other discouragements weighed on him as well. Whatever the reasons, the Lord suddenly took that heavy-hearted man to be with Him in glory on Easter Sunday morning, April 2, in 1961.

For eleven years Dad had attended the Jewish synagogue in a lonely witness to the Jews of Colorado Springs. So far as I know, only one Jewish man in the Colorado Springs Synagogue ever trusted the Lord as his personal Savior. But they respected him, and when he died, the Baptist church was filled with his Jewish friends.

In a letter to that lone believer, written April 12, 1961—just ten days after Dad's death—Tom wrote:

> [Dad's death] caught us unprepared and has been hard to fully understand, and it has been hard on us all. But, Ira, this past week has been one of the richest of my life. Three things have become so very real: one is Christ Himself. Oh, Ira, how close He has been at this time. The other things are life itself—and so closely associated with life is death. Someone once said that a man is not prepared to live until he is prepared to die.
>
> A Jewish man said to our pastor, "If this is God, what hope is there in Him?" But it is at a time like this that what we have in Christ is so very important, and means so very much. How wonderful it is to know, with full assurance, that Dad is with Him. It is thrilling, too, to KNOW that one day we will be with him and with Christ and will share together the riches of His glory. . . .
>
> Ira, you were as much a thrill to Dad's heart as any man he ever knew. So often he would tell about the times you spent together. Greatest among those times was the one in which you said that "I believe that Jesus Christ is the Messiah." You were the only Jewish man that Dad ever heard say those words (1961).

Did the depression related to his ministry and the heartache Dad suffered over Tom bring on the sudden heart attack he had that morning? We will never know. To his everlasting memory and credit though, the little Baptist church was over half full of Jews on the day of his funeral.

4
A SHATTERED VESSEL

But the pot he was shaping from the clay was marred in his hands;
so the potter formed it into another pot, shaping it as seemed best
to him (Jeremiah 18:4 NIV).

Tom's travels by car in those years were the precursor of an
unusual lifestyle that took him all over the world. Tom was an
explorer geographically. He was about to become one intellectually,
spiritually, and missiologically. One of the objectives of an early
trip with Phil Hollar was to stop at some university campuses to
see which ones might be wheelchair accessible. He had already
taken some course work at the University of Colorado Denver
campus. looked promising, and Tom and Phil enrolled there in the
fall of 1961.

The years at Memphis State were typical college fun. Tom was
not going to let school—or a little thing like quadriplegia—get in
the way of a good time. Tom quickly became known as "The Big
Wheel," and he and his many friends were always game to try
something together—even things that quadriplegics should not do.
Like careening around a roller skating rink, during which he fell
out of his wheel chair and broke his cheek bone. ("The only bones
in my body I can feel!" he complained.) Like snow tobogganing
with a group of friends in Colorado. I was with him once in Florida
when he and Morning Star, his paraplegic friend, got carried away
with a couple of good looking girls, and challenged one another to a
race with the girls pushing the wheelchairs. Tom, always the com-
petitor, leaned forward to help the young lady pushing his chair,
and sure enough, caused it to tip forward, catching the pedals, and
flipping him out onto the pavement on his face. Needless to say, he
was a mess.

While at Memphis State, when they were not partying, Tom and
Phil became a beloved part of the Christian and Missionary Alli-

ance Church where Rev. Andrew Berkner was pastor. From time
to time Tom taught Sunday school classes for the young people and
young adults. Rev. Berkner also recalls that Tom responded to an
invitation to give his life for missions at the first missionary con-
vention Tom attended there. That Tom could actually be involved
in missions, though, seemed a bit far-fetched to Rev. Berkner. He
wrote:

> [Tom] was ready to drop everything then and there and go to Bible
> college to prepare to become a missionary. After talking it over with
> me, as his pastor, he realized he should continue to get all the edu-
> cation he could, because, unless the Lord saw fit to perform a spec-
> tacular miracle, Tom would probably minister in a teaching capac-
> ity from his chair. It was already evident that he was a gifted
> teacher. Tom had such a beautiful personality and was such a
> vibrant person; it was impossible to feel sorry for him. Little did we
> know, at that time, what the Lord had planned for Tom (Berkner
> 1987).

With funds from Social Security for his disability and an insurance and Workmen's Compensation allowance for a full time
physical assistant, Tom completed a four-year program of study in
1964 at Memphis State, majoring in biology with a minor in
speech. During that time, he also served as president of the campus Inter-varsity chapter, and often shared with youth and other
groups a powerful message of acceptance and trust in the loving
sovereignty of God. "I had a distinct sense that what I was doing
was part of God's will for me at that time," he wrote, "but I also
very distinctly remember that I had no idea what the Lord had in
store for my future" (c.1969).

A New Tragedy

But it was in his final year at Memphis State that Tom endured
the hardest and saddest days of his life. After the accident Tom
had resigned himself to the fact that he would probably never
marry. After all, what woman would want to tie herself down to
the care of a paralyzed man all her life?

But Tom grew close to one particular young woman named Pat in his circle of Christian friends, and after some months of courtship, and against the advice of his pastor, Rev. Berkner, they too hastily decided to marry in Memphis in December of 1963. There were, some say, lots of warning signs of trouble that Tom chose to ignore—that Pat did not have the temperament or stability to care for and at the same time love deeply a man in Tom's condition. But when Tom met Pat, his heart and emotions took control.

Sadly, it was a brief, heartbreaking episode. A complex and insecure personality, Pat immediately found herself unable to cope with a marriage as demanding as the one to which she had committed herself. They had a month of honeymoon happiness before things started to fall apart for her—and for them.

Unable to accept the emotional pressures, Pat began to take out frustrations on Tom. She would refuse to assist him, leaving him for long hours in the wheelchair, unable to get to bed or to care for himself. At times she was violent, sometimes sending him sprawling from his chair. Acting out some deep insecurity, Pat would sometimes take Tom's hands in hers and beat herself with his hands until both he and she were badly bruised.

On their anniversary, Tom, perhaps not too judiciously, gave her a dozen roses, eleven red and one white—for the one month of peace and harmony in their home. "Next year, Tom," she said, "it will be twelve white ones." But it was not to be.

Tom graduated from Memphis State in February of 1964 and in June they moved to Lansing, Michigan where Tom planned to begin work towards a Master's degree in psychology at Michigan State. One motivation was certainly a desire to understand and deal with Pat. Perhaps he had also begun to recognize his gifts in counseling with people, and felt he could make a professional contribution in that area. Tom was able to work out an arrangement to work as a counselor in a VA hospital, comforting and encouraging mental and psychiatric patients.

Tom hoped that a new start could be made in his marriage. But that too was not to be. Things got even worse at home. At one point Pat left Tom in bed and simply walked out the door. Tom laid there for three days unable to get up, eat, clean up or otherwise care for himself. Finally able to get the attention of the garbage collectors outside, they came in and got him to a hospital. Tom had to move out. On the week ends he began staying with his friend Phil Hollar. On the two or three days a week that he had classes, Tom commuted back to school. He would attend his classes, go to the library and then get someone to put him in his car so he could sleep. Sometimes in the car. He would get somebody to get him out of his car and into his wheelchair when he arrived in the mornings. He did not believe in divorce, but he could not go home.

But the discord continued, and our sister Martha, a nurse, came to live with him and care for him. Pat came to where they were staying from time to time, always very angry at both of them. Neither could speak peaceably to one another. Martha worked part-time at the veteran's hospital while doing all she could to restore him spiritually and emotionally. Finally his wife allowed another man to move into Tom's house with her—someone else whose physical needs were less demanding. Soon after she filed for divorce.

At first, Tom fought the divorce proceedings and pleaded with the court to let them have some time together to try to work things out. The skeptical judge cautioned Tom though that if he contested it, and it was ultimately granted, he would have to pay all court costs. And he reminded Tom that "a woman convinced against her will remains unconvinced still."

Tom decided to let the divorce go through uncontested. At the proceedings he quoted to Pat, "In Acceptance Lieth Peace." It made her furious.

But Tom was also devastated in every way. For him, the tragedy of his marriage and the divorce were far harder to deal with than his broken neck had been. That was an accident for which he accepted God's sovereignty. But this was failure. Brewsters do not get divorced! He had failed his dad. He had failed God. He had failed his own convictions.

And Tom was disillusioned. He had thought he was in God's will. He was involved in Christian ministry. He had accepted a call to mission service. He had never asked God "why?" after the accident. But now he could not help it. He was convinced he was no longer fit for missionary service.

Years later Mona, herself going through a bitter marriage, asked him, "Why did you marry her?" He replied, "She was beautiful, she said she loved me and I didn't know if anyone ever would again."

After the divorce, he bravely carried on with his Masters program at Michigan State with Martha continuing to care for him. He found much comfort and solace in being able to reach out to hurting patients at the VA hospital. He was loved by the patients, especially for his ability to relate to those with depression. He could say "I understand, I've been there," and the patients knew that it was genuine.

During a break, Tom and Martha drove down to Chicago and went to the Pacific Garden Mission. Since he had no idea what the next steps were for him, he was looking for a place where he could minister and be ministered to. He was impressed with the caring spirit there, but did not see how he could fit in, and it was obvious to him that, while he needed nurture, it was of a different sort than was offered there.

(While in Chicago, they stayed at a local YMCA where someone broke into their rooms and stole their money and some tailor-made suits that Tom had just picked up. Martha recalls that "Tom had the grace to laugh heartily when we thought about how those suits were made, specifically tailored to fit a guy in a wheelchair, not a standing person. I imagine those thieves were dumbfounded when they tried them on!")

Tom managed to finish his Masters program at Michigan State in early December of 1965, but his heart was not in it. The year Tom spent there in Master's work was a sad and desperately lonely time. Like Joseph in the Bible, he had been broken, used, then broken again. Now he was a shattered vessel. This was the lowest time of his life, much worse even than the emotional effects of becoming a cripple for life. More than once he even considered ending his life. Once he faced a cabinet full of medicines, tempted to choose some to end his embarrassment and grief. At his lowest point, Tom drove his car to the railroad tracks and parked there, blinded by tears, waiting for the train to come along and end it all.

"Can You Trust Me?"

In that fearsome moment, God spoke to him again. In reality, Tom was, quite understandably, trusting in himself and his own regained abilities and not in God for his affirmations, his independence, and his future. Jesus had said to Peter after the disillusionment of seeing Jesus die on the cross, "Do you love me?" This was as though God was saying the same thing to Tom. "Do you love *me*? Can you trust *me*? The arm of flesh will fail you. You know that. I allowed your broken neck to get your attention. Now I must break your 'stiff neck' to get your trust."

It was as though God trusted Tom enough to put him through a test of a true leader. "I don't want your broken body—I want your broken and bruised spirit to be wholly mine. Sure, you have plenty of reason to die. But do you trust me enough to find a reason to live? Even life is a choice. Will you trust me now—now before you see any fruit in your life? Will you choose to live and love and trust out of love, not just obligation?"

> Though the fig tree does not bud
>> and there are no grapes on the vines,
> though the olive crop fails and the fields produce no food,
> though there are no sheep in the pen
>> and no cattle in the stalls,
> yet I will rejoice in the Lord,
> I will be joyful in God my Savior.
>
> The Sovereign Lord is my strength;
>> he makes my feet like the feet of a deer,
>> he enables me to go on the heights. (Habbakuk 3:17–19 NIV)

Suddenly Tom realized again that God had already given him back his life a second time. And there had to be a purpose! Surely God could give him back his life yet again. Surely there was something more God had for him in life, and now he had to find out what that was. Suddenly he realized what he was doing and where he was. Marvelously, in later years he was able to tell Mona of the incident with his car on the railroad tracks and how he found himself wet as a dish rag, yelling, "Yes, God, I want to live!" as he frantically fumbled with the car keys and spun off and away from the tracks.

A New Start

The process of healing was not over though. Tom still had to find himself again. To restore his confidence and sense of direction. He found solace and comfort with old friends near Memphis, Phil and Nona Carlson. He was more at peace, but what to do now? Fortunately his basic financial needs were met, thanks to his disability allowance from Social Security and insurance payments. He did not have any excess, but he was able to get by, and being naturally frugal, have enough left over for study and travel.

He decided that he'd had enough of Michigan, enough of the bad experience, and enough of the cold. He had heard about a place in Guadalajara, Mexico that was a care center for people in wheel chairs. Tom was only twenty-seven, but he felt like a crippled old man.

On December 18, 1965, Tom bought a ticket, had someone get him to the airport and onto the plane, and flew to Mexico. Alone. He had arranged for a missionary there to meet him and get him to the care center. All Tom wanted to do was to thaw out and get into a corner with God.

There was care and company at the care center, but not the kind that interested Tom. There were a lot of other guys in wheel chairs but all they could think of to do was sit around and drink beer. And talk about the girls. And gamble. No one even wanted to play chess. They had nothing in common.

One day his missionary friend told him of a language school for missionaries there in Guadalajara. Being around Christians again, and the opportunity to begin to learn Spanish was appealing to Tom, so he decided to join the school. He left the center and moved into Motel Santos that had apartments about three blocks from school. Being closer to the school was important since he did not have his car. He also did not have an attendant of any sort to care for him—nobody at all.

After the first day of classes he got someone to push him back to the apartment, and then he waited—and prayed—for someone to come along to help him. When evening came he laid his Bible on the table, opened to Matthew 6, and read aloud the passage about God clothing the flowers and taking care of the birds:

> Therefore I tell you, do not worry about your life, what you will eat or drink; or about your body, what you will wear. Is not life more important than food, and the body more important than clothes? Look at the birds of the air; they do not sow or reap or store away in barns, and yet your heavenly Father feeds them. Are you not much more valuable than they? . . . And why do you worry about clothes? See how the lilies of the field grow. They do not labor or spin. Yet I tell you that not even Solomon in all his splendor was dressed like one of these. If that is how God clothes the grass of the field, which is here today and tomorrow is thrown into the fire, will he not much more clothe you, O you of little faith? So do not worry, saying 'What shall we drink?' or 'What shall we wear?' . . . your heavenly Father knows that you need them. But seek first his kingdom and his righteousness, and all these things will be given to you as well (Matthew 6:25–33, NIV).

He said to the Lord, "Lord, you know I've got to be fed and clothed. You know I can't do it myself. I have no one."

He left his Bible open on the table and nobody came. He managed to get a pillow off the bed and put it on the table. He slept with his head on the pillow on the table. The next morning when he was rereading those verses, a young man by the name of Heliodoro Anaya (nicknamed Lolo), came to the door looking for work. Lolo was a young Mexican lad about eighteen years old. Tom spoke only a few words of Spanish. Lolo did not speak any English. Tom managed to communicate to him a request to help him wash up because it was time for school. Lolo got Tom some breakfast, washed him up and got him ready for school. Tom trusted him to come back in the evening—and he did. After that Lolo came by every day and worked for Tom for over three years.

Tom eventually led Lolo to the Lord, and he became a joyous and vibrant Christian. It was a delight to watch his spiritual growth. Lolo invited Tom to come to his house to meet with his family and relatives. At one point during the visit Lolo said to Tom, "You can talk about the Word of God here." Tom thanked him and told him he appreciated it, and carried on socializing. About fifteen minutes later Lolo said the same thing and asked Tom why he did not get on with sharing the Gospel! That began what developed into a weekly Bible study in Lolo's part of town in which several of his friends and neighbors came to Christ in spite of Tom's faulty Spanish (T. Brewster 1966).

Tom taught Lolo the chorus "Jesus Loves Me" in Spanish. That song did not fully express Lolo's feelings, so he rewrote it to express his own feelings. Soon he began writing choruses on his own. Actually, he did not know how to write either the words or the music, but he would play them on his guitar and sing them the same way every time. His songs were very country Mexican in rhythm and tune, which Tom enjoyed very much. (Unfortunately, the staff at the language school mostly found them *"demasiado Mexicano"*—too Mexican!)

5
BETTY SUE—A TRUE SERVANT

"Tom, no matter what lies ahead of us, I pledge to you my life as your loving, obedient, faithful wife, that 'whither you go, I will go, where you lodge I will lodge, your people shall be my people,' for your God is my God" (E. Brewster 1967).

"When you detest someone, even the way he folds his napkin can be an irritant. But when you love someone he can do anything—he can even pour his soup in his lap—and it just endears him to you all the more. Tom was endeared to me. It was my pleasure to serve him" (E. Brewster c1987).

Betty Sue Green was born in Cleveland on May 31, 1943, during her parents' furlough from missionary work in Venezuela. It was during the war and her parents could not get a visa so they went to Arizona for two years before returning to Venezuela. Betty Sue lived in Venezuela until she was sixteen except for furloughs. And, with the exception of second and seventh grades, she was home schooled all the way through high school.

Her parents were planting churches in a team ministry.

She knew she wanted to serve the Lord but did not know where or what and so she told her mission's professor at one point in Bible college that she thought she wanted to be a Bible translator. A few days later he came back to her. "My wife and I have been talking about you," he said, "and we don't think you have what it takes to be a linguist. We think you ought to try something else."

Betty Sue figured that must be of the Lord, so she spent quite a bit of time reconsidering and trying to find something else to do. She tried all sorts of doors and none of them seemed to be opening; so in desperation, she decided to apply to the same board that her parents were with. On March 25, 1965, she was commissioned as a missionary. At that point she did not sense a strong call to Venezuela, but that was the door that seemed to be open. As part of the acceptance process, they gave all candidates the Modern Language

Aptitude Test. Betty Sue took it, thinking she would fail it completely. But she blew the top out of it, and that changed things.

"Have you ever considered being a linguist?"

"Have you ever considered being a linguist?" her supervisor asked. She told him that she had but had dropped the idea. "I think you should reconsider," he said—and that summer they sent her to Summer Institute of Linguistics (SIL) in Norman, OK. She loved it! Then, just when it looked like she would go ahead with a career in translation work, another problem arose. They wrote her saying, "Our board has decided that we won't send any single women out as Bible translators because of the risk involved." And the door was closed to go to Venezuela as a Bible translator.

That fall she went back to school at the Baptist Bible College in New York and took a few more courses. In December the mission board wrote and told her of a language school in Guadalajara that had just opened. They asked her to attend for a term or two, partly to refresh her Spanish but mostly to evaluate the school. She was interested, perhaps mainly because she had nothing else to do.

They met at the language school on January 2, 1966, in Guadalajara. The first meeting was outside the school where Betty Sue was sitting in a car and turned around to see another car drive up behind her and park. It had a nice looking guy sitting in the passenger's seat. Betty Sue said to herself, "There's the man I'm going to marry." And then she said to herself, "Oh come on, you're getting to really be an old maid when you say that about every guy you see!" Then she saw the wheel chair and really laughed.

Tom was beginning to put his life back together. He taught a group of young people from time to time and displayed his usual creativity. Kay Arthur, now the director of Precept Ministries, was a missionary in Guadalajara at the time and remembers one of Tom's lessons. He had a jar full of watch parts which he was slowly shaking back and forth as he spoke. "The evolutionists tell me that if I keep shakin' this long enough, I'll have a watch that runs," he said. "I guess I'll just keep on shakin'. Just shakin' and shakin'." He kept it "shakin" throughout the lesson. At the end he expressed mock surprise that his watch was not running yet. "Guess I'll just keep shakin'," he said as the young people left.

Tom had not been at the school very long—he had not even finished the first term when, in the spring of 1966, the director, Nathan Booth, asked if he would set up counseling for local missionaries and help direct the school. Tom did not have much administrative experience but he had done a lot of counseling as an intern in Michigan. It was Booth's intention that Tom would eventually set up a counseling center for missionaries.

Tom put a fleece before the Lord that if he was going to do that he would need support from the States because he was running out of money. And he thought it might be a good idea to bring his car down. (When he told Betty that had a car, she thought he was joking. She did not have a clue he could drive. She was impressed!) In just a few days, he got a letter from a lawyer in the States saying that someone had been in a very similar accident to his and would he come and give testimony to the fact that it was the slide that caused the injury. They said they would pay his air fare. When he got there, it turned out that he was not needed in the court case after all, but the lawyer paid his expenses anyway. Tom asked Martha to accompany him back down to Mexico in his car.

After that first term there were a couple of months left before it was time for Betty to go to SIL, so she worked for Tom during those months. She was concerned about what she would do after SIL Tom had set up a little counseling office and she went into his office and told him how worried she was about going away to school and not knowing what she was going to do afterward. Tom asked her, "Has the Lord been faithful to you in the past? Then you don't need to worry about the present."

For you too, "In Acceptance Lieth Peace"

Tom quoted for her the poem that had already so influenced his own life: "In acceptance lieth peace, oh my heart be still. . . ."

Betty typed the poem and put it up in her own room when she went back to Norman for a second summer of SIL in 1966. Consciously she was not thinking about Tom, but sub-consciously he was all she was thinking about. She talked about him all the time. (Later she got letters from a couple of gals that she had gotten really close to that summer, and one of them laughingly wrote, "I knew all summer long that you were in love, but you didn't have a clue that you were. All you talked about was Tom.") Betty Sue says the only thing she remembers saying about Tom was that she thought he was a great guy who would make somebody a wonderful husband—if he was willing to marry.

At the end of the summer when she still did not know what to do, she wrote to the mission board and they suggested that she go back to the school and work there.

In September, Betty Sue returned to Guadalajara. She did various things for Tom, so he took her to church and arranged to go places and they were together quite a bit. Before long she was working entirely for him. They were in charge of sectioning the students, assigning the teachers to rooms, and in charge of the library. She took over the job of cooking lunch for him and doing his wash. It was a convenience for both of them. And Betty was getting to exercise a spiritual gift which she had in unique measure—the gift of helps and doing things for people.

Up to that point they had gone everywhere together, just because he had a car and she did not. But Tom's attraction to this pretty, petite, brunette was growing. Growing enough to worry him. Could he handle another intimate relationship? And even if he could, should he put someone else through the stress of living with and caring for a quadriplegic? Worst of all, how would she react when she learned about his previous marriage? Just prior to their first "formal" date, they were browsing through some pictures of Tom when he was a little boy. In the warmth of their pleasant conversation, Tom began to bare his heart and soul about his first marriage and divorce.

Just as Tom had feared, Betty was shocked. She had not realized yet how deep her feelings had become, but was beginning to realize there was something there. She cried all night. But not just for herself. She cried because she realized what deep hurts there were for Tom and his former wife.

Coming from such a conservative background, it was devastating. She remembered when her brother was dating someone who was divorced, and how she had spoken to him against it. She had given him many verses in the Bible showing why marriage after divorce could not be done.

Now, however, it seemed different. Together and alone over the next weeks they talked and prayed for guidance from the Lord. By November it was becoming clear to both of them that theirs was to be more than just a casual relationship. Because of their strong fundamentalist backgrounds, the issue of remarriage after divorce was a real dilemma for them. Both wrestled with it in their hearts and minds but more and more became convinced that God had provided a way out for them in that Pat had been unfaithful in the last months of Tom's marriage with her. God gave them the peace and release in their hearts on the matter.

One night on their way to practice a Christmas program, a John Peterson cantata, they had a few minutes to spare so drove to a quiet "talking" spot at the edge of town. Feeling rather low, Tom said something about having led her on since anything serious between them would be so complicated. To the shock of both of them, Betty Sue leaned over and kissed him. A few days later Tom said to her, "I guess I should propose to you." And Betty Sue said, "Yep, I guess you should." Tom: "Well, will you marry me?" "*Con gusto!*" [with pleasure]. After they kissed Betty Sue began to giggle and had to explain. As a child, her family had bought a brand of tinned butter called "Gusto" (literally pleasure, or good taste), but it was always a bit rancid tasting. They had had a family joke whenever asked to do anything—"Sure, con gusto—with rancid butter!" She was embarrassed at having responded to her wedding proposal with rancid butter!

The engagement was announced in early December, 1966 at a Christmas party at a friend's house, just as the school term ended. In typical fashion, they wanted to announce it in an unusual way. Tom and Betty Sue sat down and wrote a puzzle—a super secret code—and arranged a contest for the guests to find out what the secret message was. The answer to the puzzle was kind of a shock to a lot of people because they did not even know Tom and Betty were dating. Oddly enough, some were even offended.

Some of Betty Sue's friends were skeptical. One told her, "Oh, Betty Sue, you are just going to be so bored sitting in one place all your life and taking care of Tom. You're never going to go anywhere. You are just going to be so bored!" Betty says she was never bored, and she certainly did not sit in one place all her life!

It was important though for Betty to know just what she was getting into in marrying a quadriplegic. She was small, just over five feet and only 100 pounds. Tom could not get himself into or out of bed, or into or out of a car or even to his own wheel chair. He could not take care of most of his body functions by himself. She would need to be his "attendant" almost around the clock. Was she ready for all of this?

Be My Valentine!

Because the early stages of their relationship had been so casual and she did not realize how serious they were, Betty had not written to her parents about Tom until they were engaged. Now here she was, twenty-three years old, getting engaged to a twenty-seven year old divorced "somebody" they had never heard of who was in a wheel chair. It was no way to help in-laws be happy. "Come home," they urged, "Let's talk about it!" They even offered to pay her way home.

Tom and Betty Sue decided to go to the States together and first meet with some of Tom's family and friends. Again, not all were convinced that the marriage was the right thing to do. One of Tom's old friends who had married a man confined to a wheelchair but who was now separated from him advised Betty Sue *not* to marry Tom because she felt taking care of the needs of a person in a wheelchair was just too demanding. Later, Tom took Betty Sue aside and very soberly offered her freedom based on what she had said. Betty Sue told him that if he could live long term *in* a wheelchair, she was sure she could live long term *with* the wheelchair.

Betty Sue went on to New York where her parents consented to her plans for marriage. Her mother even took Betty Sue shopping for a bridal gown. They found a lovely one that was slightly torn but on sale for only $12! Someone had ripped it, and it was a little dirty, and sleeveless, which was not the style for wedding dresses at the time. But the tear was in the hem and the dress was too long for her, so a seamstress cut the ripped hem off, re-hemmed it, put in some sleeves and Betty Sue thought it was perfect.

Back in Colorado, Tom and Betty Sue got their blood tests but could not get a marriage license because they were not residents. On their return to Mexico they drove through a little town named Alice Springs, Texas, where they got a marriage license.

However, when they read the fine print they discovered that the license had to be used within fourteen days. They went to Nathan Booth who agreed to conduct a "preliminary" ceremony as long as they realized that from that moment they were legally married. They would not live together until the official wedding date of February 14, 1967. The private ceremony was conducted in Tom's office with a friend, Sharon Chisom and Lolo present as witnesses.

Booth wrote later: "[Lolo] was puzzled about his boss getting married and not taking his new bride home with him! They tried to explain, but all he could do was shake his head" (1993). Crazy gringos! They kept it a secret and exactly a month later, on February 14th—Valentine's Day—had the church wedding in the Baptist church, the only wheelchair accessible church around.

Tom knew more Spanish by then, so the ceremony, and music were in both Spanish and English. The whole wedding cost under $50. They did not have money for a fancy cake, so they had a baker make a bunch of loaf cakes, put them together and decorate it with a verse on top: "O magnify the Lord with me and let us exalt His name together" (Psalm 34:3 KJV). It had a little bride and groom on top and one of the little kids came up and stared at it for a long time before concluding, "That's not Uncle Tom—he can't stand up."

For the honeymoon they went along the coast of Mexico down to Baranquilla and Barra de Navidad, staying in hotels that had only cold water. On one of the afternoons they bravely went "swimming" in the surf. Betty Sue got Tom out of his wheelchair and they sat on the sand at the edge of the water letting the wavelets lap at their feet. Suddenly a large wave came and engulfed them. Betty Sue grabbed Tom tightly by the shoulders so he would not be washed out to sea. The wave lifted him and turned him around nearly out of Betty Sue's grasp. By the time the wave receded, he had lost his glasses and almost lost his pants. Betty Sue feared for a moment that it was going to be a quick end to their honeymoon.

"It Was My Pleasure to Serve Him"

Tom was definitely "surprised by joy" in meeting Betty Sue. When he left Michigan he was sure he had felt the last of romantic delights. He felt he was a doctrinal disgrace because of his divorce. He had thought there was nothing left.

Before his divorce, Tom had been trusting in himself. He believed in God, but in reality he had been relying on his own resourcefulness to cope, perhaps in super-human ways with his physical condition. The crushing blow of divorce had shattered his confidence.

> A bruised reed he will not break, and a smoldering wick he will not snuff out. (Isaiah 42:3 NIV)

Tom was a bruised reed. But now his focus had changed. Instead of needing "somebody," he now knew that he really needed only God. And just when he thought there was nothing left for him, when he thought that his "wick" had been snuffed out, God saw that it was still smoldering, and surprised him with his lifelong treasure, Betty Sue.

To all who have gotten to know Betty Sue over the years, she is the epitome of a servant. In a sense, Betty Sue laid her life down for Tom. She put aside (potentially at least) her education, her training, and ambition to be a translator, and, some would argue, her freedom, to be the arms and legs for a man who could not walk, dress himself, or even go to the bathroom by himself.

For the next nineteen years she dressed him every morning and put him to bed every night, and turned him during the night, every night. In their travels to over eighty countries around the world she put him in and out of his wheelchair, of plane seats, and every other form of transportation; she packed their bags and carried their luggage (and later on their young son) to and from the connections. It took them extra time to do everything they did because she had to do it for both of them.

It was not an easy task. Tom was often so engaged with what he was doing, that he could be oblivious to the feelings of others. I knew, as did anyone else who ever had the opportunity to do things with and for Tom, that he could be very demanding, persistent, and impatient. He could, in fact, be a nuisance. But if Betty Sue ever noticed that, she never let it be known to anyone else. Over the years I and others had many opportunities to work with Tom and Betty Sue over long periods of time, and I can honestly say that I never once saw her lose her temper or in any way express frustration or exasperation at meeting his varied, frequent and sometimes demanding needs.

Mona remembers a time in their home when Betty Sue was looking for something on a stool in another room in a closet. Tom dropped his pencil and called for Betty Sue to come and get it for him. She did so and then went back to the closet. Then Tom had another need and again she came running. When it happened a third time, Mona upbraided Tom for being so demanding and impatient. Betty Sue told Mona to relax—that it was OK.

Betty Sue explained later that she always tried to put herself in Tom's shoes. "Think of being in the middle of a thought," she said, "and dropping your pencil and not being able to complete it and there is nothing you can do but ask someone for help. Think how frustrating that would be. As I remember that I can pick up my pencils and he can't, I *choose* to help him. It's my choice."

In fact, for her it was a true joy. She put it this way:

> Sometimes people would look at me as though I was some saint or martyr, but it was always a joy for me to serve Tom. Some saw the work and pitied me. I saw the rewards and was content and happy. I delighted even in such little things as bringing him a glass of water. Some wives would say get it yourself, but I always *wanted* to do it (c.1987).

When they were first married, Tom had to adjust his understandings to Betty Sue's response patterns. Naturally he expected

Betty Sue to react in the same way his first wife had, and he sometimes misunderstood her good will. Once he went ahead with something that Betty Sue advised against and it did not turn out well. After a while Tom asked her, "So when are you going to tell me 'I told you so'?" He was surprised and relieved when he learned that "I told you so" was not in her vocabulary. He always felt it was so much easier listening to her point of view since he knew she was not going to make an issue of it if a decision turned out wrong.

Perhaps Tom and Betty Sue's marriage had its highs and lows. To all observers the relationship seemed always on a high. Indeed, it was a very romantic relationship. Tom was great at remembering to do and say the little things that kept their marriage fresh. He even instituted a celebration of each "month-iversary" and they had big celebrations with friends on their 50th and their 100th.

Later in Tom's life he and Betty Sue would be instrumental in forming a new mission organization called "*Servants Among the Poor.*" But long before God put that into place, Betty Sue was modeling servanthood on a personal, day-to-day basis. The Lord had prepared Betty Sue for just such a role. Her idea of Biblical womanhood was to find someone she could pour her life into. Betty Sue knew that the essence of love is to serve, not to be served, "*for even the Son of Man came to serve and to give. . . .*" (Mark 10:42). She had an understanding of what it meant to be a true servant, to gain fulfillment not from independence but in dependence and service. She chose to lay down her life so that Tom could be successful.

And in fact, they both were able to use the training and skills that God had given them in marvelous ways. For Tom, the speaking, counseling and psychology training always served him well. And Betty Sue's linguistics background provided the professional spark for much of their later teaching and writing. But more than this, they both chose to give of themselves—to incarnate themselves as servants among the poor.

Jesus was the model for servanthood. But in my mind, and in the minds of many others who knew her, Betty exemplified that servanthood as well as anyone we ever met.

PART II
THE MINISTRY AND THE MESSAGE

6
MINISTRY FOUNDATIONS

> Before long it was clear. Tom and I were both like prospectors
> looking for gold. . . . Each was quick to recognize how much there
> was to learn from the other. . . . Tom quickly recognized ways and
> means of "demystifying" some of TIL's technical detail, and giving
> greater attention to aspects of learning which we had neglected to
> see (Larson 1994).

The years 1967–1971 were formative in shaping a career that
would follow in language learning and missions strategy.

For the first year after their marriage, Tom continued the counseling program for the missionaries at the Spanish Language
School, and helped administer the school while Betty Sue also
helped with administration and teacher training. He made friends
with the students and they accepted him as their friend. Tom was
in his late 20s, just like most of the missionary learners, and there
was a warm camaraderie. He did not dwell on his wheelchair and
did not expect others to either. "Tom accepted his condition grace-
fully and wanted others to do the same. Once he said, 'When
somebody begins calling me the 'wheel,' I know he has accepted me
in my situation'" (Booth 1993).

During that time Tom and Betty got to know some friends outside of the language school, who would play an important part in
Tom's further rehabilitation and understanding of what was really
possible for him as a quadriplegic. "Buzz" (real name Gerald)
Lugenbeel was himself a quadriplegic with even less recovered
movement than Tom had. He had moved to Mexico after his own
injury and married Mica, a sweet and, like Betty, infinitely patient
and caring young "señorita." In spite of his handicap, Buzz was
very active and extremely creative in learning to do things that
quadriplegics "could not" do.

When they first met, Buzz and Mica lived in a little *hacienda* outside of Guadalajara to which, with the help of others, he had attached an aviary with a huge variety of native birds. In the back of the house he had a workshop with a lathe, casting molds for bronze, and lots of clay figures he had sculpted. He shaped chess pieces on the lathe with tools and stabilizers he had designed, did wood carving, sculpting, casting and other creative pursuits.

Tom was active before meeting Buzz, but it was Buzz who had opened up a wide range of other interests for Tom that he never dreamed he could do. Tom respected and admired Buzz's independence (one time he even refused to accept a raise in his government disability check), his acceptance of his handicap, and his innovative approaches to dealing with his limitations. He loved to share his projects, and taught Tom how to hold and manipulate wood and clay. Tom tried his hand at other creative arts as well. He did not have the artistic skills Buzz did, but Betty still wears as a necklace a beautiful wooden heart which he spent scores of hours shaping, sanding and polishing to smooth perfection.

Tom and Betty spent lots of time with Buzz and Mica. Tom and Buzz loved playing chess together, and used it as an opportunity to discuss issues of every sort. In fact, they disagreed about many things, but would often take different sides of an issue just to have a good strong argument. Perhaps their greatest area of real disagreement was on spiritual issues. In the years that followed, every time they got together, the discussions turned to spiritual issues, but Buzz never budged from his firm humanistic convictions.

Tom and Betty stayed in Mexico having their ideas shaped by their involvement with the Spanish Language School of Guadalajara. Tom said later that while they worked diligently at that time, they discovered that they did not know what they were doing. It was clear, he said, that they had to go back to school.

The University of Texas was their first choice, but they would not accept Betty Sue's undergraduate credits from the Baptist Bible College in Johnson City New York. ("Sure we'll take you if you will enroll as a freshman!") After shopping around for the right place, they inquired at the University of Arizona where the registrar was a bit kinder to Betty Sue. He said they could only accept her on probation, since the U of A did not recognize the Baptist Bible College credits. But, given her academic record, she qualified for a full academic scholarship. So she was in the unusual position of being on academic probation but with a full scholarship. They settled then on the U of A, and returned to Guadalajara for a further term at the Spanish Language school, planning to return to Tucson in January of 1968.

The Toronto Institute of Linguistics

While they were in Mexico, they read a short little ad about the Toronto Institute of Linguistics, a unique one month long language and culture learning program for missionaries about to go overseas for the first time. The principal, Don Larson, says it may have been the only advertisement TIL ever published. Tom and Betty felt that this was what the language school in Guadalajara was lacking. Betty wrote and asked for the culture learning book list from TIL so that they could use it in Mexico. Larson said they did not have a book list but that they would be welcome to come and "observe" during the coming month of June.

Perfect! The month long format would give them just the amount of exposure they wanted, and the timing before the next sessions at the school would work out fine. TIL was to become one of the most significant building blocks for Tom and Betty Sue's future ministry.

They went to Toronto assuming they were just going to observe. But they did not know Don Larson. For him, "participant observation" meant being part of the process, to teach, experiment and challenge learners to face themselves and the realities of language and culture learning. Numerous creative minds such as Eugene Nida, Bill Reyburn, Bill Smalley, and Chuck Kraft had been involved in making TIL an innovative and stimulating environment for new missionaries. Under Don's brilliant leadership, experimentation continued all the time, and "observers" helped make it happen. Lessons were developed and modified practically before each session. Tom and Betty Sue, along with sharp new thinkers such as Dave McClure and Dwight Gradin, made TIL an environment bubbling with language and culture learning ideas, and a fertile place to experiment and test theory and practice.

Tom had never taken a phonetics course but as part of the faculty, he was expected to teach phonetics. With her studies at SIL and her natural aptitude, Betty Sue was an expert. And in a beautiful demonstration of their relationship and her servant spirit, every night she taught Tom the next day's phonetics lesson and made sure he was ready to teach it. On weekends he listened to the tapes and they would try to get two or three lessons ahead.

The "Learning Cycle," "Becoming Bi-lingual," and other resources which in future years would be a mainstay of the course work at TIL, were still being developed. Every afternoon the teachers met to practice phonetics. The evenings were filled with discussions on the content and methodology for teaching language and culture learning. Improvisation and instant responsiveness to student needs was all important.

In this hectic but innovative environment, Tom and Betty Sue learned much about missionary language learning needs as well as how to address them. The Don Larson concepts of "awareness of squareness," (awareness of ones own culture and biases), "bi-passing," (thoughts on moving and communicating effectively between cultures), and the "Learning Cycle" became important tools in their tool kit for teaching and counseling language learners in future years.

Tom and Betty Sue loved Don's insights on the barriers to effective missionary language learning, and his quirky but always creative ways of expressing them. Don cautioned against "narrogance," the combination of narrow-mindedness and arrogance that prevents many Americans from taking people of other societies seriously and hampers involvement with them in ways that would build trust and friendships. And he lamented the "insulperiority" of many missionaries—the combination of a superior attitude and the resultant insulation that once again inhibits involvement.

They agreed with Don that most missionaries have bad cases of "monolingual myopia." Don called this a "disease of the tongue that affects the vision"—the unwillingness or inability of many missionaries to learn the languages of the people with whom they worked, with the result that they must lower their sights for effective communication of the gospel.

Tom and Betty Sue became part of the team with Don and the others in pioneering "relational" language learning approaches by having students go out into the ethnically diverse communities of Toronto, learning introductory phrases in some of the many languages found in abundance there.

In that first of what became eleven consecutive summers at TIL, they learned much about how languages ought to be learned, and confirmed their impressions drawn from experiences with the Spanish Language School in Guadalajara, about the ineffectiveness of most approaches to language learning. Much of their early emphasis on language learning tools and techniques grew out of the rich environment of TIL during their years teaching there with Don and his colleagues. They also got a taste of missions and missions thinking through interaction with the many missionary candidates who came through and in discussions with missions' representatives. Perhaps just as importantly, there was a foreshadowing of a need that they could meet.

Paying Their Academic Dues

In the fall of 1968, Tom continued his doctoral course work at the University of Arizona while Betty Sue worked on her Masters. Tom was still interested in the difference that attitude can make in the lives of individuals, and his dissertation drew again on the writing of Victor Frankl. Tom had originally wanted his dissertation topic to compare the attitude and personality characteristics of born-again Christians vs. non-Christians, but his committee would not tolerate such a religious topic. They had him change it to a study of giving versus. receiving-oriented individuals.

He got what he wanted anyway though, by choosing as his giving-oriented test group, missionaries, missionary candidates and Christian nurses. He chose welfare recipients for his receiving-oriented group. His premise was that "[d]eep satisfaction in life does not consist in what we receive, but rather, in what we give. Conversely, to pursue satisfaction, happiness, or meaning for one's life amounts to a self contradiction, for the more one strives the less he attains" (1971:1). He agreed with John Gardener that "[young people] today . . . [are] misled by the juvenile interpretation of the 'pursuit of happiness'" (1963:96), since happiness must be a byproduct of life endeavors rather than the end in itself. Tom believed what Paul writes in 2 Corinthians 5:17, "Therefore, if any one is in Christ, he is a new creation . . ." and set out to prove it in his dissertation. His purpose was to test whether the difference that Christ made in a person's life was psychologically measurable, according to the widely used and accepted Minnesota Multiphasic Personality Inventory (MMPI).

Along with their classes, Tom and Betty Sue both worked, Tom in the Rehabilitation Counseling office, and Betty Sue as a phonetics teaching assistant in the Anthropology department.

Betty Sue finished her Masters work at the University of Arizona in May 1969, majoring in Latin American Studies, Spanish literature, and Linguistics. Tom also completed his doctoral course work that spring. However, they still had a language requirement to meet, and decided to do it in French.

Quebec seemed an ideal place to study, being French speaking and close to Toronto. I was in college at Colorado State University at the time, and that summer, Tom asked me if I would like to join them in Quebec. I could learn a little French myself, help them out with some of the "tossing about" that might need to be done, and have a nice vacation as well. I was happy to join them then, that summer of '69. Our time in Quebec was characteristic of Tom and Betty's many "mini-vacations." In spite of a very busy schedule practically all the time, Tom never hesitated to take time off, especially if there was something new or unusual to see or do. He knew how to balance life's demands. We drove together to the little town of Ville Marie in the Quebec wilderness where we rented a small cottage on the spectacular shores of Lake Temiscaming. There we listened to French tapes from the Defense Language Institute, and used our minimal French with the occasional visitors.

That month of July, 1969 was also filled with unforgettable early morning excursions out on to the lake for incredible fishing. In late July, we moved to a very small motel that had what passed for a TV and watched in awe the fuzzy pictures of a man named Armstrong take man's first steps on the moon.

That fall, they moved all their belongings in a small trailer to Austin, Texas, where Tom could finish up his doctoral thesis and Betty Sue would enroll in her own doctoral program. Betty Sue had reapplied to the University of Texas to do course work for her doctorate in Foreign Language Education. They had not accepted her bachelor's degree, but one and a half years later she was there with a Master's degree in Latin American Studies with concentrations in Spanish Literature and Anthropology/Linguistics, and no questions were asked.

On the way to Austin, pulling a trailer with all their belongings, (just as had happened with me years before), Betty Sue nearly flipped the car. Tom was driving, and he asked her to take the wheel for a moment. Betty Sue misinterpreted the urgency of the situation and grabbed it too quickly, jerking the car to the right and violently swinging the trailer from side to side. Overcompensating back to the left, the trailer started to fishtail. Tom grabbed the wheel again and somehow managed to get the car and the trailer straightened out. There was no harm done, but it was a reminder again of Tom's limitations and vulnerabilities as a quadriplegic.

A Medical Glitch . . . and Shadow of Things to Come

Soon after their arrival, they got another reminder. After the bags were unpacked, they took a trip down to Houston to watch a baseball game in the Astrodome. Tom started having chills and running a fever during the game and it became clear that he was getting very sick. Betty Sue took him back to Austin and the next day he was admitted to the hospital. It was their first week in Austin, and Betty Sue did not know anyone to call on for prayer or help. It was a lonely time for her.

It was also a dangerous time for Tom, and it reinforced a growing dislike of the medical establishment. The medical care they received during that crisis began to shape an impression of the medical establishment that stayed with Tom for the rest of his life. The doctors found they had to operate to remove some kidney stones. The difficult procedure required them to cut off a piece of rib and split open the kidney. Betty Sue waited in the hallway outside the operating room for hours, her anxiety increasing with every passing minute.

Finally she found a nurse who told her that the operation had been over for over an hour. They had already transferred Tom to the intensive care unit by another route. After another long delay, she was finally able to see him—but for only five minutes an hour. Tom was very uncomfortable and wanted Betty to be allowed to stay in the room to give him more frequent and loving care. Betty had by now been caring for him twenty-four hours a day for more than two years, and Tom felt that she could be more responsive than many of the nurses to his particular requirements. But the hospital had rules, you know! Eventually they did let Betty stay with Tom in a large recliner, through the remainder of quite a difficult recovery (E. Brewster 1970).

It was this sort of thing that began what later became a firmly held and often expressed distrust of doctors and of the medical establishment in general. Tom always felt that even though he was paralyzed, his body was his own and he should have a say in what doctors did to it. Tom knew he needed doctors and their skills and advice. But he also believed in himself and trusted his own judgment. He could not manage much of his body, but where he could be in control, he wanted to be truly in control. He strongly resented doctors who acted as if they were the only experts and they need not share their diagnoses or decisions with him. Over the years, he developed a remarkable sensitivity to the workings of his own body, and could fairly accurately detail what was going on. Occasionally, and more frequently in his later life, he understood better than the doctors the nature of problems he was experiencing.

They completed the school year in Austin and then in the summer of 1970 returned to Tucson where they rented a cottage to continue Tom's dissertation work. During that visit, Tom nearly died. Betty Sue relates the story:

> One day I went to do some research for him at the library and he stayed home to study, as he often did. As usual, I called him after an hour or two to check on him and see if he needed me for anything. The phone rang and rang with no answer. I figured he might be temporarily unable to reach the phone, so I waited a few minutes and tried again. Still no answer. The third time I tried and didn't get him I became very concerned. I went right out to the car and drove home as fast as I legally could, praying all the way. I kept telling myself that there was a simple explanation, but I wasn't satisfied with any that came to mind. When I drove up in front of the house I could see Tom lying on the lawn with his head under a chair.
>
> Tom had gone to get the mail from our box at the street. On the way back he had gone off the edge of the sidewalk, been pitched out onto the grass. He had managed to pull his chair toward him to give him a slight bit of shade, but he had been lying there in the very hot Arizona summer sun for quite a while. I quickly got him back into his chair and rolled him inside to cool off with cool washcloths. He had a fierce headache the rest of the day, felt very weak, and was rather sunburned, but otherwise was not harmed. It could have been much worse considering how unstable and volatile the temperature-regulating mechanism of a spinal cord injured person can be (E. Brewster 1992).

Good-bye Guadalajara

After spending the Fall of 1970 in Austin, they returned to Guadalajara in December. Tom and Betty Sue had been invited to return and got the distinct impression that the Dr. Booth was wanting to be relieved of the responsibilities of running the school. They offered to administer the school, a move unfortunately viewed by some of the board members as a kind of take-over.

Not surprisingly, they made some enemies. It may be an understatement to say that (like Dad) Tom could be quite abrasive.

When he had something in mind, he often was not subtle. When Tom felt strongly about something, he was very forthright, often with little regard for people's sensitivities. And this was one of those occasions.

Tom said that there was to be an audit. This made a few people very nervous. Later on they found out why that made them nervous. Tom and Betty Sue were new faces now, and did not know whose toes must not be stepped upon. The sensitive toes turned out to belong to the same person who had objected to the audit.

Regardless of what the audit revealed, it was time to move on and close the door on a formative five years of involvement with the Spanish Language School. Surely it was God's sovereignty that had taken Tom to Mexico in his hour of despair, and led him to the school. He had not gone there to teach, much less to be involved in the leadership of the school nor to draw from his experiences there the insights and inspiration for a lifelong ministry of helping new missionaries communicate more effectively through better language learning and communication. But, just as surely, that was part of God's plan.

Their leaving was traumatic and for a time they felt almost abandoned by the Lord. An old missionary man in Guanajuato, Mexico ministered to them. He urged them to have an attitude of reconciliation and remember that the Lord was in control. Quoting Hebrews 12:15, *"Beware lest a root of bitterness spring up and thereby many be defiled,"* he brought them back to equilibrium and encouraged them both to forgive deeply no matter what had happened or what the motives.

Their experiences at the Spanish Language School and at TIL led Tom and Betty Sue to begin thinking about establishing language schools in many parts of the world. They incorporated and set up the Evangelical Language Institutes for Missionaries (ELIM) at that time. At the time they felt they might like to set up language schools all over the world using adaptations of the Defense Language Institute materials. They sent out questionnaires to mission boards all over the world inquiring about their language learning needs, methods, and interest in new possibilities. The response was promising. Under the umbrella of ELIM, Tom and Betty Sue were asked, but declined, to set up a language school in Indonesia.

As they prayed about it, they began to realize that in many languages of the world there would not be enough learners to run a school. Moreover, in many unevangelized areas of the world, there would be no freedom to establish one. They realized that their emphasis needed to be on training learners *how* to learn, rather than just setting up schools. Learners could then work in any environment regardless of the availability of an actual school setting. Both the incipient concern for the unreached peoples, and the insight about teaching learners how to learn were crucial keys to the ministry doors that God was opening for them.

"Ph.uD.y Duddys"

Though their lives were in turmoil during these months, Tom was still able to complete his work for his doctorate and defended his dissertation in May of 1971, and promptly labeled himself a "Ph.uD.y Duddy!" His research showed that there *were* measurable attitude and personality differences between giving and receiving oriented individuals and that these are statistically significant. Tom was interested in the characteristics of successful missionaries, and as part of the dissertation developed a seventy-two item questionnaire to measure these differences. He hoped that mission boards and personnel offices might be able to utilize his findings to help in missionary selection.

After finishing his dissertation, Tom decided to reward himself and Betty with a trip on a Poseidon line freighter loaded with heavy equipment up the St. Lawrence Seaway. They started in Quebec, went through various locks, picked up heavy equipment in Toronto, and wound up in the windy city of Chicago. It was a delightful and very relaxed time. It brought back to Betty Sue fond recollections of similar trips to the mission field when she was a child, and planted a desire to take an ocean trip together one day, an idea they inquired about in some of their ports of call, but for which they never found another opportunity.

In the Fall of 1971, Betty Sue still had her dissertation to finish. Her thesis was titled "Personality Characteristics Relevant to Intensive Audio-Lingual Foreign Language Learning." In it she compared the language aptitude of language learners with their actual language learning performance, and, using the Sixteen Personality Factor Questionnaire (16PF), she related the sixteen personality characteristics to language learning performance. Her objective was to help explain the fact that some learners with high aptitude did well in language learning, while some others with lower aptitude did better that expected. She had arranged with the Defense Language Institute of Monterey, California to do testing on students there. (Traveling to set up testing with those learners for a week was one of the very few times in their nineteen years of marriage that she was away from Tom.) Through her research, she found that there were significant personality differences between language-learners who performed well and those who did not, and concluded that these could also be used to predict language learning success.

She already had most of her data gathering and library work done when she found that if she could finish writing the dissertation in a month, she could graduate that year. If not, she would have to wait until the next year. They decided they would shoot for it. When they got the testing results back from Monterey they went to a little motel on the edge of a lake in Texas. There they coded the responses of hundreds of people who had responded to her questionnaire into a way that it could be put into a computer.

Betty Sue had typed the rough drafts for Tom's dissertation and now he typed hers. She wrote it all out in long-hand and he typed the rough draft—with one finger, on an IBM Selectric. And in a manner that set a pattern for the rest of their lives together, they decided that the best time of day to work was at night. In the day there were errands to run, phone calls to answer, and three meals to eat. They found at night they could work longer with fewer interruptions and did not feel they had to stop to eat. Better to get up late in the day and have their dinner and then work right through the night, going to bed about dawn. That way, too, they would only have to have one meal. They did this for a number of days, and they finished right at the wire.

Her research, too, provided significant insights into the work and directions for their future ministry. The research demonstrated that people who have certain personality characteristics tend to learn languages better than persons who do not have those characteristics. Tom and Betty felt that this research too would be valuable in the selection and training of personnel who have to learn foreign languages. If this personality test, combined with other tests such as aptitude and ability tests, indicated that a person would have difficulty in language learning, then a personnel office might be able to assign the individual to work in a location where he did not have to learn a new language.

Betty Sue defended her dissertation on November 23, 1971. The next day, they received a phone call from Bill Bright, the director of Campus Crusade for Christ.

7
MAKING THE GOSPEL MAKE SENSE

> Tom was fully aware, as most scholars were not, of the feasibility,
> of the possibility of thought for thought translations. Because of
> Tom and Betty Sue's friendship and encouragement, I was affirmed
> in going ahead with translation plans, despite much skepticism on
> the part of the missionary world, as well as opposition from many
> pastors (Ken Taylor).

Bill Bright was in Dallas and asked if they could come up and
see him and talk about their translation department. Betty Sue
had hardly heard of Campus Crusade.

On the other hand, Bright did not know much about Tom and
Betty Sue either. He had heard of them through a language school
director whom they had met in Cuernavaca, Mexico. Bright asked
them if they would be willing to take on a challenge—to see that
the *Four Spiritual Laws* booklet and other important Crusade
materials were translated into all the languages of the world!
When Tom asked him (respectfully) if he realized how many languages that would be, Bright replied that he did not but that it
was their business to find out.

They knew that the challenge was a lot bigger than they could
accomplish, but the visionary Bright appealed to the visionary in
Tom. Tom was always a visionary. It was something that both
attracted Betty Sue to Tom and also scared her to death. Over the
years, many of their projects were originally his conception and
many of them he brought her into "kicking and screaming." She
would say "we just can't do that, it's impossible, it's too big," and
he would convince her very carefully and very patiently over a
period of weeks that they could, and that the project could be
"theirs." Then she would help put the legs on the idea.

They agreed to pray about Bright's challenge. They were on
their way to Campus Crusade headquarters in Arrowhead Springs

by early January. Thus began the "translation" phase of their ministry which brought them into contact with the other (along with the Spanish Language School and TIL) significant people and organizations foundational to their later ministry.

The Literal Four Spiritual Laws

The Crusade translation task as they understood it was to develop translation workbooks to help structure and simplify the translation process, train the individuals who would actually carry out the translation in the other languages, and staff the translation department with whatever linguists, language specialists or cultural anthropologists might be needed to do the job.

Unfortunately, Tom and Betty Sue did not know what the Crusade translation policy was. They were dismayed when they learned about it.

The intent of the policy was to preserve faithfully not only the meaning of the Scriptures used, but also the meaning of the particular "Campus Crusade" type of presentation of the message to the unsaved. In order to preserve this meaning, it was assumed that every item had to be translated word for word, page for page and, yes, diagram for diagram from the original. The policy required then a very formal word-for-word translation. While Tom and Betty Sue had not learned much about translation yet, they both knew enough about languages to know that *meaningful* word-for-word translation was impossible. They knew that literal, word-for-word translations from one language to another will almost always be stilted and foreign and usually the meaning will be lost. To preserve the meaning, the "forms"—the way the material was presented—have to be changed.

It was not long before their fears were confirmed in a discussion with Andre Wrench concerning the Haitian translation from the French of the *Four Spiritual Laws*. Before she had had a chance to read it, she had given the booklet to 25 professional Frenchmen as an example of what Crusade was doing in French. Later she read it and "was horrified to think that she had given that booklet to them as an example of Crusade" (T. Brewster 1972).

Other similarly embarrassing examples emerged as they studied samples of Crusade translations from around the world. Tom and Betty were discouraged. What had they gotten themselves into? They did not feel they could be responsible for a program they did not fully believe in. "We can't do that," they said. "We'll just have to leave."

They went to Steve Douglas, their supervisor and told him that there was no way they could work with such a policy. "We cannot ethically live with a policy like this. It needs to change or we've got to leave." Steve said, "Just wait. We'll see what we can do."

This approach to translation was not unique to Campus Crusade. Word-for word literalness was perceived to equal accuracy in many ministries at the time. Ken Taylor's "Living Bible," with which Tom and Betty were soon to get involved, and which went much further than most translations in changing the "forms" to preserve the meanings and impact, was severely criticized in many circles. Virtually anyone who used it loved it (a group of millions of people), but learned to be careful to acknowledge that they knew that it was *just a paraphrase*—not a *real* translation.

Tom and Betty began two weeks' orientation and training with the Crusade staff. Immediately following the orientation they participated in a cross-cultural communications workshop for Campus Crusade, led by Don Smith. Don was the founder and Director of Daystar Communications, a unique research and consulting ministry which he had begun in Rhodesia and then moved to Nairobi, Kenya. Daystar was dedicated to helping missionaries and national church leaders do their job better, especially in the communication of the Gospel. One of the early emphases was to help missionaries and church leaders involved in the media such as radio broadcasting, Bible correspondence courses, literature production and translation work. The focus was on learning who your audience was and how to make your message understood. "Communication is what is heard—not just what is sent," Don would say, and participants learned to understand what was being heard by their listeners, rather than just focusing on the content of what they wanted to communicate.

Daystar was unique in Africa. The staff there conducted four week long training courses for people focusing on communications systems, cross-cultural communications, research techniques, the theory of missions and missiology, and statistics to enable them to analyze data that they would gather when they began their own research. Then they would be given assignments to apply what they were learning by tackling their own communication problems. Don's work had tremendous value in cross-cultural ministries, since the verbal and written language barriers are only two of the many communication barriers that confront the persons communicating the Gospel in cross-cultural contexts. For Tom and Betty Sue, this was seminal work that provided a wealth of insights.

Don's presence and lectures were used by the Lord to help Steve Douglas understand more of the nature of the concerns being raised by Tom about the Campus Crusade translation policies.

Non-Verbal Communication

It was immediately clear that Tom and Don were on the same wave-length. He was saying the exact things that they were trying to say—to communicate you cannot stifle form and expect communication. He stressed that communication is much more than written and verbal messages—he talked about ten different "symbol systems," with which we communicate, including verbal, kinetic (body language), tactile (touch—Latin Americans often hug and kiss in public, but Africans almost never do), space (yes, the size and location of our offices does communicate!), time (as any one who has been in the Latin American "*mañana*" societies knows, time is interpreted differently in different places), and even smell (what smells good to persons depends on cultural preferences).

For example, while we may use Brut to make ourselves attractive to the opposite sex, a Maasai warrior may use rancid butter to accomplish the same purpose. (*Con Gusto!*) The striking thing is that the more subtle the communication system, at times the more influential it is. The powerful smell of body odor of a job applicant, for example, simply communicates more about him than what he may be trying to say!

What made the lectures really timely were the obvious implications for cross-cultural communication. If virtually everything about us communicates something (which it does), and if virtually every society interprets these "symbols" differently, then it is very important to be sure that every aspect of the message, both verbal and non-verbal is understood and communicated in ways that are understood within the target society. The importance of using symbol systems that make sense to people cross-culturally was obvious. Reflection on the symbol systems enabled them to say some of the same things they had been saying but with a bit more credibility. Just as we might have to use a different "form" (i.e., a smaller house on the mission field to communicate concern for and identification with rural tribal people), in the same way we must alter the "forms" of our written communications in translation work to communicate the same message.

Don was articulating some of the concerns that Tom and Betty Sue were aware of but did not yet have the theoretical language to describe. Bells started ringing in their heads not only about the significance for translation work but also about language learning as well. Just as interesting perhaps, Don invited them both to come to Kenya to what was then called the International Institute of Christian Communications (IICC). At the IICC, all participants were Christians involved in some form of cross-cultural ministry. There they would take workshop classes from well-known Christian experts in cross-cultural communication of the Gospel, and study cross-cultural communications theory and practice.

Off to Africa!

However, the most important feature was that they brought with them the particular communications problem or challenges they were working on and received consultation and guidance from the experts. There were translators, radio station personnel, literature producers and others. Tom and Don thought it would be excellent for Tom to participate and bring the challenge of translation of the Campus Crusade materials. Bill Bright agreed. So practically without batting an eyelash, they both said, "Sure! Let's do it!"

But wait! Africa? Tom, go to Africa! You're paralyzed!! People around them said, "You're crazy! How will you get around?"

Tom replied, "Like I always get around—in my wheelchair!"

"What if you get sick?" And Tom said, "What if I do get sick? I get sick all the time. I'll survive."

Clearly, Tom was not going to be denied the chance to travel abroad. He felt that not only was the conference just what he needed, this would give him an opportunity to meet with others facing the same kinds of challenges he was.

Don Smith thought Tom would want to hurry over and hurry back in order to minimize the stresses of the travel, so he wanted to arrange a ticket for them from L.A. to Nairobi and back again without any stops. That would make sense for a quadriplegic, would it not? But Tom figured differently. He had traveled by plane. This trip would just be a little longer than most. They had time, so why not stop off in Europe and do some visiting? It took considerable persuasion, because Don Smith and Bill Bright, both experienced travelers, could not believe Tom would want to extend the trip and make it any harder on themselves than they had to. Neither Tom nor Betty Sue had ever been to Europe before though, and they did not want to rush back. So they arranged the trip so they could go through Holland, Greece and Israel.

The time in Israel was exceptional. Tom had some friends at the Institute of Holy Land Studies who arranged for a friend to be their tour guide. The guide was an Arab Christian, and it was his day off. He was going to paint his house that day but he decided it would be more fun to give this eager American in a wheelchair and his wife a tour. So they got in his little VW and went to Jerusalem, Bethlehem, Jericho and the Dead Sea, and then to Galilee, Capernaum and Nazareth, through Samaria, to Tel Aviv and back to Jerusalem. Visiting Israel was especially meaningful for Tom, for in doing so, he was fulfilling his own dream, and vicariously, the dream of his father, the missionary to the Jews in Colorado, who often prayed that someday he could visit Israel himself.

For Tom, the Nairobi, Kenya conference was also all that he hoped it would be, and he came away with lots of ideas and a new approach to the translation project. But there was an added bonus as well. Just a year or so previously, Ken Taylor had completed the whole of *The Living Bible* which had sold millions in its first months after publication. He had formed a new organization, Living Bibles International (LBI) to help translators all over the world create living translations in their own languages. And, he had arranged with Smith to have Daystar coordinate the recruiting, training and supervision of translators and testing of translations in projects all over Africa.

The *Living Bible*, of course, was and is an excellent example of the kind of translation that Tom felt was needed for the Crusade materials. Easy to read, emotive, chock full of contemporary, meaningful idioms and colloquial speech, it communicated well then and now to readers of all ages in a language that all can understand. Ken Taylor had traded a close, literal conformance to the words and structures of the original biblical languages, for a close attention to the meanings and emotions of the text, presented in a way that reflected the way English speakers actually speak today. For millions of readers, the *Living Bible* opened the windows of understanding of that ancient book with customs and cultural practices so different from our own.

The LBI work was at the stage where they needed a manual of translation principles for training translators and lots of consultant time to spend with Christian writers all over the world; to teach them what the "Living Bible" concept was all about and review with them the progress and suitability of their work. Don Smith was already working with Taylor to analyze the features that made the *Living Bible* unique, and incorporate these into principles and procedures for translators in other languages. The objective was not, of course, to translate the *Living Bible* into lots of different languages, but rather to translate faithfully the meaning and message of the sacred texts in an easy to read and interesting style, at the same time duplicating in those other languages the effect and impact that the *Living Bible* had in English.

Ken Taylor appreciated Tom and Betty's understanding of what he had tried to do in his paraphrase of the Bible. "Tom and Betty

Sue were real friends of The Living Bible International, especially in their desire to produce easy to read translations of the Bible in the major languages of the world" (Taylor 1993).

Tom and Betty Sue worked closely with Don Smith and the Living Bible people in Nairobi. It was clear to them, and later to Bill Bright, how appropriate it was for Tom to work on Living Bible projects along side of their Campus Crusade translation activities. So before they left Africa, Tom and Betty Sue, with Bright's approval, had agreed to work with LBI translators and projects wherever they traveled for Crusade work. In fact, they began to split up their time and devote about half to the work of each of the organizations.

On their return from that first trip to Africa, they landed in Amsterdam at the time of the flower festival. They saw the acres and acres of tulips planted in special formations—circles and squares and mounds and the huge hanger-like buildings with orchids and indoor plants.

Tom and Betty Sue may not have known it then, but they were hooked on traveling. That first trip to Africa gave them the confidence to travel anywhere in spite of the difficulties in taking along a wheelchair, the problem of transferring in and out of airplanes and every other form of conveyance imaginable, the amounts of special medical provisions they had to carry along with them, and the uncertainties of Tom's health. That first trip was the start of a traveling lifestyle that over the next thirteen years took them to over eighty countries.

Dynamic Equivalence—Not!

When they got back from Africa they started reading through the Crusade files trying to find if there was any feedback in the files that would encourage a change in policy and, sure enough, they found a lot. Things like the translator from Brazil who had had his Portuguese translation rejected because in his translation the "G R O W T H" acrostic on the back of the Four Laws had too many letters. The literal translation policy in place at the time virtually required that the acrostic be reproduced in the target language with six characters. In fact, that was one of the ways the translations were checked and approved. To preserve the *meaning* of course, the *forms*—the spelling of the word, and thus the number of letters in the word—would have to be changed to correct Portuguese. The Portuguese translator wrote back and said, "I'm sorry but you can't spell '*Crescer*' with only six letters, it just happens to be spelled with seven!"

There were other examples demonstrating that more flexibility was needed in the translation policy. Since even the size and color of the booklet was specified, the type size in some languages had to be very small. One frustrated translator pointed out that since those he was working with were new readers, they would never be able to read a booklet with such small print even if the translation was perfect. Another staff person wrote that a particular Bible verse used in the materials was translated so poorly in their language that it did not say anything. "Why can't we change it to another verse?" Or, "The diagrams mean nothing," or "The colors are wrong!" In one place they said that the color was pornographic. All the talk about Don Smith's "symbol systems" came to life!

Tom and Betty certainly never questioned Bright's motives or those of any one in Campus Crusade. They were challenged and inspired by the vision and the energy being invested in actually winning people to Christ in many countries around the world. They found too, that it was not just Crusade that had such formal translation policies. It was the prevailing understanding of "good translations" at the time, especially among those who were not involved in actual field translation work or those who had no understanding of the true nature of languages.

In the summer of 1972, Tom and Betty Sue went to their fourth TIL, where they continued refining their ideas about language acquisition, and the communication of the Gospel across cultural barriers. Then they flew from Toronto to Medicine Hat, Alberta, Canada, for a translation seminar to be led by the "master" in translation, Eugene Nida of the Bible Societies.

The conference had perhaps twenty-five participants but Nida put as much energy into it as he would into a big conference. There

Tom and Betty learned the terminology for the principles they believed. Most important was the idea of "dynamic equivalence."

Dynamic equivalence was the term used to describe the fact that the range of meaning of individual words varies from language to language, and that to translate *meaning* accurately from one language to another, the *forms* must change. A "word-for-word" translation can never be fully accurate in the "target" language, and will, moreover, always be stilted and unnatural. The nearly word-for-word KJV, for example, which says in Philippians 1:8, "For God is my record, how greatly I long after you all in the *bowels* of Jesus Christ," literally translates "bowels" from the Greek, but that word in this context makes no sense in English. To communicate the *meaning* more accurately, this *form* (word) must change to one more appropriate in English, as all modern translations have done.

Nida had Tom and Betty research as many Crusade translations as they could find, and "back-translate" them literally into English in order to demonstrate what they really said. To do so, they went to Fuller Seminary often because there were so many international students there, and once again hit on a gold mine of insight and understanding of the task before them. It was on their forays to Fuller that they met Chuck Kraft, Art Glasser, Ralph Winter and others who were later to have a notable influence on them. Kraft had been talking about the distinction between forms meanings in communication of the Gospel and would soon create considerable waves in theological and missiological circles for his extension of the dynamic equivalence concept to theologizing across cultures, spelled out most fully in his *Christianity in Culture*, first published in 1979. Dr. Kraft offered lots of valuable suggestions about translation and effective cross-cultural communication. "What is the purpose of translation," he asked, "to impress, or to communicate?" If it is to communicate, he argued, then the language used must be readable, idiomatic, and emotive.

> God wants to be understood not simply admired. God, of course, is
> impressive. He is, of course, to be admired. But there is a sense in

which if we focus on merely admiring God, His ultimate purpose in interacting with human beings is thwarted (Kraft 1979b:5).

A dynamic equivalent translation is one that aims to be, as Kraft later wrote, "so true to both the message of the source documents and the normal ways of expressing such a message in the receptor language that the hearers/readers can . . . derive the proper meanings" (1979a:269). The concept of dynamic equivalence was the tool they needed to convey the idea of being faithful to the meaning of the original materials while making whatever changes of the forms (words, structures, idioms, etc.) were required or appropriate in the new language.

They began as soon as they got back to the Crusade headquarters at Arrowhead Springs in California. Steve allowed them to travel around Southern California by car, finding native speakers of many languages at the universities and seminaries to back-translate many of the *Four Spiritual Laws* booklets that had already been translated. What they found was that the meanings were definitely *not* dynamically equivalent.

One piece of material being translated talked about the "love that Bill Bright sensed in that auditorium," which happened to be a ball room. The unfortunate translation in one language came out referring to making love in the dance hall!

Tom and Betty Sue were constantly finding examples of illustrations or stories which, in English or in the American culture, are easy to understand and help to explain the Gospel message, but which in other languages and cultures are meaningless or convey a totally different meaning. Imagine the confusion to a group of Kenyans, if Bill Bright's story (in one of his booklets) about "standing in Chicago and a 'Black Panther' came up and put his hand on my shoulder!" were translated word-for-word!

It was fun work, because of the insights into other cultures. Before long they had reams and reams of very revealing material.

To do the back-translation, Tom would ask a speaker of the language into which the material had been translated to read the material in his own language and then relate in English, sentence-by-sentence, what it said. Betty Sue would write furiously to try to get it all down. She also had the English version in front of her and sometimes could follow it word for word and comma for comma. But when Tom would ask the person what it meant, he or she often said, "I understand all the words, but it doesn't really mean anything."

They worked at the back-translation project for several months, with helpers in French, some African and Indian languages, Chinese, Arabic, Japanese, Korean, and others. As much as possible, they tried to get people who were not familiar with Campus Crusade—people who did not already know the jargon of Campus Crusade or of evangelizing.

By the end of December 1972, they felt they had gotten enough material, and made a three page summary of the findings, giving a few examples. Unfortunately, much of the leadership of Crusade had not been aware of the problems and were reluctant to believe that things could be so bad. The findings were so appalling, they were almost unbelievable.

Tom decided that it was not just Bill Bright's problem; the Directors of Affairs of the different regions needed to know about the findings too. There were four such directors—Latin America, Africa, Asia and Steve who was their supervisor. Tom decided to send them a copy of the summary.

That was perhaps not a smart thing to do. In the furor that followed, they were told *not* to correspond with individuals and to suspend their translation activities. Tom and Betty thought that was the first step in being fired. To preempt what they thought was the inevitable, they prepared themselves to move on, though they had been with Crusade for only a year. They mentioned to a couple of national directors that they were considering leaving but both pleaded with Tom and Betty Sue not to leave. "We've been praying for a breakthrough on the translation policy for years," they said. "Hang around and help us push this through."

So they stayed on, guardedly hoping that they could still make a contribution.

A Crusade International Advisory Council conference in Mexico in January of 1973 including all the Area Directors and some of their Country Directors provided the forum to resolve the impasse. Bill Bright said, "This issue is important enough to discuss with the whole group. I can't believe that it's possible for the translations to be as bad as you say, but let's get it settled."

At the conference, Tom was given the opportunity to teach some of the principles of dynamic equivalence in translation that he had learned from Nida and Kraft, and the communication principles he learned from Don Smith, which he felt threw open doors of understanding as to the nature of and means to effective translation. He urged translators to consider the importance of asking the question, "What does it mean to *insiders*?"

They had also prepared a first-edition of a programmed workbook for translators of the *Four Spiritual Laws* to show more concretely what they were aiming at. Both the presentations and the workbook were very well received.

Making Sense in Our Own Languages!

The response, especially among the national directors was electric. "This is exactly what we want," they said, "a translation policy that allows us to make sense in our own languages!"

The decision was made to re-write the Campus Crusade translation policy. Together, they changed it from one with insistence on very literal word-for-word translation to one that allowed a dynamic equivalence approach at the discretion of the Area Director. The national Nigerian director, immediately invited them to Nigeria to hold a translation seminar. Then the Ghanaian director said, "Hey, if you are going to Nigeria why don't you come to Ghana and hold one for us?" Before long representatives from Kenya, Liberia, South Africa and others had asked them to come to their countries as well.

Thus began almost non-stop traveling around the world for the rest of Tom's life. Crusade funded most of the actual travel expenses, but Tom and Betty covered most of their living expenses. For the next several years, they used much of their own funds from disability coverage to supplement costs for their travel. Tom and Betty got ready for what looked like a three month trip. They were away almost three years. (When they were unpacking their stored goods three years later, Betty Sue wondered why she had saved tea bags, and a whole host of other semi-perishables. Then she remembered that she had expected to be gone only three months.)

Along the way, Ken Taylor learned that they were going to be near some of their translation projects and asked if they could check the progress of some of the Living Bible translators and do some training. Bill Bright agreed that this would be a good use of their talents, and was happy to have them spend time (and share the travel costs) with LBI.

On that first trip to Nigeria in March of 1973, a young Crusade worker named Bulus Tauna, working in his own unwritten Katab language, was trying to invent his own alphabet as he went along. Having had no training in linguistics or orthography, he was not making much progress. He had not discovered how to write things consistently, so he had to decide anew how to spell each word as he came to it. He often spelled the same word differently in different contexts. Tom and Betty Sue sat down with him and asked him to tell them a legend which Betty Sue, using her considerable linguistic skills, wrote out phonetically as they were going along. When he was finished she read it back to him. His eyes got big, and he exclaimed, "You can read my language!"

Together they worked out the basics of a consistent orthography. Tom and Betty Sue learned that about 8000 people speak Katab, and about one-third of these are Christians. The other two-thirds followed their traditional animist religion. The chief, though, was a committed Christian and supportive of Bulus Tauna's translation work. A light went on in Tom's heart about a "people movement" among the Katab. In a report to Bright that foreshadowed his passion for the unreached, Tom wrote:

> Bulus [Tauna] has the opportunity to work under the direction of the chief and with the chief's authority, in a way that could result in very large groups of his people making decisions for Christ. It is not at all unreasonable to expect that this entire tribe could place their faith in Christ. If done in an African way, the numbers trusting Christ could be far greater than if the strategy required ... indi-

vidual decision. It seems to us that we need to learn much more about what is involved in doing things in an African way (1973).

"Kai! He Must Be Important!"

The time in Nigeria was Tom's first opportunity to get into rural areas and Tom and Betty's first real taste of African life. As they went through a village in one day with Herb Klem, a veteran missionary, Herb informed them that all visitors from the outside should visit the chief. That's the polite thing to do. Herb set up an appointment for them to visit the chief. As was to be the case many times in the future when they walked through a village, they drew a crowd of curious children and adults, all fascinated by the long flowing beard Tom wore at the time, and, of course, his wheelchair.

They created quite a commotion. They had to walk right through the center of a market, trying to skirt around the ladies sitting on the ground with their pots and goods spread out for sale. Tom and Betty tried to stick to the aisles but the crowd of people stepped on the ladies' things, and some children, walking backwards, fell into the pots. Many of the market ladies were very angry at them because of the crowd.

Finally they arrived at the chief's house and the crowd gathered around. A number of the elders of the village sat around the edge of the porch and the chief sat in the middle. "Now we have to just sit," Herb said. So they sat and nobody talked.

The crowd was watching. Soon the crowd became too noisy and the chief made a motion with his fly whisk and shooed the kids away. They sat in silence for a few more minutes until Herb indicated to Tom to wheel up to the chief. Tom spoke to him in English and an interpreter translated into the local language, (though the chief probably understood everything). Tom introduced himself and Betty and told him why they were there. The chief said he was pleased that they had done the right thing to come and visit him. They exchanged more pleasantries and then took their leave.

As they left, Herb overheard somebody saying, "Kai! That bearded old man must be really rich and important because he doesn't have to walk and he has a woman to push him!"

Taking a cue from Herb, Tom had a tailor in Igbaja, Nigeria, make him an African suit—a flowing purple top and trousers and a matching purple hat. Did he look regal in that outfit! Betty Sue had an inexpensive African outfit made too, and at the first opportunity they wore them to dinner. Betty Sue felt as conspicuous as a sore thumb, but Tom, with his characteristic boldness, wore it proudly and smiled at the surprised guests in the guest house. All through the meal Betty felt the African people were staring at them. She feared they had really offended them.

She was relieved then when several Africans, even some wearing western dress, thanked them for wearing "their" clothes! It was a confirmation for Tom that most people appreciate it when outsiders show interest in their culture and lifestyle—a useful lesson in cross-cultural identification they would share often to language learners using the community as their classroom. From then on, Tom and Betty often wore the native dress in the countries they visited, and often to dress-up functions in the US as well.

They were also careful to eat whatever food was served to them. Tom always liked to experiment and rarely found a dish that he could not enjoy. Such willingness to try never failed to add warmth to the friendships they were building. While in Ghana they decided to take a Ghanaian friend, Ben Adjei, out to lunch to show appreciation for Ben's help. They planned to take him to the Black Pot, a nice Ghanaian restaurant, but found it closed, so decided on a Chinese restaurant across the street. Ben did not know what to order so Tom suggested his own favorite, sweet and sour pork. Ben took one bite and could not stomach another. "I couldn't figure out why some missionaries didn't want to eat our Ghanaian food," he said, "but now I see that some food really is not edible!"

From Ghana they went to Liberia and then Zaire. Then on to Swaziland, a tiny, beautiful country that Betty Sue loved.

They enjoyed South Africa too, but as is the case for any sensitive visitor at that time, the visit there was a bitter sweet experience. The racial nonsense of apartheid appalled them. They enjoyed the whites. Many were delightful Christian people. But so, of course, were the blacks. Not to be able to be around both races together was so unnatural. One day as they returned to their hotel, they invited one of the African men they were working with to join them for a cup of tea. "I'm sorry but I'm not allowed in that hotel," he said, pointing to his skin color on his arm. But then he gave a big grin and said, "Never mind. Since I'm carrying your suitcase I can go in as your porter!" So he went in with them and had a surreptitious cup of tea with them.

Such was the reality of South African life in the 1970s. Tom would have many later opportunities to experience and bring a small measure of healing to that problem.

Taking It to the World

Tom and Betty Sue's travel in 1973 was constant, and took them to every major area of the world. Even before they returned from that first consulting trip to Africa, they began receiving other invitations from other Crusade national directors for other workshops in other parts of the world. They traveled to Europe and through Latin America and then back to Africa again conducting translation workshops for both Crusade and Living Bibles. They also began to conduct language learning workshops for new missionaries from a variety of mission groups who heard about them either through their work at the Toronto Institute of Linguistics or by word of mouth from other agencies.

In June of 1973, they were back at Toronto where Tom served as acting principal of the Toronto Institute of Linguistics in the absence of Don Larson. That summer, they took an after-TIL excursion on the Ontario Northland Train north to Moosonee, just south of the Hudson Bay. On the train trip up to Moosonee they met a Christian businessman who was going to Moosonee to visit with a missionary there. When they told him they had been teaching at TIL, he became interested in the concepts of language learning through relationships. Thinking that his local missionary friend would surely also be terribly interested, the businessman made arrangements for Tom to spend some time with him to share about these principles. In the process, Tom learned some lessons.

Tom made arrangements to get a Cree speaker to serve as a helper so they would not just *talk* about language learning but *do* some together. When they arrived at the missionary's they spent five or ten minutes discussing general principles of language learning and then began eliciting a basic greeting in the Cree language. After just a few minutes the missionary dismissed himself saying he would be back shortly. Tom and Betty waited quite a while but finally decided to go ahead and learn some Cree with the helper. But the missionary never returned!

Later they learned that the missionary had been given an opportunity that afternoon to make a flight over the area in a small plane and so had gone on the flight without letting anyone know he had left. Lesson One: Make sure that people have a *personal* felt need before offering a free seminar. Lesson Two: Do not invite yourself to give unsolicited language classes!

At any rate, the time was not wasted. Tom and Betty had enjoyed learning a little Cree and had fun using it around town with waitresses and other townspeople.

The last half of 1973 was just as ambitious as the first. In July and August, they began their first trip to South America, visiting Peru, Chile, Argentina, and Bolivia.

In September, they went to Ecuador, Colombia, and Venezuela, where they visited the small town where Betty Sue lived as a child.

October found them in Curacao, Panama, Costa Rica, Guatemala, and Nicaragua. Finally to Mexico City for a Crusade conference, then to San Bernardino for two weeks of training the new Agape missionaries.

Astonishingly, there was still more travel that year. By the end of November they were back in Trinidad and St. Vincent and then on to Rio de Janeiro, Brazil for Crusade and LBI regional conferences. Before the year was out they were back in Africa for work in Liberia, Ivory Coast, and Nigeria in West Africa.

A Welcome Affirmation

The travel was fun and rewarding. But as might be expected, it was wearisome, and, eventually, spiritually and emotionally draining. Just before the Congress on World Evangelism at Lausanne, Switzerland in July 1974, there came a kind of low spiritual point for both of them. They had been traveling for about two years. Perhaps it was emotional as much as spiritual but, not surprisingly, they felt the schedule had been too intense. Moreover, they had not been able to go back and follow up on much of the training they had done. Had they made a difference? Were there any long-term accomplishments? They feared that perhaps there were not. Perhaps traveling around the world and holding one-week seminars was too superficial?.

One night just before the Lausanne Congress on World Evangelization, Tom and Betty talked together and prayed seriously about their concern. "Are we doing anything worthwhile, Lord, or are we just having fun with the job and with our time running around the world? Please make it clear to us that we are where you want us to be, and that we are in your will and accomplishing what you want us to."

A refreshing affirmation and confirmation came just a few days later when they were able to spend a few days at the Congress. There they were surprised to meet scores of people from all over the world that they had trained or with whom they had consulted. They missed meetings because they were so busy talking to people. At times there were actually lines of people waiting to talk.

Person after person said, "Guess what has happened since we met with you!" and would then relate some adventure in successful language and culture learning by being involved with the people, or how their new translations were having much better impact. Their confidence was restored. They felt reassured that God was indeed allowing them to make a difference in many lives around the world. As they thanked the Lord that night Betty thought, "This is a foretaste of heaven. Think how it's going to be when we get there. There will be people from all over the world and we will have a small share with them in their ministries."

God's timing was perfect to provide the lift and encouragement to go on. It turned out that they needed that assurance and confidence only a few weeks later. Their time at Crusade's enormous evangelism extravaganza, "Explo 74" in August in Seoul, Korea was not nearly so affirming. While they felt they had made good progress not only with actual translation of Campus Crusade material, but also in equipping people with a much more sound approach and philosophy of translation, not every one in Crusade agreed with the new direction. In fact, Tom had challenged the conventional wisdom within Crusade so much that some old timers doubted their loyalty to the cause and to the vision of Bright.

Tom thought he and Betty Sue were going to Seoul to train and further explain the new translation policies and procedures to groups of staff meeting there. Instead, in a rather ambiguous fashion, they were relieved of their responsibilities as directors of the Crusade translation activities. Initially it was not clear if they were being fired or if they were expected to resign. But before it came to that, Larry Poland, the Director of the new Agape program, asked Bright if Tom and Betty could work with him, training the new Agape missionaries. One of the old-timers objected uncharitably grousing that they "had been poisoning thousands, and now would poison ten thousands." In the end, cooler heads prevailed and arrangements were made for Tom and Betty to be responsible for much of the language and culture learning activities of the Agape missionaries.

Tom and Betty's tenure as Directors of Translations for Crusade came to an end, but Bright's influence on them certainly did not. In Bill Bright, Tom saw a man whose heart beat for the unreached people of the world, and whose every waking hour was devoted to communication of God's plan for every person. Tom had caught that tremendous vision for winning the lost to Christ

The Agape Movement of Campus Crusade was a kind of Christian "Peace Corps" which sent vocationally and spiritually trained people who desired to share Christ through their skills to various parts of the world. Their appointments were usually for two years. This short time allowed little, if any time for formal language training, yet in many countries, the Agape team members needed to to use a new language. Tom and Betty Sue were asked to help solve the problem by teaching members *how* to learn a language.

At the same time, they continued "free-lancing" with language and culture learning workshops with various missionaries and mission groups. Returning from Explo 74 in Korea, they conducted workshops in Tokyo and Indonesia, and then in Bangkok, Calcutta and New Delhi. The workshops in Thailand and India had a much more far reaching impact than most. There they had opportunities to visit with missionaries working among the poorest of the poor. The shock of learning that some of the children of Calcutta were handicapped by their own parents out of love for them was almost a shock beyond belief. (Parents break the children's arms, burn them, or mutilate them so they can be more successful in their begging efforts and thus be more apt to survive.) The fact that any parent could be forced into that kind of a situation was mind-boggling and heart breaking.

Later, they both saw the visit to Calcutta as instrumental in piquing their interest in and concern for the poor—the calling that consumed much of their heart and energies the rest of Tom's life.

"Where Is the Church?"

Working with the Agape team provided an excellent opportunity to test some of the total immersion, self directed language learning theories that they had talked about and promoted at TIL, and elsewhere in shorter workshops.

They had put together manuals and they were working on what was to become *Language Acquisition Made Practical*, (*LAMP*), but it was not yet ready. They were always after ideas for resources and ways to experiment and test their ideas. The opportunity to test some important concepts on language learning came in early 1975 with a group of Agape language learners in Kenya.

Tom and Betty Sue were to have the first two weeks with them for language learning. They decided to take all of them to the Kamba town of Machakos, about forty miles outside of Nairobi.

The goal was to test the strategy of total immersion, living more or less at the level of the people themselves, learning *how* to learn a language on their own, by learning some of the Kikamba language using only the resources of the community itself.

When the group arrived in Machakos, they found the accommo-
dations in the cheap hotel they had chosen, were very basic
indeed—they had a bed. The communal bathrooms were pit toilets
where one had to step up about knee high to get to the toilet. Betty
Sue said they all felt like they were "on stage." The showers were
just a bucket of water which they used to pour water over their
heads. There were some little tables out in the courtyard so they
bought food in the market and made their own meals.

Each learner was to find his or her own helper, and using techniques taught by Tom and Betty, elicit from the helper some basic
greetings. The learners were to record the "texts" and memorize
them. Then they would fix it in their minds by going out and using
what they had learned in the community. In the process, they
would get ideas about new texts that they needed in order to con-
verse more with the people they met. More important however,
were the friendships being established. The whole premise of the
approach to language learning was that it could be done by learning from the people themselves without having to do formal language training. And more important still was the prospect that
ministry could begin with the people with whom they were establishing relationships. The learners would not have to put off
friendship evangelism until they had the language learned well.
They could begin immediately!

Tom and Betty Sue taught by modeling, going out into the
community like everyone else and learning the language with
them. Following the strategy of getting what they needed, practicing it, and then going out and using it with as many people as
they could find, they all first learned how to introduce themselves
and greet another person. Then they walked around and said what
they had learned to as many people as they could find. Their
learner role diffused suspicion, and, as the Africans say, "slowly by
slowly" they were building friendships as they met people.

One young lady learned the phrase, "Where's the church?" and
walked down the street asking everybody that question. A local
girl walking on the other side of the street going the same direction
noticed that she kept asking everybody the same question so she

came across the street and said, "Look, if nobody else will take you there, I will." That encounter produced a friendship just like what Tom and Betty Sue envisioned, and the two girls were friends for the rest of the time that they were in Machakos. She became the learner's language helper for those two weeks.

The group stayed in the little hotel for almost a week. They began to realize, however, that it did not have a good reputation. A local pastor advised them not to stay there lest they too might get a bad reputation. So they moved across the street to a kind of community house that had rooms. It did not have any eating place but was actually a lot cleaner, very pleasant and even cheaper than the hotel—about $2.00 a night per person!

Even that though, was expensive for the local people. Tom and Betty Sue's helper said to them one day, "You know, if I were staying here, I wouldn't stay in such an expensive place." He took them to his room, which had only enough room for his bed and a little walk space, where he lived with his brother and a cousin and a cousin's friend. "Where does everybody sleep?" they asked. "Oh, we take turns. Sometimes two sleep in the bed and two on the floor and then we swap. It's a little crowded but that doesn't matter."

8
LAMP

We never went to language school. We learned Spanish using Tom and Betty Sue's book. From day one we were involved with people. Language learning never meant books and tapes to us. We were able to reach a high level of proficiency as we became involved with people" (Cirafesi 1993).

Tom's life and ministry were characterized by his commitment to Christ and sharing the Gospel with unreached peoples around the world. Tom believed in the Great Commission and took seriously Christ's command to "go into all the world."

Tom is best known for his emphasis on language learning through building relationships with the people whose language needs to be learned. By far his best known writing is *Language Acquisition Made Practical*, or as it has become known around the world, simply *LAMP*. *LAMP* was born out of Tom and Betty Sue's early years at the Toronto Institute of Linguistics.

The point of the training at TIL was, as Don said, to "de-school" language learning. So many adults feel that they are not able to learn a language, or that they do not have the aptitude. The only way they know how to approach language learning is to "go to language school." This means that the new missionary language learner will spend at least a year or two in full time language school, before they are able to begin their ministry—a long and costly process with a high attrition rate. Many potential missionaries are "weeded out" of missionary service because of their conviction that they ca not learn a language, or the time and financial costs of such training. The process also makes it highly unlikely that learners will be able to go to some of the more remote or unreached peoples, because language schools do not exist for those languages.

It is not that they were against language schools. Tom and Betty often visited and consulted with them regularly. What dismayed them though, was a schoolish approach to language learning and the resulting dependence of the students on the teachers and books. It was becoming obvious and very important to them that language learning was a social activity, not an academic one.

Learn a little—Use it a lot!

TIL sought to address all of these problems by teaching the students how to learn a language with or without the help of a language school or formal language training. The core of the material they used was what they called the learning cycle, conceptualized by Bill Smalley, Larson, and the other TIL staff members. It was a four step procedure that later was later labeled the "GLUE method" by Dwight Gradin and David McClure who was also an instructor at TIL. "GLUE" stands for:

> Get what you need,
> Learn what you get,
> Use what you learn, and
> Evaluate what you have done as you envision what you need to do
>   for the next stage of learning.

Getting what you need puts the learning responsibility into the learner's hands to choose the area of language to focus on for that day's cycle. To do so, the learners have to be where the speakers of the language are. Thus the need to live in the community. The closer the new learner can live with the people whose language he is trying to learn, (and presumably trying to minister to), the more effective the learning will be. Once in the community, the learner usually needs to find a helper, a native speaker of the language who can be a resource person to help the learner get what he needs. The learner works with the helper to elicit a text—the phrases or dialogue that are needed at that stage of the learners' program. Naturally the learner first gets basic greetings and introductory "pleasantries" which help them get around in the new community. A phrase Tom always recommended in the first few days was something like, "That is all I know how to say right now."

Or, "I'll come back tomorrow and say the new phrases I've learned."

Learning what you get involves just that—memorizing it thoroughly and making sure that you can say accurately what you have elicited. This often involves practice with the helper, or from a tape recording.

Using what you learn is the most important step. It means getting out into the community and using the newly acquired portion of the language with the native speakers. A lot. Tom used to recommend that learners use their practiced text with at least fifty persons each day. "Learn a little, use it a lot," was Tom's constant exhortation. He could guarantee that the learner would never forget it if he or she used the text in conversation that many times.

But other benefits are even more important. Establishing oneself as a learner diffuses suspicions among the target community. Almost everyone is interested in and open to people who are interested in them. This is especially true in the area of a people's language. Almost never is there resentment towards a person doing his best to learn to hear, mimic and speak your own language.

Even more important is that relationships can begin to be built on the first day of such language practice—relationships of people who, because of the non-threatening learner role, are more able to trust you, want to help you, and before long may even be willing to listen to what you have to say about your faith. Over and over through the years, as Tom and Betty promoted language learning in this way, new missionaries have been able to lead people to Christ *while* they are learning the language, sometimes even early on in the process, because of the trust and friendships built in the first stages of the language learning process.

Evaluate what you use makes the learner responsible for self-evaluation and for planning and record-keeping. After a day of communicating his text, the learner usually can have a pretty good idea of what he needs to learn to say next day. His new friends are talking back to him, asking questions that the learner cannot understand, trying to engage him in further conversation. In the evaluation stage the learner assesses the progress of the day and decides the next phrases that he needs to move the process along. He has his helper work with him to get more of what he needs, learn what he gets, use what he practices, and once again evaluate his progress.

Don Larson, the creative principal, was always looking for new and stimulating ways to challenge and equip learners along these lines. In the summer of 1973, he encouraged all of the TIL staff to try their hand at writing things about language learning, at a popular level. Tom took him up on that challenge.

At first Tom simply wanted to get some basic learning cycle procedures and helps in use at TIL, written up in a simpler way. Tom was using materials developed at TIL with his Agape language learners, and other missionaries with whom he was involved. He wanted something a little more simple to bring them along in their learning so he and Betty wrote an extended introduction to the learning cycle. They called it *"Language Acquisition Through Manageable Procedures,"* and this was the basic material they used in many of their subsequent workshops until the "real" *LAMP* became a reality.

After using the introduction, various learners commented to Tom that they needed a lot more ideas on how to continue on with language learning. Following suggestions from "on the job" learners, they decided to expand it, first with chapters on eliciting texts, and then with comprehension, pronunciation, and structure sections. They decided on a daily learning format, rather than a topical arrangement which they hoped would be interesting and less confusing to learners. They changed the name of the project but preserved the LAMP acronym by calling it *Language Acquisition Made Practical.*

While they had a general outline in mind, they did not write the chapters of *LAMP* sequentially. When either of them got an idea for dealing with some aspect of a topic they would work on it together to get something down on paper, and then put it in the file folder that corresponded to that part of the outline.

Tom did much, though not all, of the initial conceptualizing, and then both he and Betty would hash out the format and wording together. Sometimes he would dictate his thoughts and then they would re-work it together. Other times each would work on writing a section and then trade sections for one another's input and editing. Usually the re-working by the other was mutually agreed upon, but sometimes one or the other would get defensive about something he or she had written and not want to accept changes. Their solution was to put that section away for a couple of days. They usually made progress when it was brought out again.

Betty Sue wrote (and rewrote) almost all of *LAMP* various times by longhand. In their frequent travels they always had with them paper, stapler, scissors, and glue stick, so they could cut their writing apart and rearrange the parts more easily. They often joked at the time that they could not write without scissors in hand. (Obviously, this was before their days with computers.)

Writing on the Run

While *LAMP* was actually conceived during their teaching stint at TIL in 1973, it had a very long and well-traveled gestation period. We have already seen the arduous schedule for 1973. Incredibly, 1974 and 1975 were filled with just as much travel. In those two years they visited over thirty countries in Africa, Asia, Europe, and the Middle East.

During all of their travels, Tom and Betty Sue always had their writing materials and idea folders with them. Following the pattern established during the writing of their dissertations, they always looked for bits and pieces of time, sometimes in some of the most exotic places, to write a few more lines.

One such place was Aqaba, at the extreme southern end of Jordan where they spent time after a workshop in Jordan in 1974. There they rented a small resort cottage for a few days of some glorious sun, and some attention to the growing manuscript. Another "exotic" writing location was a *bure* (a thatched roof house with woven bamboo walls) on the south coast of Fiji in October of that year. Like many of their "mini" vacations, this one was designed as a working holiday, but it turned out to be something out of the ordinary. On arrival in Fiji, Tom told the owner of a small hotel that they were looking for a quiet place on the beach where they could relax and write. The man went into his office and proudly brought out a photograph album of a beach resort he was planning to build. At the moment there was only a Fiji style "bure." But in the absence of anything better, he said, they were most welcome to stay there.

The bure was just beside the beach on a large piece of grassy land with lots of coconut palms, banana trees, papaya plants, and hibiscus flowers; just the kind of place they were looking for! In the bure, they had to "camp out," cooking over a one-burner kerosene stove and sleeping on a bed which was a mattress placed on the floor. But it worked, and they felt it was perfect.

On their first evening though, they began to feel they were living in a zoo. First, as they were sitting working, an enormous frog plopped across the floor chasing a large moth. He had some trouble catching the moth, so Betty Sue helped him by chasing the moth toward him. A few minutes later a very large rat went running across the rafter overhead. A variety of lizards, bugs, and even crabs went skittering around the floor from time to time.

Some time after they had gone to sleep, both were awakened by a noise beside the bed. Tom thought it was the frog, and Betty Sue was sure that it was the rat. She shined the flashlight toward the noise and found herself face to face with a huge crab. The crab must have been attracted to the light, for he started crawling towards the bed. Betty Sue did not like having a crab a few inches from her feet, so she bravely got up to see what she could do about chasing him out of doors or catching him. She finally managed to catch him by dropping a large, square, plastic pan over him. Then she put the typewriter and the stool on top of the pan so the crab could not get out, and they went back to bed. They managed then to sleep, in spite of the disagreeable scratching inside the pan!

In the morning, a groundskeeper came around with two large lobsters. He thought it strange that she did not know how to fix them, but delightedly offered to be their cook. He dropped them in a pan of water, and while they were boiling, found a dried coconut and shredded the meat with a handy little scraper. He poured a

little water on the shredded coconut and squeezed it with his fingers until the water was white from the coconut juice. Later he
cooked the lobster meat in a little of the coconut milk, and the
result was delicious!

Sometimes it was the exotic settings that provided inspiration
for their writing. At other times it was people they met along the
way who provided helpful insights. It was at the end of their second 1973 trip to Nigeria that they met Joyce Flint at Igbaja who
gave them lots of excellent critique on their early writing of *LAMP*.
She was the one who encouraged them to lighten it up with pictures and to rewrite it in a less formal style.

Learners vs. Students

Tom and Betty Sue were convinced that successful relationships
were the key to successful language learning and to successful
evangelism. What they were striving for in *LAMP* was a how-to
book to equip people to structure their own language learning program. They had seen how ineffective and short-sighted the traditional approaches to language learning were. They had seen the
"schoolish" mentality to language learning, and many instructors
and mission administrators who felt that a new language should
not be used until people had learned it well. (Paul Pierson, Dean of
the Fuller School of World Mission, later confirmed this prevailing
language learning mentality. "In my language study for Portuguese," he said, "I was advised not to even try to use the language
until I had it mastered" 1987.)

Tom and Betty wanted to change all this. They wanted something which would enable any learner to proceed at his or her own
pace, and at the same time motivate and enable the learner to
begin to build the relationships that are crucial to successful language learning and to successful ministry. "We have become convinced," Tom wrote, "that relationships are the most important
factor in language learning and in mission."

> Isn't it interesting that millions of people have studied languages
> without learning them, but billions of people have learned lan-
> guages without studying them. What's the difference? I think it is

one simple thing. Regardless of how good a school program is, if the student doesn't fully recognize his full responsibility, then he will not learn the language. The responsibility rests firmly on the learner's shoulders. A language is *learned* rather than taught, but some people in school don't know that. They think that they just put in their time—you know, like serving a prison sentence or something—and endure it to the end, and then they'll come out being able to use the language. But it just doesn't work that way (T. Brewster 1983:45)

Tom was also convinced that the difference between successful learners and those who failed was in the extent to which they were willing to take responsibility for their own language learning program. He saw significant differences between what he called "students" and "learners." "I don't want students in my classes," he often said, "I want learners. I'm a bit of a rebel in this regard. I'm kind of a non-school person. I think it was Mark Twain who first said 'never let school get in the way of your education,' and I can relate to that." Tom, drawing again from Don Larson, and with help from Dwight Gradin, compared students versus learners in the following ways (T. and E. Brewster 1983:61–62):

"LEARNERS"	"STUDENTS"
The learner is primarily involved with the people of the neighborhood—in a normal context.	The student is primarily involved with the books and studies of his or her course.
The learner revels in the immersion of the real-life experience.	A student is fearful of immersion—"Land drills" are more his style.
The learner learns the language—and the very process is a *means* of communicating his interest in the people.	The student studies the language in hopes of preparing himself to some-day be able to communicate with the people.
The learner's goal is to know the people.	The student's goal is usually to "learn" the language.
The learner's attitude enables him to implement a strategy that will communicate a love for the people.	The student's attitude often results in a strategy of isolation that's interrupted with occasional forays out to the people.

The learner values the cultural knowledge of the people. When sensitively understood, God may use that knowledge redemptively as a bridge to Himself.	For the student, the local culture may be viewed as a barrier (not a bridge) in the way of accomplishing his ministry goals.
The learner decides what he is going to do next.	Others decide what the student will do next.
The learner learns because of personal wants and needs.	A student's learning becomes oriented to passing an exam or course.
The learner "learns" the language in order to *use* it.	The student studies the language in order to know it.
Learners learn a little and use a lot.	Schools typically reverse that. In schools, you're exposed to lots of material with a minimal opportunity to master it.
Learners do not get uptight about getting behind. For learners, the relationships are in focus. The learner is almost never behind.	Students almost always are behind. And, students get "behinder and behinder."

Tom and Betty learned much from Don Larson's ideas about "barefoot language learning." Who learns languages barefoot? Children do, and tribal people in many parts of the world where some people who have never been to school can speak two, three, or even half a dozen languages. Part of the reason for their proficiency is the fact that they put themselves into learner roles (not student roles) and acquire the languages in the context of relationships, learning what they need as they go along, and using it a lot. Young children are also learners rather than students, and they learn their first and sometimes second and third languages long before they know what a verb or a noun is, and without ever doing a grammar drill or memorizing a vocabulary list. Chuck Kraft was also very familiar with this phenomenon. He noted that as children when we learned our first language, the

> ability or lack of ability was not very important. . . . Nor was the quality and training of our teachers a major factor. The ability and

training of our parents and the many others from whom we learned our language was characterized by considerable variation. . . .

Some of the reasons for our early mastery of English relate to the fact that our youth and inexperience cast us completely in the role of learner. We pretended to be no more. We expected to make mistakes, did, and received correction with a minimum of embarrassment. We were unashamed to be utterly dependent and often wrong (1973).

A Long Labor and LAMP Is Born

Tom and Betty's idea for *LAMP* was to create a tool for learners to successfully manage their own language learning experience whether or not language schools or materials were available in their chosen language. But getting the manuscript finished, while constantly on the move was a major challenge. For over two years Tom and Betty carried parts of the *LAMP* manuscript around the world. In July 1975, they finally got a chance to take some extended time off to work at it in Chicago. It was nearing completion, but this was the first time they got to see in typewritten form the whole work in one place. Chapter Five was written at that time, and the rest totally reworked.

For language learning without language schools, they certainly did not want a stale "schoolish" book, so they had constantly kept an eye out for cartoons ideas. They hired Dick Wil liams, a Colorado Springs artist, who had a style and a flair that captured the spirit of what they had been hoping for. Each time they went to Colorado Springs, they took with them a fat file of cartoon suggestions to discuss with him. He had a file of standard characters which became the "stars" of the *LAMP* book. Sometimes he would dash off a quick rough cartoon to illustrate an idea. Other times they would talk through an idea and Dick would come back with some drawings later. He was a delight to work with, and he came up with something far better than they had dared hoped for.

The typesetting of *LAMP* was one of those ordeals you never want to have to repeat. Tom called a few typesetting companies to see what they could learn about that side of things. The company they engaged did not really know their own equipment. The need for phonetic characters as well as for bold and different type sizes for headings and footnotes stretched them to the limit and beyond. Tom and Betty kept getting galleys full of typing errors. They bought a small portable light table for layout and Betty Sue spent many hours over that table making one line or even one word corrections or having to piece parts of words together. Sometimes she wondered if her back and eyes would hold out.

In November of 1975, they were back at Crusade's Arrowhead Springs headquarters for training with the new Agape team. While there they found a Christian-owned typesetter, Via Type, nearby who had the same type of equipment as their Colorado typesetters. When Clarence and Mae Kiphart, the owners of Via Type, saw the kind of layout Betty Sue was having to do they could not believe that commercial typesetters could operate so unprofessionally. They set chapters 4 and 5 and were a joy to work with.

Tom and Betty were pretty particular about how they wanted the book to look. With all the special phonetic fonts and cartoons, they wanted to supervise it closely. They prayed about how to publish and decided, to ensure that all the details were right, to do it themselves. To do so they had to start their own publishing house. They called it Lingua House, and in November of 1975 Lingua House published *LAMP*, its first book.

It was time for a celebration when the manuscript was finally off to the printers. They had lived, eaten, and slept that project for so long that even though they made back-up copies and sent it insured by UPS, they were still uneasy lest it somehow not reach the printers and all those hundreds of hours of work be lost.

Initially, of course, Lingua House was just a name and one book. Tom and Betty were in Colorado in the Fall of 1975, staying with our Mom, discussing with each other how they would go about the warehousing, distribution, and management of the operation while traveling. Tom's mother suggested that she would like to do it.

Perfect. Tom was glad to hire her. Tom felt a real sense of responsibility for Mother, as did I, and tried to visit her as often as possible. (At Mom's house one day, Tom had leafed through her *Living Psalms*. He noticed which verses she had underlined, and many of them dealt with trust and safety and loneliness. Tom shared this with Betty and suggested that they should be spending as much time with her as they could.) Since Dad's death, she had gone to nursing school, learned to drive, and begun supporting herself working in nursing homes. Most of the work available to her was swing or night shift, but she hated being out at night. It was hard work at minimum wage. Also a new driver, she especially disliked driving in the wintertime.

Tom knew a little of how she felt, since he hated being out in the cold as well. He looked for a way to provide work for her in Lingua House that would enable her to stay at home. But there were concerns. Could Lingua House pay her enough for part-time work to give her a living wage? Would working at home be good for her, or did she need the stimulus of getting out to go to work? Was it safe for her to try to carry the boxes of books up from the basement and out to the mailbox? They decided it would work, and she became the manager and distributor of Lingua House Publishers.

As it turned out, the arrangement worked well for over five years. The mailman became a friend and picked the books up at the door when she left a note in mailbox for him saying she had boxes to mail. It also ensured that Tom and Betty would get to see Mother at least once a quarter as they needed to do the accounting and file Colorado accounting reports. I'm sure she was sometimes glad for the peace again after they left as the visits were often rushed and hectic, but she always appreciated having them come.

LAMP sales were brisk and Lingua House quickly sold out its first edition. It was picked up by numerous mission boards and many were keen to initiate *LAMP* style language learning among their missionaries right away. Most people appreciated its lightheartedness and obvious attempt to make language learning fun. But not everyone felt that way. While Betty Sue was attending a book table at the IFMA/EFMA conference in Kansas City that following year, an older missionary leader picked it up and thumbed through it briefly. Not realizing that Betty Sue was the co-author, he dismissed it saying, "Young people think everything has to be fun nowadays."

Both the procedures and strategy phases were fairly well understood when Tom and Betty Sue wrote the *LAMP* book. Over the next decade it became reasonably successful, with nearly 25,000 copies sold and used by many missions and missionaries. The *LAMP* book is still used at TIL, Missionary Internship, SIL, and virtually every other missionary language training center. And whether or not the approach and procedures are actually followed closely, virtually all new missionary language learners at least know about "the *LAMP* Method" as one of their language learning options. It is still among the best books available to help learners with language learning strategies and procedures.

While *LAMP* was and is a success among missionary language learners, its appearance was not without some concern on the part of Don Larson. While Don had suggested that the staff at TIL participate in the production of materials, he was quite surprised at the extent to which Tom had used ideas from TIL and his own in-process manuscripts. Don had given what he termed "generic" permission to quote from his materials, but was surprised, he said, at the volume of the borrowing (correspondence to Tom Brewster from Don Larson, November 20, 1985). Tom argued that though the motivation for writing *LAMP* grew directly out of their teaching of Don's materials in the classes at TIL and at the Agape Movement of Campus Crusade, they were actually standing on many people's shoulders.

Tom and Betty Sue always felt they were being careful to give credit to Don for the ideas and inspiration for *LAMP*, as well as for much of their other work. Nevertheless, Don felt confused at the appearance of *LAMP* and delayed the publication of some of his own excellent work until much later (Larson 1985). Sadly, this troubled the relationship between Tom and Don for the rest of Tom's life.

9
"I'VE NEVER BEEN SO FULFILLED
IN ALL MY LIFE!"

> My job is evangelism and church planting, yet each of these learners spends more time involved with people during any given day than I do in a week (as quoted by T. and E. Brewster 1978:101).

After all that work, Tom and Betty were not present at the actual "birth" of *LAMP*. In January of 1976, before the book was back from the printers, they were off to lead another group of Agape language learners in an intensive live-in program in Cochabamba, Bolivia. While there, they met a visiting missionary who informed them that she was enjoying their book! Their own copies arrived by mail several weeks later. Tom was excited about the book—just like a new father—but he was not enthusiastic about the cover. Instead of the glossy black he had requested, the cover had what he thought was an unpleasant green tinge. "It looks like a Girl Scout Manual," he groused. Girl Scout Manual or not, they put it into use immediately in Bolivia.

The three month experiment from February through May 1976 in Cochabamba, Bolivia, was another opportunity to explore the total immersion and language learning cycle concepts with a second group of Agape team members.

"That's all I know today;
I'll tell you more tomorrow."

Before the team went to Cochabamba, Tom had the learners trust the Lord for the opportunity to live with Bolivian families. They were expected to get involved with Spanish speakers from the day they arrived. By the second day there the team members were to learn to say something like, "We will be learning Spanish for about three months here in Cochabamba. We hope to locate a Bolivian family to live with. Do you know of a possible family?"

Following the *LAMP* method, one learner, her husband and two little girls began riding the city buses. She said her memorized text about wanting to find a Bolivian family to live with to everyone on a bus. Then they would get off and board another one. One man took them seriously and invited them to stay in his home. In fact, within less than two weeks all of the team members were living in Bolivian homes, eating with the families and sharing in family life. Warm bonds developed as each learner became a member of his or her adopted family. And, as if in confirmation and affirmation of the commitment to ministry and love for the people, one or more family members trusted Christ during the three months in almost all of these homes.

During their stay, the team members began learning to tell a story about their own personal relationship with God. Each learner planned the total story he wanted to be able to tell in the new language, and then subdivided it into parts that could be memorized in one day. Then he or she would hit the streets sharing that part of their testimony with the contacts on their regular communication route. When he finished, he would say, "That's all I know today; I'll tell you more tomorrow."

Tom and Betty Sue wrote about the success of the program in an article titled, *"I've Never Been So Fulfilled in all my Life!"*

> One girl shared her story with a young man and then asked him if he wanted to invite Christ into his life. He responded affirmatively and she found herself in the awkward position of having to say, "That's all I know today." She encouraged him to wait there while she ran home to get her husband who knew more Spanish than she. He came and led the fellow to Christ.
>
> In fact, over 30 people came to know Christ as a result of the involvement ministry that these new language-learners were able to develop during those three months. . . .
>
> A result of this involvement with people in the community was that ministry opportunities developed, even for these new language-learners. These opportunities prompted [one] learner to comment "I've never been so fulfilled in my life" (1978:101).

In addition to the confirmation that the language could be learned quite effectively and quickly in a total immersion context, all the participants confirmed that ministry did not have to wait for a year or two until they became fluent and confident in the new language. Rather, ministry could begin on Day One.

Tom observed that typically, "the new missionary's year of language study often robs him of the enthusiasm, excitement and zeal for God that he first brought to the field. His vision and expectation are no longer the same as when God placed his call on his life" (1978:105).

In contrast, he noted,

> The Agape team's experience in Bolivia demonstrated the value of new language-learners being independently involved with people in the community. Their skill in using Spanish progressed as they responded daily to their communication needs. And, even more significant, as they enjoyed spending informal communication time with people they found that involvement also resulted in many ministry opportunities. Even the first few months of language-learning can be very fulfilling for the person who knows *how* to learn and who is *involved* with people (T. and E. Brewster 1978:102).

Tom and Betty returned in May from the exhilarating Cochabamba experience convinced anew that the *LAMP* approach to language learning was not only feasible, but it was the best way to really learn a language. Most learners enjoyed a high level of confidence in themselves as language learners and made rapid progress. They confirmed that the time needed to actually get involved in ministry was significantly shorter using this method than for missionaries using other programs. They observed too that the degree to which the missionaries actually engaged in relationship building and evangelism—the job most missionaries are sent out to do—was immensely increased. It was far higher than that achieved by most missionaries.

Moreover, here was an approach to both language learning and evangelism that could take place almost anywhere, whether or not there was a language school in the area, and whether or not traditional church-planting mission activity was allowed. This was much more significant than simply a new way for missionaries to learn languages. This was a serious new strategy for mission that deserved wide attention and support. They began to view their own calling as not just helping language learners, but in facilitating much more effective and appropriate mission activity in furthering God's Kingdom.

Invitation to the "Big Leagues"

Even before the Cochabamba experience, one person who had believed in Tom and Betty Sue was Chuck Kraft, at the Fuller School of World Mission. Chuck had been an advisor to them when they were doing the back translation project for Campus Crusade, and they had developed a friendship and mutual respect. Chuck was a firm believer not only in the importance of missionary language learning, but, long before it became known as "the *LAMP* method," was convinced that the best way to do so was in the context of relationships.

Tom once invited Chuck to speak to the missionary candidates when he and Betty Sue taught the language acquisition seminars for Crusade in San Bernardino. As he often did in his own classes, Chuck "blew some of those people out of the water." In his teaching he loved to challenge traditional missionary attitudes, often deliberately overstating a case to get people's attention and cause them to face critically their assumptions and stereotypes. Sometimes at first, some students were not sure if he was an evangelical, a "liberal" or even if he was a believer. But Tom and Betty Sue loved his style and creative thinking. The discussion of the distinction between form and meaning had been a crucial insight for their translation consultations. And as Chuck expanded the idea, it was clear that it challenged all cross-cultural workers to look at the way their religious forms and meanings were understood in any target culture.

Just as they were finishing *LAMP*, in November of 1975, Chuck invited them to his house for Thanksgiving dinner and to spend a day with him and his wife Meg. They talked at length about their experiences and vision. Chuck was especially interested in their background in translation work, and had been looking for someone to head up a translation program at The Fuller School of World Mission. Late that evening, he surprised them with the question, "Would you be interested in teaching at Fuller?"

Betty Sue was floored. "Why would Fuller want us, of all people?" she asked herself. "We are just in our mid-30s. Why, we're just peons," she thought "and Fuller is the Big Leagues. What do we have to offer?" But Chuck was serious (even though at that moment it was just his idea; he had not discussed it with the rest of the Fuller faculty).

Betty and Tom stayed up another couple of hours discussing it. And as was often the case with the two of them, she was the foot dragger. "I just don't think we can handle it. I am not sure we're Fuller material. Besides, we have our travel commitments. I'm enjoying traveling and I don't want to quit."

Tom thought it was a wonderful opportunity. He thrived on change, and he needed challenges. He saw the possible invitation to Fuller as a challenge and something that could be significant for the Kingdom.

"Come on," he reminded her, "I thought you wanted to settle down?"

It was true that she had wanted to settle down. She was at the time thirty-two years old, and looking a little wistfully at motherhood and perhaps a little slower pace:

> I had somewhere in the back of my mind figured that we had to have our first child before I was 30. The summer that I turned 30 was traumatic for me because I didn't have a baby yet. Maybe I should get on with it. Among other things that really bothered me about turning 30, was that part of my self image was being young, I was the youngest person to do this and the youngest to do that and all of a sudden, here I was middle aged. The first year I went to TIL I was the youngest teacher and now we were some of the older teachers. That kind of bothered my self image so I had to find a new self-image, not as a little kid anymore but supposedly as an adult. (I never have quite come through that one. Someday I'm going to be a

lady.) But perhaps it was time to think about a change. Not a sedentary lifestyle, but something more "normal" (E. Brewster 1994).

The next morning they told Chuck some of their hesitancies, like the fact that they wanted to continue traveling, at least part time. He said he did not think that would be a problem. They could join on a part time basis leaving plenty of time for travel and consultations. (And Chuck, of course, did not think they were "peons" at all!)

They accepted the invitation and agreed to begin teaching in the Fall of 1976.

The Fuller School of World Mission was a stimulating environment of innovative people who respected Tom and Betty Sue's own creativity and innovativeness, who wanted to challenge and provoke further investigation of language learning and translation principles. And, they were passionate about exploring new strategies to communicate the Gospel of Christ and further His Kingdom. That was where Tom wanted to be!

The initial agreement with Fuller was to teach two quarters per year, leaving two other quarters free for traveling. In fact, Chuck did not get the translation specialists he thought he was getting. Dean Gilliland had also recently joined the Fuller faculty and took over the new Cross-Cultural Studies Program, the School of World Mission's first for persons who did not have missionary field experience. More and more, Tom and Betty were turning their attention to the language and cross-cultural communication needs of new missionaries, and this program was ideal for this emphasis. Though they taught a few courses in translation theory and practice, they resisted being drawn more into that field. Kraft was disappointed at first, but recognized that their input would be stronger in the area of greatest interest, and was always delighted at their contribution.

With the publication of *LAMP*, Tom and Betty Sue had the tools they needed to provide intensive, on-site, language and culture learning workshops to missionaries and missionary candidates. With a home base at Fuller, they could continue with a modular lifestyle alternately teaching there and consulting or training in other far-flung destinations. And that is just what they did for the next eight years. Their foreign travel decreased slightly, though hardly noticeably, but they did consultations with more groups within the US. In 1977, these included Missionary Internship in Michigan, The Southern Baptist's Journeyman program in Raleigh, the LINK Care program in Fresno, Agape team training in Tijuana, and at the Summer Institute of International Studies, (which later became the popular "Perspectives on the World Christian Movement" course) in Colorado, in addition to their usual TIL. For the next few years, they generally taught two quarters per year at the School of World Mission, and arranged to travel for the other two terms out of the year. This fit Tom's physical needs nicely as well, since he could generally arrange to head south for the winters, since he loathed cold weather.

Blow Out!

Overseas travel in 1977 included a trip to India and Bangladesh in March, and in November to Central America. The first stop was in Costa Rica to do two workshops for Peace Corps people, in conjunction with the Center for Human Potential from Chicago.

The last Sunday they were in Costa Rica they went for a walk and noticed Tom's wheelchair tires were low. They found a gas station and Betty Sue proceeded to fill them from an air pump. The hose was hanging from a large gauge, but as she was filling the second tire she noticed that the gauge was acting a bit strange. Just then the tire she was filling blew up, and seconds later the other one exploded. Upon more careful observation they found that the hose was indeed hanging from the gauge, but was not at all attached to that gauge—it was just a handy place to hang the hose. What to do with two flat tires? Betty Sue sat down on curb close to tears. They had no spare tires, and were not at all confident they could get new ones anywhere in Costa Rica. Tom, a bit more practical, flagged down a cab to get them back to the hotel.

The next day they wandered around looking for a bicycle shop where they could buy new tires since the old ones were beyond repair. Finally they found one, but, naturally, wheel chair rims are off-size and bicycle tires do not fit well. (Tom was convinced that the manufacturers wanted to be sure that the size was slightly non-standard so they could control the supply and charge higher prices.)

After a great deal of pulling and tugging and oiling the rims, they were finally able to stretch tires onto the rims.

They went from there to El Salvador, Belize, and then to the Wycliffe Jungle camp in southern Mexico. While there, Tom's "jerry-rigged" tires quit holding air. So the jungle camp maintenance man put a plastic hose inside each tire to give them something to roll on. It worked fine on the trails in jungle camp, but sure did sound funny, creaking and squeaking in the airports when they left.

The blowout incident helped Tom make a decision about his personal needs that changed his life considerably. Fuller had made an apartment available to him about three blocks from campus, and modified it to make it more wheelchair accessible. The sunny warm climate in Pasadena suited Tom, and he enjoyed the "walk" to and from his classes. There were smooth sidewalks all the way, and he realized that if he were "motorized" he could get back and forth by himself. He looked into various possibilities and decided on a chair with small motors on the two small rear wheels. (The wheels were made of solid rubber so he would not be in danger of further blowouts!)

The motors were powered by a battery that fit between the wheels and could be easily removed for recharging and for travel. Tom had just enough hand and arm movement to steer the chair with a little joystick. It worked well for him. The chair and battery were heavy for Betty to lift when she had to put it into a car, but Tom's increased mobility, freeing her up from time to time, made the tradeoff worthwhile for both of them. From then on, the battery and a charger was an essential part of their travel gear.

In early 1978, they were once again teaching their very popular class on language and culture learning at Fuller. Even in these classes, the students were expected to find one or more speakers of some language of interest and work with them to learn initial phrases in that language. The Los Angeles area is blessed with a large number of ethnic communities, and forty or so learners were able to work in fifteen languages: Arabic, Dutch, French, German, Indonesian, Japanese, Korean, Mandarin, Portuguese, Samoan, Spanish, Swedish, Tamil, Thai, and Tiv.

In July they spent a day at the Wycliffe North American Branch conference and had a workshop on learning the North American Native American languages. Some of the translators responded positively, while others seemed to think it impossible to really learn American Indian languages in the *LAMP* way (or any other way, for that matter). "Besides that," some argued, "it is a side-track/distraction from our true goal of Bible translation." Just how they did effective translation without thoroughly learning the language is a bit of a mystery! (Betty Sue overheard one woman say "No missionary has ever learned an Athabascan language well except one Roman Catholic priest a long time ago, and perhaps stories of his language learning are exaggerated—who knows, a hundred years from now they might even think we learned to speak it!")

Fortunately, the attitude is much different today in all branches of Wycliffe.

LEAP!

The rest of 1978 was spent in the US in various workshops and a heavier than usual load at Fuller. It was not until December that they did any travel outside the US, and that was to Cali, Colombia for what they called the "Language Exploration and Acquisition Project" (LEAP) They were exploring a new role for themselves there, that of "coaches" for the learners. Once again, all the participants stayed in the homes of Colombians, including Tom and Betty who stayed with a widow lady and her son (around ten) and a couple other boarders. Nancy Chillingworth, Carol Littlejohn, Jan Metzger and Sandra Banasik (now Seaton) went with them as assistant coaches.

The participants again learned a good deal of Spanish, and had good success in building the kinds of relationships that resulted in opportunities to share the Gospel. Tom was not as pleased however with the "coaching" role for himself and the others. He felt it was too high-powered and caused more dependency in learners than was healthy. Tom felt that they should think the role through further and try to be less conspicuous in the training but still provide the insights and encouragement for learners to learn languages on their own.

Interestingly, just at that time, God was arranging another model to explore.

"We're Pregnant!"

It was while in Colombia that Tom and Betty discovered that "they" were pregnant. (Tom never let people forget it was a joint project!) They left the LEAP project in the hands of the assistant coaches, and returned to Pasadena.

At the time Tom was reading II Samuel, and encountered the name Jedidiah—Beloved of the Lord—in II Samuel 12:24. He told Betty that if they had a son (and he was pretty sure they would), he wanted to name him Jedidiah. At first Betty laughed, thinking he had made up the name, but after he explained the meaning, she agreed.

Obviously, for a quadriplegic, the very possibility of fathering a child is not at all certain. It is possible, though unusual. And for Betty Sue, for whom caring for Tom was as big a task as caring for several children, the prospect of caring for an infant as well as Tom should have seemed a daunting challenge. Given the enormous challenges already inherent in their traveling lifestyle, most would have thought that having a child would surely mean an end to the travel and consultation that they enjoyed so much. Betty thought they could probably carry on more or less as they had been doing, maintaining a heavy travel schedule, and continuing to teach in various locations around the world. Amazingly, that is exactly what they did!

I must admit that, as his brother, I was not sure how a child would fit in to their lives. Tom was a very caring and loving uncle to my own young son, but he certainly was not overly tolerant of the neighborhood children going about their normal, noisy business of being kids. Tom was always aware of the usefulness of children in language learning activities (they do not seem to mind being asked the same questions over and over again, or having someone endlessly repeat phrases to them, but frankly, he did not seem to have much use for them otherwise). Tom was always very intense in his teaching and I remember him encouraging learners coming to TIL to leave their children at home. Indeed, before Jed came along, I always thought of Tom as "putting up" with kids, as long as they did not interfere with their parent's language learning activities.

It is amazing how a child of your own changes your perspective!

My wife Alice and I had the privilege of living next door to Tom and Betty Sue during their first two years at Fuller, from 1976–1978, and, no doubt, we had a big influence on their decision to have a home birth. When the news came in 1977 that we were expecting our second child we started looking for alternatives to the traditional hospital birth. One of the main reasons was the overwhelming cost; we were seminary students living on a shoestring without any childbirth insurance and would have found it very difficult to cover those costs.

Most importantly, however, my wife had a mind of her own about being responsible for her own body and wanting to be in control of what she viewed as a natural process. She was concerned that doctors sometimes had their own schedules and agenda in mind, and that they treated childbirth as a sickness. Not surprisingly, those sentiments resonated positively with Tom. The result for us was our finding a chiropractor in Southern California who, along with his nurse, did "almost legal" home deliveries. When the time came, in February, 1978, we invited Tom and Betty Sue and Alice's parents to share that delightful "birthday party" for our second child, in the front room of our apartment. Julisa's birth was a joyous and exciting time for all of us, and the all natural experience was beautiful and exhilarating.

Our extremely rewarding and exciting home birth, made Tom and Betty serious about home birthing. But clearly, with their own

general distrust for doctors, they did not need much encouragement from us to be enthusiastic about a home birth themselves.

On more than one occasion Tom believed he was badly mis-
treated by doctors, and in some cases, he felt his life had been in
jeopardy as a result. He was very concerned that doctors seemed to
conduct their work in secrecy, to make assumptions without consulting the patient, and often intervene unnecessarily or improp-
erly. All of these things contributed to their thinking about home
birthing alternatives.

Given the medical establishment opposition to home birthing in
California at the time, they had to shop around fairly aggressively
just like we did to find a midwife whom they felt good about and
who was willing to do the job. Just when Betty was getting discouraged, they met Joan Doland who agreed to be their midwife.
Betty's June 19 entry in her diary read: "First felt the baby move
for sure—and Tom felt it, too! Shortly after that left to see *Brother
Sun, Sister Moon,* felt baby move again. Was on a high all
evening!"

Language Learning "Midwifery"

Tom was always on the lookout for illustrations and analogous
processes, and the pregnancy was a gold mine. He was convinced
that language learning was a social activity, not just an academic
one, and that the socialization process had to be with native
speakers of the language—not classroom teachers or missionaries.
It led to a very creative but perhaps somewhat angry (or intense?)
time of writing and reflection, resulting in the publication of the
unusual article "Language Learning Midwifery."

It is clear that "midwifery" was written during their frustrating
time of searching for alternatives to typical hospital birthing practices which would humanize the process, and give them more
control over it. The California laws at the time made it very difficult to go around the system, and their frustration grew at every
turn. However, ideas about the analogies of midwifing the birthing
and the language learning processes flowed freely.

Both pregnant women and new language learners, he said, "are assumed to be in desperate need of all the technological and institutional help that can be provided for this poor individual who has gotten herself into this horrible situation" (1983a). In an analogy that was perhaps a bit overextended, Tom compared the "patient" with the typical language learning student in a classroom:

> *The patient* in childbirth routinely endures the sterile environment, rules to be followed, routinized interaction with professionals, imposed schedules, internal exams, enema and prep, intravenous infusions, chemicals to induce labor, anesthetic and analgesic narcotics, breaking the bag of water, electronic fetal monitoring, stirrups, forceps and (with alarming frequency) cesarean section. When delivered the drugged child is separated from the mother during the recovery process. Accompanying all these privileges is the privilege of paying an exorbitant fee. Altogether a dehumanizing and degrading experience violating the individual's dignity while lowering self-esteem and fostering dependency on the system.
>
> *The student* in language study routinely endures a sterile learning environment, rules to follow, routine interaction with professionals, imposed schedules, assignments, homework, drills, paradigms and grammar rules, dialogues and vocabulary lists, electronic tape recorders, laboratories and even computers, textbooks, artificial sequencing and examinations. When the course is completed, the student's compatibility with the system is evaluated and a grade is given. Though costs are normally exorbitant, seldom does the process result in the student's ability to communicate in a new language. It is typically a dehumanizing and degrading experience ignoring the individual's dignity and lowering self-esteem, while fostering a dependence on the system (T. and E. Brewster 1980:204).

Tom and Betty Sue were concerned that many language learners start out with a defeatist mentality, having been convinced, usually through school experiences, that they cannot learn another language. The key to normal, natural childbirth or language learning, they argued, was first to believe that it was possible, and second, to adopt an attitude which says, "I bring plenty of God-given capability to a manageable, indeed exciting, challenge. Thus

I don't particularly need technology, but I do need to implement a course of action to keep me in harmony with the natural . . . processes" (1980:205).

As language learning "midwives," they affirmed that language learning is a normal, God-given capability. Their argument was that dependence on the "system" was crippling for both patients and students and that there was a better way for both the birthing and the language learning. The alternative Tom said, is a return to normality:

> Women have been giving birth since Eve just as though they were uniquely designed for the process. Most women of the rest of the world find it a fulfilling and manageable challenge. Similarly, languages are learned spontaneously by virtually all children, and more than half of the world is multilingual. They learn language in the context of relationships and find their learning to be meaningful and manageable (1980:205).

On September 2, 1979, their son was born in the front room of their apartment. They named him Jedidiah. On September 3, Tom bundled one-day old "Jed" onto his lap and strolled off in his electric wheelchair to the Fuller campus to show him off to the President, the late David Hubbard, and other faculty. Tom was always enormously proud of Jed—the ultimate of proud papas—and loved to have him with him no matter what he was doing. At two weeks, Tom took him on his lap to the barber shop, to show him off to the barber. On September 29, at just four weeks of age, Tom and Betty Sue bundled him up and took him with them to a second LEAP project for a month in Guatemala and Honduras!

This Second LEAP was with Wycliffe mission personnel and new missionaries. As usual, Tom had the participants spend their days on the streets in relationships with people. But this time, Tom and Betty Sue went as "midwives" to facilitate the natural process of language learning—not as coaches!

10
BONDING AND THE MISSIONARY TASK

I believe that if your goal is to learn a language, you'll probably fail. On the other hand, if your goal is to know people—to deeply love people, to be involved in their lives—then success in language learning is predictable. If your goal is to be deeply involved in a network of relationships with people, then language learning will be almost spontaneous. It will not be a goal in itself—it will rather be a means to an end (T. Brewster 1983:192).

Some people come to me with a whole basket full of reasons why learning a language through relationships won't work for them. You don't need a basket full of rationalizations and reasons why you can't do it. Just one is enough. If you have one excuse that is legitimate from your frame of reason, that's all you need. That's enough to weigh it 100% against all the reasons why you can (T. Brewster 1983:377).

You don't get a duck to become imprinted on you at any old time (1983:69).

They were back in Los Angeles in November where they taught an intensive course at Fuller. In December they decided to go to Hawaii, for a long vacation. Clearly they needed the vacation and time away to enjoy their newborn son. But there was much more to this trip. Our younger sister Ramona was at a crisis point in her life, and desperately needed some counsel and spiritual nurture, Mom too, needed a break and time for renewal. Tom and Betty made the arrangements and paid the fares for both to join them in Hawaii. The time there was a profound turning point in Mona's life as we will see. It was delightful for Mom as well, and satisfying for Tom too, for as it turned out, Mom was never able to travel again.

But it was pivotal for Tom and Betty as well, for two reasons. One, they met Loren Cunningham, the International Director for Youth With A Mission (YWAM) which became one of Tom's favorite mission contacts, and resulted in far-reaching consultations for him and Betty over the next few years. Secondly, it was a creative time and they were able to write an article that became a signature piece—"Bonding and the Missionary Task."

The Imprinting of Ducks . . . and Missionaries

Tom and Betty Sue were preaching bonding long before they had the vocabulary to talk about it. They had spoken often of their dismay at the isolation of most new missionaries from the people to whom they were sent to minister. The response to the problem began to emerge from the practical "living among the people" experiences that they had at Machakos, Kenya, Cochabamba, Bolivia and Cali, Colombia. Their observations and study after Jed was born brought it into focus.

Again, Tom's mistrust of the medical establishment fueled the writing process. From the time they learned they were pregnant, they had begun to read all they could on the subject of childbirth and related subjects. One of those subjects was the work of Nobel prize winning naturalist, Konrad Lorenz. He studied and wrote about the phenomenon of "imprinting" which took place among ducklings and a variety of other animals, including goats, cows, and monkeys. He showed that at a critical time, immediately after hatching, if Lorenz and the ducklings were alone together, they would from then on respond to him as though he were their parent. A photo of ducklings following Lorenz was widely published, drawing attention to his work.

As is now well known, infants and mothers also have an early period of extreme sensitivity right after birth. If the mother and infant are together at this time, a close bonding results which can withstand subsequent separations. However, if an infant and mother are separated immediately after birth, the infant can become attached to a surrogate or substitute mother—a cloth doll, a different adult animal, or even a human. Then, if the infant and mother are later reunited, one or both may reject the other or at least not respond with the normal attachment.

Dairymen have known about the imprinting phenomena for generations. A newborn calf will be taken from its mother and attached to
a substitute mother and the substitute will care for four or five different calves. There have also been experiments with monkeys in
which a newborn monkey can be attached to a rag doll. Later on
when the real mother was put into the cage with the baby, it was
startled and frightened. Where does the startled infant run for its
security? To its mother? No, to the rag doll because of the imprinting and the sense of belonging that it has established (T. Brewster
1983:68, 69).

Tom felt that the abnormal attachment to a surrogate or substitute mother, in this case other missionaries, was precisely what
happens to most new missionaries when they arrive on the field.

They read Marshall H. Klaus and John H. Kennel (1976) who
extended the concept of animal imprinting to human bonding in
their book *Maternal-Infant Bonding* (1976). In the bonding article,
Tom argued that the typical hospital birth was not conducive to
normal bonding between mother and child for at least two reasons.
First, hospital-born babies are often drugged and therefore groggy
from a variety of medications typically given to the mother during
labor. Neither the baby nor the mother have the opportunity to
experience a period of acute alertness immediately after birth.

Second, normal bonding sometimes does not occur within the
hospital establishment because the baby is "typically snatched
away from his family and straightway placed in the isolation of the
nursery" (T. and E. Brewster 1984a:4). "It's not uncommon," Tom
wrote, "for the first bonding experience of the infant to be not with
the mother, but rather with the hospital personnel." Tom viewed
this as almost a criminal intrusion on the family privilege
(1983:67–68).

Of course Tom saw many analogies and comparisons with this
process and the typical "birthing and bonding" experiences of new
missionaries—the experience of new missionaries being "snatched"
away for orientation by their more experienced missionary colleagues the moment they arrive rather than being with the people
they come to minister to. Tom felt that this was one reason they

never form the strong relationship bonds necessary for successful language learning or successful missionary work.

> Just as the infant is snatched away by the hospital establishment and put into the isolation of the nursery, so the newly arrived missionary is typically snatched away by the expatriate missionary contingency and, thus, isolated from his new language community (T. and E. Brewster 1984a:4).

The Bonding of "Joe Missionary"

Tom used a striking illustration of the typical way that missionaries are received into the new country. They were on a plane in southern Africa, and stopping in Malawi the plane pulled up to the terminal where there was a large group of white faces (American missionaries) holding a long banner from the observation deck. The banner was welcoming a new missionary family and had the name of the mission board written under it. The new missionary family got off the airplane, and the huge crowd of missionary residents soon gathered around to meet them.

Tom speculated what was going to happen during the next couple of weeks to the newly arrived "Joe Missionary and his family."

He guessed that they would be taken to their homes and have a big festive welcome party. They would stay in the homes of the missionaries during the next couple of weeks while they got their other living arrangements sorted out. Then they would take some trips to the game park and down to the lake and all the other places that the tourists go with their cameras. And then they'd have to start settling down because they have their umpteen barrels arriving soon at the port of entry. And they only know one way to settle; they only know one way to live. They've always lived in a western way and they see the other missionaries who have been hanging around with them during these weeks also living in a western way. Besides, their mission board required them to raise so much money that they have to live in a western way.

> And then they get established. And after about the first month you get a prayer letter from "Joe Missionary and his family," telling about how wonderful it has been to be welcomed by the missionar-

ies and all the wonderful orientation that they've been receiving. The letter ends with a prayer request that they might now get to have some relationships established with the local people; that they might meet some of the local people and get to know them (T. Brewster 1983:71).

That was "a noble desire," Tom said, "but, unfortunately, a concern that is being expressed about three weeks too late!—and now without a viable strategy to achieve the goal" (T. Brewster and E. Brewster 1984a:8).

It would have been far better, he argued, had those new missionaries come and gotten deeply involved with the people God had called them to, and begun to enjoy a sense of belonging with them and had their priorities straight.

Tom was not questioning the motives behind the welcoming committees that greeted new missionaries around the world. He understood the motives. But he was definitely questioning the results. "People get locked into a lifestyle right from the beginning. It happens so subtly that they've never had the opportunity to question 'what is this going to mean in terms of my effectiveness for what I've been called to do here?'" (1983:72).

Tom and Betty felt that much of the orientation established missionaries offered to the incoming new missionary might in fact be a mistake for several reasons. First, they argued that when the new missionary's sense of belonging was established with other foreigners, it was predictable that the new missionary would carry out his ministry by the "foray" method:

> . . . he will live isolated from the local people, as the other foreigners do, but make a few forays out into the community each week, returning always to the security and isolation of the missionary community. Without bonding he does not have a sense of feeling at home within the local cultural context. Thus, he does not pursue, as a way of life, significant relationships in the community (T. and E. Brewster 1984a:6).

They continued:

> When normal bonding is not established, rejection of the people, or even abuse, can occur—it is often reflected in the attitude behind

statements like "Oh, these people! Why do they always do things *this* way?" or "Somebody ought to teach them how to live!" or "Won't these people *ever* learn?" (1984a:6).

Second, Tom felt that sheltering new missionaries from immediate exposure to the local language, culture and people would cause them to miss out on a unique window of opportunity for learning and acceptance. He recognized that newcomers would experience disorientation which could lead to culture shock, but argued that it is better to plunge right in and experience the new situation from the insider's perspective, while the sense of excitement and newness and adventure is strong. During the first two or three weeks the newcomer would be especially able to cope with the unpredictable situations encountered in the new culture. Indeed, he would probably even revel in all the variety. Better to live with the people, worship with them, go shopping with them, and use their public transportation right from the start. *"From the very first day* it is important to develop many meaningful relation- ships with local people" (1984a:8).

> You don't get a duck to become imprinted on you at any old time. You don't decide that it would be nice if this duck would follow you around just any old time. You have to start right at the beginning. And I'm convinced that there is a right time also for people going into a new culture. It is extremely important how the first two weeks are spent. Usually by the end of the first two weeks, the group—the ethnic group that the missionary feels comfortable with—will be firmly established (T. Brewster 1983:69–70).

Third, though Tom recognized the risks of bonding with local people, he felt that the stress and risk components might themselves be essential to the formation of the unique chemistry that makes imprinting and bonding possible (T. and E. Brewster 1984a:14). Moreover, he felt that *not* being willing to bond with local people had its own, much more serious, long-term risks:

> I'm convinced that newcomers into a culture with the kind of orien- tation that puts a focus on relationships can get deeply involved in very, very meaningful relationships, and they not only can but they must do it from the very first day, right from the outset. If they

don't, then they're going to be a tourist. They're just going to be viewing all the sites and dancing around the fringes of things rather than really getting involved in other people's lives. They may be very busy in "ministry," but they may not be ministering when viewed through the eyes of local people (T. Brewster 1983:95, 96).

We see an awful lot of that in missions today. Missionaries are being recruited to do all kinds of different things—technological things, run print shops and run camera shops and run automobile repair shops and build buildings and all the rest. And unfortunately, a lot of missionaries are defining their work in ways that exclude themselves from meaningful, deep relationships with the local people. I think this is a weakness in western missions. But I think we've gotten into it largely because we don't know how to get deeply involved in relationships with peoples of another culture (1983:97, 98).

We Have This Treasure in Earthen Vessels . . .

Finally, Tom argued that the very vulnerability of a new missionary when he first arrives on the mission field, is a strength—it helps the missionary to be dependent on the nationals. Tom could speak about vulnerability. His every body function needed assistance. He had known many times when he had to ask people, even some he hardly knew, for assistance in some embarrassing or humiliating things. And Betty provided the same assistance on a daily basis. A willingness to be vulnerable, so contrary to our culture, was, Tom felt, the key to successful bonding, and a key to acceptance and effectiveness in missionary work.

Unfortunately, we have a cultural perception that causes us to believe that dependence and vulnerability are weaknesses. On the contrary, the one who authenticates his life-message is the one whose strength lies in his willingness to be vulnerable. . . . The Lord told the Apostle Paul "My power shows up best in weak people" (2 Corinthians 12:9 Living Bible). "We have this treasure in earthen vessels, that the excellence of the power may be of God, and not of us" (2 Corinthians 4:7). Jesus' willingness to go all the way to the cross is the supreme example of vulnerability being a strength (T. and E. Brewster 1984b:7).

Vulnerability, Tom knew, is a willingness to put oneself in a position where others learn of your weaknesses, might find you out, or even take advantage of you. He lamented the fact that sometimes missionaries don't want to come across to the local people as ones who are needy, who have shortcomings. They want to come across as though they have it all together; with the attitude that if others would just do it their way, then they would have it all together as well. "But the fact is, we all have our struggles, and if we share with people the very struggles we go through, the growing processes that we experience might enable people to have a pattern for growing themselves" (1983:100).

Tom saw western independence as being a barrier to missionary effectiveness. Society prepares people to be dependent on institutions, dependent on teachers, dependent on curricula, dependent on professionals, but it doesn't prepare us to be dependent on other persons. "[Our western] society does not prepare people to independently take responsibility" (1983:40). Tom was aware that his own physical dependence had taught him how to really be vulnerable. He knew too that it is much harder for non-handicapped people to put themselves into such dependent relationships. But he felt that the difficulty or inability to do so resulted in reduced effectiveness of western missionaries. He asked the YWAMers,

> What does it mean to be dependent on other people rather than living in independence? . . . I wonder if we don't rob people of the privilege of having God bless them because we don't put ourselves in a [dependent] relationship with them. I'm convinced that our independence and our self-sufficiency gets in the way of God using us.
>
> Remember Elijah? God directed him to the poorest woman in the whole village, and she said, "We only have a little bit and we're collecting some wood to cook it. It's going to be our last meal. We'll eat it and die." Isn't it interesting that this was the family the Lord directed Elijah to be dependent upon. Because she had the privilege of giving that which she did have, she also had the privilege of receiving that which God wanted to pour out into her life (T. Brewster 1983:98, 99).

Tom was also aware that the successful "bonding" of many new missionaries with national cultures required significant preparation and a very different mindset than that of new missionaries or mission boards. A significant prior decision and commitment to do so is essential. Without that prior commitment, it simply will not happen. Part of the preparation that Tom required for those he supervised during their initial immersion and bonding times, such as that in Machakos and Cochabamba, included meeting four conditions: (1) Being willing to live with a local family; (2) Limiting personal belongings to twenty kilos; (3) Using only local public transportation; (4) Expecting to carry out language learning in the context of relationships that the learner himself would be responsible to develop and maintain (T. and E. Brewster 1984a:14).

Language Learning Is Communication—Is Ministry

The concept behind bonding was not new in missiology. Much had been written previously about the related idea of "identification" by missionaries with target cultures. What was revolutionary in Tom's teaching was *when* bonding needed to be done. Missions had done so much to develop field training and orientation programs to ease their missionaries into the target cultures and language learning activities. Now Tom came along saying that much of that might not be necessary or even counter-productive. The notion was disturbing to some. To others however, it was a startlingly refreshing door opener for radically more effective cross-cultural ministry. For several missions, it changed dramatically the way they thought about missionary preparation, orientation, language learning and even the way they "do" missions. Don Stevens, Director of Mercy Ships, wrote in a personal letter:

> I think that the single most profound concept that Tom was able to communicate was his understanding of "bonding." This word has so been used, not only within Mercy Ships, but also within Youth With a Mission International, that it is currently a buzz word. Tom gave us the understanding that identification, empathy, and being culturally sensitive and being willing to live on an equal standard with any people or any culture were all a part of the bonding process.

We often now refer to different individuals as, "Yes, they were deeply bonded; or no, they missed something in their bonding process." All of this came to us through Tom and Betty Sue's understanding of identification and compassion with the people they were trying to reach (1987).

Bonding also fit seamlessly into the teaching and writing that Tom and Betty had always done. The focus on the importance of building cross-cultural relationships permeated their ministry from the beginning. Their first professional article, printed in *Practical Anthropology* in January/February 1972, called "Involvement as a Means of Second Culture Learning," was a preview of their message and ministry for many years. In it, they spelled out the importance of being involved with others if one was to have any genuine opportunity to effectively learn a second language. The rest of their dozen years in ministry reinforced that point, and expanded its application to all aspects of cross-cultural evangelism and mission.

They observed that whenever people are members of a social group, they speak the language of that group. They had gotten to know many tribal people in Africa and elsewhere who spoke two, three, and sometimes half a dozen or more languages but who had little education and no formal language training. They had learned the languages by being with the people, listening to them and being part of the groups that spoke those languages. Tom said the real challenge for learners then, was not "How do I learn the language?" but rather "How do I join a social group of the people God has called me to?"

In fact, they were convinced that language learning itself should be secondary to getting to know the people:

> I believe that if your goal is to learn a language, you'll probably fail. On the other hand, if you goal is to know people—to deeply love people, to be involved in their lives—then success in language learning is predictable. If your goal is to be deeply involved in a network of relationships with people, then language learning will be almost spontaneous. It will not be a goal in itself—it will rather be a means to an end (T. Brewster 1983:192).

The more Tom thought about it, the more it became fundamental to his ministry that language learning was not something done in preparation for cross-cultural ministry but that language learning *is* (or at least should be) ministry. Chuck Kraft was convinced of the same thing, and had been thinking of writing an article spelling that out. In discussion with Tom, Chuck mentioned the idea and suggested that Tom write it. The result was a powerful complement to the bonding article called "Language Learning is Communication—is Ministry!" published in the *International Bulletin of Missionary Research* in 1982.

The point was that language learning was not simply a means to prepare for ministry to the people but rather, the language learning, when done in a highly involved way and by building relationships right from the start, was itself ministry.

Chuck Kraft had often said that the most effective way for even a short-term missionary to spend his time is in beginning to learn the language:

> Chuck was once asked the question, "How much time should one who goes to serve as a two month short-term missionary spend in language learning?"
>
> Kraft responded: "Two months."
>
> The questioner continued, "What about one who stays six months?"
>
> "Then spend six months in language learning."
>
> "And if he stays two years?"
>
> "There is nothing he could do that would communicate more effectively than spending those two years in language learning." Kraft continued, "Indeed, if we do no more than engage in the process of language learning we will have communicated more of the essentials of the Gospel than if we devote ourselves to any other task I can think of" (T. and E. Brewster 1984b:1).

Thinking Missions?—Study Abroad!

Tom suggested that one response toward overcoming the bonding to one's own culture that anyone crossing cultural boundaries faces is to think about studying abroad as part of their preparation. One of the major reasons why people do not go to the mission field, he said, is that they finish college in the United States. What is wrong with that?

> Each year North American graduates enter a materialistic society where a cacophony of voices thrusts its advice: "Better get a job." "Get some experience first." "This is the time of life to get married and settle down." "You need a seminary education before you can become a missionary." And later, "You owe your children a good start."
>
> A subtle trap. Debts pile up as young families accumulate houses, furniture and cars. The "cares of this world" get heavy. Each new commitment reduces flexibility and options. Each year takes the edge off zeal to serve God in a foreign country. Availability to God becomes subject to "ifs"—"If only I could . . . then I would follow through on my commitment to be a missionary (1985:21).

One new missionary who listened to him on this was Carol Nerge. She and Tom met in a short language learning course Tom and Betty taught in San Francisco in July of 1982. At the time Carol was trying to decide whether to go to seminary for two years in the states to meet a requirement imposed by her mission before going to Nepal, or to pursue the possibility of ministry in Hungary by studying the language and literature of Hungary in the university in Budapest. One evening she had a long talk with Tom, telling him of her dual interests. She writes:

> [Tom] seemed to have keen insight into my real interests and into the question of trying to reconcile my choice of schools and the goals I had. He said simply, "Carol, I nearly always advise that if a person has the choice of living in a new culture and learning there, it is far superior to schooling in one's own culture." My heart exploded with joy. Here was the first person who seemed to be saying, "It is okay for you to choose to go to Hungary even if there will be no degrees to show for it and there may not even be any practical or concrete skills gained" (Nerge 1987).

There's little doubt that the concept of bonding was the most talked about and controversial component of Tom and Betty Sue's teachings. Many embraced it wholeheartedly, and they gathered many endorsements from both new missionaries and established missionaries who began to take it seriously and move into bonding relationships with national people.

But there is also little doubt that it worked. It gave people a confidence that they could, in fact, learn a new language, and it equipped new missionaries to relate positively to the people to whom they were called to minister. In a report done by the Wycliffe mission after the October 1979 Guatemala LEAP program in which learners hit the streets and bonded with nationals, the mission noted:

> . . . each of [The LEAP participants] . . . [is] less affected by the "ghetto mentality" than any of our other missionaries.
>
> The LEAPers feel relatively "at home" in Latin culture. The Language Schoolers, even those who have been here for years, do not.
>
> The LEAPers have not only learned some Spanish, they have learned how to continue learning by relating to people. Most Language Schoolers, when asked about further Spanish learning, have ideas of "taking an advanced course," or "working through a grammar book."
>
> Those in the control group have, on the average, one Guatemalan friend. The LEAPers each have fifteen or more.
>
> Each LEAPer has had contacts with dozens of people in Guatemala. There are at least 1,000 Guatemalans who have had positive experiences with the mission in the twelve weeks of this program . . . (Echerd 1980:27).

Scores of individual missionaries also testified to the effectiveness of the bonding approach and to the depth of the relationships made possible through bonding

> During our first year, my wife and I bonded with a family in the Tugen hills (in Kenya). . . . It does work! When we returned from "bonding," someone made a joking sort of comment about the Kalenjin people (those with whom we were bonded). We both cringed at the comment—as if they had said something about our mother! We then realized what bonding was! Since then, our love for the people has only deepened. I really enjoy their things, activities—even their language is somehow fun and sweet to hear and use (Meeks 1983).

11
INSIGHTS AND HEARTACHES

Tom helped me to discover that there is so much we can learn from blacks, and in that way South African society can be changed into a society in which people are willing to learn from each other—both blacks and whites (Smith 1993).

The message was clear and strong—God and His Kingdom is the motivating force. "Give priority to building relationships with people (bonding). View language learning as part and parcel of ministry. Take personal responsibility for getting the language. Make a commitment to a simple lifestyle. . . ." Those who have put this into practice have reaped the fruits of it in such a rich and satisfying ministry (Gradin 1985).

After the publication of the article on bonding in the *International Review of Missions* in 1980, Tom and Betty spent most of the remainder of that year in the US. They taught at the School of World Mission, and with Link Care in Fresno; they consulted with the Navigators in a short-term missions project on a Navaho reservation and did a month long workshop in Quesnel, British Colombia, with the "Missionary Development Program," the training and orientation program of the North American Indian Mission.

Early in 1981 however, they were off again to Africa.

Tom and Betty spent their 14th anniversary, February, 14, 1981, flying to Johannesburg. There they had a two week seminar in Hammanskraal, a conference ground near Warmbad, South Africa.

Apartheid

It was at that seminar that they first met Nico and Ellen Smith.

Nico Smith was a professor at Stellenbosch University. He was concerned about the pass courts' system in South Africa. This evil system required blacks to present a pass for permission to move about. Blacks were allowed to travel or live in only certain places, often apart from their wives and children. The hardships created forced many blacks to violate the pass laws, and an entire court system was established to control and prosecute violators. Nico was outspoken about the evil of the pass system and spoke often of it in his classes. His frustration was at a boiling point when he first met Tom.

Tom suggested that Nico take some of the students to the courts to have them see for themselves the injustice and grief the laws imposed on the blacks. Nico said that by law he could not take them nor assign them to go, but could tell them what he had seen and encourage them to go on their own and he determined to do that. And he became more and more vocal about his views on the appalling system of apartheid. He began to be watched, by the media, and by the administration at the university.

Some time later a well established coloured squatter town was being bulldozed and the women and children were being forced to go to a "homeland," one of the mostly depressed and impoverished "independent countries" carved out of South Africa by the apartheid government for blacks to avoid having to share power with them in South Africa. Nico told his students he was going to go and see if it was as bad as they had heard. A number of the students decided to go with him. The ride to the township in the bus began like any other school outing with a lot of laughing and joking. But what they saw was no laughing matter. It was much worse than they ever imagined. They were dumbfounded at the callousness with which the homes were destroyed, and the pain inflicted on the residents, most of whom had nowhere else to go.

For many of the all white students, this was their first real exposure to the horrors of the oppressive systems within apartheid. The students saw the women and children weeping, their things being thrown out on the ground, and the women sent away without even the opportunity to notify their husbands.

The trip back to Stellenbosch was a somber one. The students were stunned by what they had seen. And by the time Nico and the students got back to Stellenbosch, the media were waiting for them. What is more, the administration of the university was also there to meet Nico. Their advice to him was to keep quiet if he wanted to keep his job. "If you do talk," they threatened him, "we will have to relieve you of your teaching position."

He and Ellen spent a couple of days praying about it. Could he in good conscience keep quiet? What would they live on if he did lose his position? What did God want them to do? While praying about it, a black congregation from Mamelodi, another township outside of Pretoria, contacted him to see if he would be their pastor.

> The name [Mamelodi] means "place of melody" because a brook runs through the center of town, but there is nothing very melodious there. The government began building the township in the late '40s as a sort of dormitory-warehouse for black workers needed in Pretoria. The standard houses are four-bedroom huts, each with an outside water faucet next to the outdoor privy. For years the people shipped to Mamelodi were forbidden to own their homes or make improvements. That was supposed to make them look forward to eventual relocation to remote tribal homelands (Hawthorne 1988:42).

For Nico to even consider the offer was very unusual. Tenured professors did not "step down" to be pastors. If they left a professorship, it was to move up, not to take a pastorate! And for a white to pastor a black congregation? That was indeed unusual—and illegal. Not only would he be the only white minister in the township, he and his wife would be the sole white residents in this township of 300,000 persons.

Just after they had accepted the invitation they attended one of Tom and Betty Sue's classes at Hammanskraal, South Africa. Nico talked extensively with Tom and through the discussions his decision to take the pastorate and try to live among the people in Mamelodi was confirmed. Nico relates Tom's influence in the decision:

> Tom awakened in me the sensitivity for the personhood of others, especially for blacks in South Africa. My decision to eventually go

and stay amongst the black people in a time when blacks were not allowed by law to live among whites, and whites not to live amongst blacks, was directly and indirectly the fruit of Tom's attitude—that there is something to learn from every person, no matter how poor, uneducated, or of whatever state in life (Smith 1993).

Smith's decision to take the pastorate at Mamelodi was so unusual, and dangerous, it was picked up by *Time* Magazine. Reporter Peter Hawthorne wrote:

> To the professor, Nico Smith, it meant a complete change in his life, a rejection, in fact, of everything that his life had been until then and everything fundamental in Afrikaner society and Afrikaner belief.
>
> [Since he took the pastorate] no Pretoria parish in the Dutch Reformed Church has invited him to speak. . . . People he thought were friends have turned away. There are telephone calls in the night. "Now that you're living with the Kaffirs," said one caller, "when we come to shoot them, we'll shoot you too" (1988:40).

In spite of the threats, Nico and his wife continued to live and to minister in Mamelodi. He wrote further of Tom's influence:

> His life was a real inspiration to me. The Lord used Tom at a stage when I started to be a lonely voice for the personhood of black people which was violated by the demonic system of apartheid. My encounter with Tom assured me that I wasn't totally out of step as my fellow white South Africans made me to understand. I will ever be thankful to the Lord that he sent Tom my way (1993).

Mom's Cancer

Tom and Betty Sue returned from Africa in March of 1981, and taught again at Fuller That summer, they were again in Fresno, did a seminar for InterVarsity in New Orleans, and then were back in British Colombia for another workshop with Missionary Development Program. It was late that summer that Tom's mother was diagnosed with cancer.

Mom and Tom were alike in that neither seemed able to attract the best doctors. One doctor treated Mom for some time for hemorrhoids and bronchitis until another discovered that she was actually suffering from advanced colon and lung cancer. In the hospital for the tests they managed to collapse her lung which caused much discomfort. Given his aversion to normal medical practice, reinforced by this misdiagnosis and poor care, Tom did not want Mom to receive chemo or radiation therapy.

Tom did however recommend to her and the rest of the family, some rather unusual diets and foot soaking treatments. These were considered somewhat bizarre by our family and especially to my sister Martha, herself an experienced registered nurse. In the end, however, probably nothing would have made a difference.

Mom was at the time living alone in Colorado. With her children scattered around the country and the world, the family decided that Martha could provide the best care for Mom, so she moved into Martha's home in Tulsa, Oklahoma. Tom and Betty Sue taught at Fuller that Fall, and were able to spend Christmas 1981 with Mom at Martha's home. Given Mom's very serious condition, they struggled with the decision to continue with a planned trip to Asia, knowing that if they left, most likely they would never see her again on this side of eternity. It was Mom who urged them to continue. "There is nothing you can do for me here," she said, "and there is so much good you can do if you carry on."

They reluctantly followed her advice and left for another extended trip beginning in India. Their fears about her condition were confirmed. Just a few days after they left, on January 1, 1982, Mom died, five months to the day after the cancer was diagnosed.

Too far away to return for the funeral, Tom and Betty mourned alone, and then carried on.

From India they went to Kathmandu in Nepal where they held a workshop for the Union Language School run by the United Mission to Nepal. Tom was, of course, very accustomed to culture differences and did not often experience real "culture shock," but he wrote from Kathmandu that he had never been to a place where everything was so strange and unpredictable. The pervasiveness of Buddhism in every aspect of life brought into bold relief the profound spiritual warfare of that hidden and unreached place.

Next, after a stupendous flight along the southern edge of the Himalayan Mountains—"even breathtaking for a Colorado boy" (T. Brewster 1982b)—they presented their language learning workshops at a language school in slum ridden Dhaka, capital of Bangladesh, and then again across the subcontinent in Multan, Pakistan.

Tom and Betty and Jed left Multan at 3:15 in the afternoon on February 20 and arrived back in Colorado Springs via Amsterdam, Chicago, and Denver late on the 21st, so tired they were hardly coherent. For some reason that flight was the hardest they ever took. They rested for a few days in the States and then in March took a holiday in Mazatlan.

In late April they went once again to Hawaii to teach a seminar for the regional directors of YWAM. This further contact with YWAM resulted in opened doors for ministry with YWAM all over the world during the next three years.

The summer of 1982 was spent in California with the Link Care workshop in San Francisco, and then in New Orleans in training for short-term summer projects with InterVarsity. In late August, it was back overseas, this time to Thailand, again with YWAM. After the YWAM conference they got a very special treat—a vacation at Royal Cliff Beach Hotel, Pattaya, Thailand—paid for by others. The hotel was so fancy that at first Betty was reluctant to stay. Their benefactors reminded her that "the Apostle Paul knew how to abound and so should you"—so they stayed and enjoyed it. While there Jed celebrated his third birthday. To help in the celebration, Tom ordered a small birthday cake for Jed from the hotel restaurant. But the Royal Cliff Beach Hotel birthday cakes are not your usual birthday cakes. When it arrived it was so huge it had to be shared. Betty cut it and Jed proudly carried pieces around to all the other tables.

The Horror of a Refugee Camp

On September 4 they arrived in Hong Kong for another YWAM language learning seminar and while there got the chance to visit another refugee camp, this one for Vietnam refugees. It was a powerful life changing experience.

The refugees were housed in what were perhaps old airport hangars—extremely hot, and extremely crowded. Each family had the equivalent of one plywood sheet of living space but they not only covered the floor space of several such buildings, but were stacked in layers five or six high. There was not even room to stand up between one layer and the next—only enough room to walk between the rows. Some of the refugees had set up little cooking pots between the rows, and laundry and other personal effects were stored everywhere.

"How would people survive if there was a fire?" Tom and Betty wondered. There was almost no space between the buildings, no space for the children to play, and very little community space. It was a "closed camp," meaning that the men and women could not leave to look for work or ways to support or feed themselves. Worse, outsiders were not allowed in to work with them. Tom talked with many of the refugees and found that refugees who had sponsors had been able to get out—these were the ones who had no sponsors and no way of escape. Not surprisingly, there was a very high suicide rate in the camp. Obviously it was a very depressing place.

Tom and Betty both felt the pain, the hopelessness, the dreariness. They had just learned the chorus, "God of righteousness and without injustice." Betty Sue could not help thinking of the words as they walked through the camp. "If God is 'righteous and without injustice,'" she agonized, "how can there be a place like this?" YWAM's presence and ministry there was a small part of the answer. God's justice and mercy had sent them to ease the pain and to minister His love.

YWAM workers pleaded with authorities to be allowed to help. Finally, perhaps out of spite, and certain that no one would take them up on it, YWAM was told that they could work with the refugees if they first cleaned out the latrines. Calf deep in human excrement, even the Vietnamese were shocked that they would do it. That stunning act of servanthood opened the door for YWAM ministry there. They were eventually able to start a day care center, a day school for the children, and began to provide assistance and ministry to the adults. It was the beginning of hope for the people in the camp.

Servanthood had been an effective strategy to open the doors for ministry.

China

Tom and Betty had often talked of trying to enter China, and so were pleased to have a few days free to spend there after the stay in Hong Kong. They wanted to go on their own, but individual visas were not being issued at the time. Only tour groups were being allowed to travel. They were concerned that they might get on a tour of "ugly Americans" who would be culturally insensitive, but were pleasantly surprised with the delightful group with which they were to travel. It included a titled British lady and a woman born in Rhodesia/Zimbabwe, both of whom had lived in the orient and were quite knowledgeable. There was also a young American couple who were believers working for an American airline company and who had traveled extensively, a UN representative, a well-traveled Latin American couple, and a man from Saudi Arabia with his Canadian wife and their two small girls rounded out the group. All showed genuine interest in the culture and history of China.

On their first afternoon in Xian they were taken to the ancient walled part of the city. The walls are at least two stories high. Tom looked at the height of the walls and the steep stairs and decided it would be best for him to stay at the base while Betty and Jed climbed up with the others. He remained behind "socializing" with some young Chinese men—who wanted to try out their little bit of English with him.

Betty and Jed were wandering around on top of the wall looking at the view when someone from the group mentioned that Tom was "over there." "No," she replied, "He decided to stay at the base." "No, no," the man explained. "I just now saw him over there." Sure enough, the young men he had been talking with had decided he should not miss the view at the top and had carried him up in his chair. From then on, someone always helped Tom up or down whatever barriers there were. He even got up on the Great Wall of China. The Great Wall made quite an impression on Jed, and even now seems to be the biggest highlight of all his travels.

One of the days in China they were riding a tour bus and the tour guide got restless. She asked if anyone wanted to sing a song over the PA system. There was a brief pause during which no one responded, then to Tom and Betty's surprise Jed raised his hand. He told the guide he had a song he liked. He sang:

> I met Jesus at the crossroads,
> Where the two ways meet.
> Satan too was standing there,
> and he said, "Come this way,
> Lots and lot of pleasures I will give to you today."
> But I said, "NO,
> there's Jesus here. See what He offers me:
> down here my sins forgiven,
> up there a home in heaven.
> Praise God that's the place for me."

Tom did not know how his tour guide would respond to such an overtly Christian song, but she was just delighted that a little tyke would offer to sing in front of people. Several times after that, when the tour met other tours she would tell the other guides that she had a little three year old boy that would sing. They would put a megaphone up to his mouth and he sang boldly about Jesus in various places in China.

The tour was quite extensive: Xian, the Terra Cotta Warriors, the Summer Palace, the Ming tombs, Peking with Red Square and the Forbidden City, Huaquing as well as the Great Wall.

After returning to Hong Kong from China, they decided to go to Macao and back by hydrofoil. Tom had long been fascinated with the concept of hydrofoil travel and was delighted to try it. They wanted to spend a few hours in Macao to look around, but when they arrived in Macao they were told that from that side back to Hong Kong every return trip was booked except the foil that they

had just arrived on. So they had just a few minutes and then had
to turn around and return—but as usual, enjoyed the ride anyway.

Once again, they spent the fall in the US, mostly teaching at
Fuller, but with occasional forays elsewhere for short courses or
workshops.

Incredibly, in January of 1983 they were off again to Africa, this
time to conduct seminars with language learners supervised by
Johann Louw. Louw had been a missionary in Malawi and then
joined the faculty of University of South Africa (UNISA). But first,
as was so typical for them, they took time to enjoy their surround-
ings. They went by train from Johannesburg to Durban to
Scottsburgh where they spent a few days on vacation. Then they
went by train again on to Capetown, where all three of them went
up the cable car at Table Mountain in Capetown.

In Capetown Tom spoke at two Bible colleges. In one of them it
was customary for the faculty to put on black academic preaching
robes before entering the classroom. They wanted to find one for
Tom but he declined the "honor." While his hosts were very gracious and many perhaps as opposed to apartheid as he was, still
Tom did not feel he could dignify the occasion in the midst of the
oppression and sinfulness he saw in South Africa.

An African Lesson

Later, they did a second workshop at Hammanskrall, and there
was a defining moment near the close which touched them all.
Tom and Betty were teaching a two week course, not just to grap-
ple with philosophical perspectives of language acquisition and
culture learning, but also to develop skills in building relationships
in order to learn a language, and in order to communicate the Gospel. Each morning Tom lectured on some aspect of mission through
involvement, and each afternoon the participants would go out into
the African community to explore and share in the language they
were learning.

Using such an approach anywhere is shocking to the psyche of
westerners. But in apartheid South Africa, where all contact with
other races and cultures is discouraged and whites simply did not

go to their black brethren to fellowship or share their beliefs or perspectives, the approach was radical.

In the middle of the course, Tom was invited by a black school principal to address his students. The school was about half a kilometer back into the trees across the cow pasture from the seminar grounds. Tom went there at 7:30 in the morning and gave his testimony. He was told later that he was the first white person to visit the school in its twenty year existence.

On the hectic last day of the course, when things were winding down and arrangements were being made to catch a plane later in the day, the principal came over again. "I've come to give a word of greeting to the learners in the project," he said and mentioned that the children were coming to sing for them.

The group was in a hurry to get home after fourteen days of absence and hard work. In a matter of fact way, but with the awareness of all that had to be done, Tom said, "I wish I had known sooner."

The principal turned and walked out the door, and Tom knew that he had blown it. He rolled across the room to the back window of the classroom, just in time to see him waving the children back to their school. And he realized that he had caused the man to lose face among the children and the teachers for whom he was responsible.

Twelve o'clock came, and Tom was thoroughly convicted about what had happened. The last thing he said to the learners was that he was going to that school and apologize for his rudeness in rejecting their gift to them. And he invited the learners to go along if they chose to, which most of them did. So off they went, with Betty Sue pushing the wheelchair across the pasture, making their way down the cow trail. The principal had gone to his home, and someone was sent to fetch him. The younger children were just being let out of school and the older ones would be let out shortly.

While they were standing and waiting, different ones of the children from the school began bringing chairs and benches, expecting that the group would sit down on them. And a few of the learners did sit down. "Stand up!" Tom told them. "We've not come here to be honored, we've come to ask their forgiveness."

When the children came out they sang some songs for them and then Tom explained to them his shame that they had come to give a gift to them, but that Tom had been more concerned about the schedule. Tom told them that while they had brought out chairs to honor them, they had come not to be honored, but to give honor.

Later, when they were packing, the principal came over and said, "I want to pray for you in my own language." It was a special time. It reminded Tom again of how easy it is for us to be so busy that people do not count. "But ministry is being involved with people, ministry is touching people, coming into actual contact with them and their lives, understanding what it is to live life from their perspective. Because it's from their perspective—within that real context that the Lord Jesus wants to come and minister" (T. Brewster 1983).

Nico and Ellen Smith were at that workshop, and were again moved by Tom's concern and love for all people and all races. Tom's was a timely message for South Africans, and Nico Smith was a willing listener. "As white South Africans, black children were not that important that they could disorganize our program," he explained. "To Tom, those children were important—more important than our program" (Smith 1993).

Partly on reflection on the things Tom had communicated, Nico and his wife had moved into Mamelodi, having gone all the way to the federal government to get permission.

> After I met Tom, my own convictions about the ideology of apartheid were confirmed and strengthened. I met Tom during a time of my own pilgrimage away from apartheid as a violation of the human dignity of blacks. Since I entered the ministry in the Dutch Reformed Church in 1953, I was a staunch supporter and defender of apartheid—and even justified it from Scriptures. In 1973, I made a final break with the ideology and was immediately rejected by the white establishment in South Africa. I then, as a result, went through a period of severe loneliness. It was during those years after my departure from apartheid that God sent Tom my way. I

strongly believe it was God's way of affirming the decision I had made. Tom became a real inspiration to me to continue on the way I had chosen (Smith 1993).

Later Nico and Ellen started a group called Koinonia for Blacks, Whites, Coloreds and Asians, feeling that tensions would be eased if the different races would just get together to eat in one another's homes in the different communities or even stay in one another's homes.

Nico reflected further on Tom's influence:

> Tom introduced a totally new approach towards learning a language to many people in South Africa. During the high time of apartheid, very few whites considered it necessary to learn one of the African languages spoken in South Africa. Tom contributed towards making people aware of the necessity to learn to speak people's language in order to understand their mind and culture. Through his method, those who started learning a language came into very direct relationship with blacks. In that way, many whites discovered that blacks are also "people," that they have a rich culture, and most of all, that we as whites have much to learn from African people (Smith 1993).

Open Doors with YWAM

The doors for ministry continued to be opened to them with YWAM and the spring of 1983 was crowded with YWAM seminars all over Europe. They left Africa on February 25, 1983 and traveled to Heidebeek and Amsterdam, Holland for seminars with the European YWAM staff, closely followed by another in Lanarca Cyprus.

On March 9 they flew Cyprus-Vienna-Zurich-Munich for yet another YWAM seminar, this time in the old castle "Schloss Hurlach" in Hurlach, a short distance out of Munich, Germany. From Hurlach they took the train to Buchloe, Switzerland, where they took a step toward extending their ministry and addressing the many requests for their services that they would never be able to accommodate—the *Language Learning & Mission* video series was taped. Actually it was not Tom's idea, and at first he was reluctant to use the medium. YWAM wanted the tape for their own use, but Tom was afraid that the needs of the video equipment would put too many constraints on his teaching style—exact ending times and perhaps limit or inhibit group discussions.

Moreover, Tom was not feeling at all well—fever and kidney troubles. Tom was never completely free of nagging health glitches, but in general felt extremely fortunate that God allowed him to travel so much and minister so extensively with relatively minor difficulties. Sometimes, of course, he ministered in spite of fevers or other problems, and was usually able to accomplish what he needed to. Now in the middle of 1983 the times when he felt miserable were more frequent and more severe.

While refusing to put himself under doctor's care, he did consult with them from time to time. Tom felt that his ureters must be kinked or otherwise blocking the normal flow of urine. He could not find many doctors who would agree with him, and none who seemed to Tom to have any good ideas of what to do about it. These were the kinds of problems, he was told, that were inevitable for quadriplegics, and there was not a lot that could be done. In any case, he usually recovered sufficiently to carry on, so that is what he did.

After returning to the US in late March, they went on to Hawaii in early May to participate in the YWAM strategy conference and a much needed three days of rest.

During July, after teaching the first of two summer courses at Fuller, they demonstrated once again their love for and interest in their family by inviting along three of their nieces—Susan and Shari Douglas, and Betty's niece Suzette—all pre-teen or early teen, to InterVarsity's Overseas Training Center orientation in the Dominican Republic for a short seminar on language learning. It was fun to have them along and to introduce them to the third world.

In August they were overseas again, this time in London for training with Operation Mobilization. Afterwards, my wife and I had a delightful four day holiday with Tom and Betty in Scotland where we were instrumental in the YWAM acquisition of the Overton House near Glasgow which they used until recently. We had been traveling south from the north of Scotland looking for a bed-and-breakfast which was accessible to Tom's wheel chair. After stopping at several places in the outskirts of Glasgow, we finally found a small place that looked like a small castle. It was wheel chair accessible, so we took it. After we had settled in, we took a walk in the late evening light. Walking up a paved path, we came to what was indeed a castle, and heard the sweet sound of Christian singing from within. Exploring further, we found a choir. We learned that castle was vacant and that the owner of the castle wanted it to be taken over by a Christian ministry. Tom knew of just the ministry. He contacted YWAM and in the exquisite tradition of God providing marvelous and unique properties for them, they were able to acquire it.

Health Crisis Down Under

On returning to the US in September 1983, Tom was due for a health check up and he heard that his uncle Harold was in the same Craig rehabilitation Center in which he had rehabilitated. Tom had long been burdened for the salvation of Mom's brother Harold. Harold was a crusty old gentleman, a former cabinet maker, who had been blinded in a car accident some years earlier. Tom tried to visit with him whenever he was in Denver. Tom arranged to get a bed in the same room with his uncle. For three days they reminisced together, with Tom sharing the Gospel with him in a gentle, caring way. Harold resisted, and we do not know that he ever accepted Christ. The time together was special, and indicative of Tom's burden for the lost, especially among his own family.

Tom also took the time to meet with the staff at the Craig Rehabilitation Center to discuss with them their rehab programs and provide his advice about it's directions and effectiveness. His assessments were blunt in their honesty but shared with a sincere desire to help the staff help others with similar disabilities. Dennis O'Malley, the director of the Craig center recalled:

The thing I always admired about Tom was that he was always willing to share some of his experiences with us for the benefit of other patients here at Craig. Some of his criticisms were not pleasant to hear, but I felt they were always rendered with Craig's best interest in mind. In fact, I was about to write him again to inform him that we now have a demonstration ABEC wheelchair available for our patients. We had an extensive demonstration done for all of our therapists here at Craig, based primarily on Tom's prompting. . . .

It is rare that we find people like Tom who remain committed to Craig and its mission over time. We could always count on you and Tom to keep us "honest" in terms of how a program was or was not preparing its graduates for the real world. For that spirit, we are eternally grateful to you (O'Malley 1985).

That fall, though Tom's health began to deteriorate significantly, they continued to minister even though it meant once again long periods of travel overseas. On November 7, 1983 they flew from Los Angeles to Auckland, New Zealand where they held two concurrent one-week intensive seminars.

It was in Auckland where God arranged a meeting with Viv Grigg—a person who changed the rest of Tom's life. Viv is from New Zealand and was the founder and leader of Servants to Asia's Urban Poor, a mission that sponsored teams for incarnational ministry in the slums of Manila, and other Asian cities. That vision and model for incarnational ministry to urban poor later became a very important part of Tom's own ministry vision.

On November 18 they flew on to Wellington for a seminar with the Navigators there, closely followed by a five day seminar at Featherston with SIL. They then went back to Auckland for another seminar with YWAM. Finally however Tom's health problems became too severe to continue.

His kidneys were not working right and, incredibly, his skin took over that function to some extent. He was constantly dripping wet, literally sweating his urine. So when he got up in the morning Betty would put a couple of towels inside his shirt and a couple of hours later literally ring them out. They had to change towels constantly all day long. At night, Betty would put him to bed lying on some towels and within a couple of hours the towels would be soaked. Tom was miserable. The temperature was cool and because Tom was so wet, he was constantly shivering.

They had to cancel a planned seminar with YWAM up north in Pahi, New Zealand, because Tom was doing so poorly. They spent one of the worst nights of their life there in Pahi with Tom's urinary system barely functioning. Betty was up all night trying to get some drainage. Tom knew that his kidneys were not functioning properly but was concerned also that his bladder was not doing what it was supposed to. He began to have severe spasms—so severe that Betty could see the muscles contracting under his skin on both sides of his kidneys. And he had one of the severe headaches he would get at such times due to his blood pressure shooting sky high. He was feeling nauseous and miserable.

Betty could see that he looked bloated. She rubbed his back and his side to see if she could get something flowing. She sat him up in bed and rocked him back and forth kind of like a baby—front to back and side to side. She elevated his feet, and then his hips. And they prayed and prayed and prayed. That whole night there was almost no flow.

By morning they were both worn out, but he was just like a dish rag. There was nothing left of him. Obviously, neither one of them had the strength to teach, but even so they briefly considered it. But for the first time they had to back out on a workshop. They canceled the course and drove back down to Auckland. The drive seemed to take forever, but they made it down and got some rest in Auckland.

Obviously they were quite discouraged and weary, with Tom feeling very weak. Nevertheless, they spent December 2–4 in a missions weekend seminar at a campground near Auckland with about sixty participants.

Then they went on to Australia and conducted a one week seminar for YWAM in Canberra.

In Canberra, they took a Christmas "vacation" in a house that YWAM provided for them. Tom was quite sick and weak, spending most of the time in bed. There were a number of nights during that time when they did not sleep at all. They spent Christmas there but it was a miserable time because Tom was feeling so bad. There were lots of days that he did not get out of bed because he simply did not have the energy to get up.

Betty and Jed tried to make a happy Christmas. They made decorations and went shopping and did whatever they could but it was very obvious that Tom was in bad shape.

Both in New Zealand and in Canberra they consulted a doctor and both doctors said, "We don't know what to do for you." They simply had not seen anything like it. Tom had been saying for some time that it felt as if his urethras were kinked up. But every doctor he talked to had told him that it was just not possible for them to kink up. Rather, they said, "Something is wrong with your bladder, or you have kidney stones or a bladder infection."

Since the main problem was that his urine was barely flowing, Tom was afraid to drink because it would not go anywhere or finally come out through his skin. But if he did not drink, an infection would take over because his kidneys could not take the lack of fluid. He was miserable, and in danger, whatever he did. That was the first time that Betty ever saw him really discouraged and depressed. And naturally, Betty grew depressed.

It was very rare for Tom to get discouraged over anything, but his health was so bad they were doubtful they could continue with their schedule. But both also knew that it was very possible for this to be terminal because Tom was going downhill so fast.

Shortly after they had arrived in Australia, they received a call from Cathy Schaller, their prayer partner in the "120" class (after the 120 gathered in the upper room in Acts, chapter one) at Lake Avenue Congregational Church in Pasadena, California. Cathy, an experienced and faithful intercessor, says that God had given her an "assignment" to pray for Tom and Betty Sue—not necessarily for their ministry but for their lives, health and spiritual battles. She was prompted to make the first international call she had ever made in her life to say to Tom, "I don't know what has been going on but today in Sunday school class we had a word of knowledge for you—against discouragement" (Schaller 1994).

While they were not actually on the YWAM grounds, a YWAM lady nevertheless came over regularly to pick up laundry, bring groceries, and provide transportation. That hospitality on the part of YWAM was so typical of their caring personnel.

By the end of that vacation time Tom was feeling a bit better. They canceled another course to extend their vacation and Tom started to feel better.

I asked Betty if they did not consider just canceling the trip and coming back to the States for treatment. Betty responded: "We considered coming back but we didn't really want to because we still had two courses in Indonesia, one in Irian Jaya, two in Papua New Guinea and another course in Australia and we didn't want to cancel all of them."

> "So he attended classes and taught in that condition?"
>
> "Yes, it took a great deal of gumption to do it."
>
> Dan—"Did the learners know about his condition or his suffering?" Some knew. They could tell something was wrong because you don't look at a man who is soaking wet all the time without knowing something strange is happening. Everybody else was wearing sweaters while his face was drenched in perspiration. As he taught he was constantly rubbing his face to get rid of the perspiration— and yet he was shivering. So obviously there was something different about this fellow" (E. Brewster 1993).

Tom began to sense that there was some kind of spiritual battle taking place around him, since he often noticed the onset of new problems just before or during workshops in which he regularly urged more thoughtful attention to the spiritual needs of the unreached peoples around the world. He began to share this with his colleagues and other prayer partners who stepped up their prayer support when they knew Tom was traveling or ministering. But Betty made it clear that Tom often taught when he was miserable—and that Satan had a hand in the suffering:

> For years we could almost clock it that the day or two days before a course, he would have a fever and feel sick. He would get a kidney

infection or bladder infection and if he would go ahead and teach the next day even though he wasn't feeling well, usually he started gaining strength during the day and by the next day he was usually OK. But if he didn't teach, he would usually end up sick in bed. We began to feel like it was just plain old spiritual warfare. The devil didn't like his teaching. And he would do what he could to keep us from teaching.

In spite of not feeling well, Tom had an incredible amount of energy. He would very often teach a full weekday course, then a week end course and teach the next week as well. And there were times when he did that two or three weeks in a row. I did some of the teaching but not nearly as much as he did. And a lot of the time it was done when he wasn't feeling well. Tom was just energized by teaching. He loved to teach and the more he taught he would get more and more energetic (E. Brewster 1993).

12
TOM'S SPIRITUAL JOURNEY

> I knew the spirit world was real and taught it. I knew also that the Holy Spirit was more powerful. But I felt like I was teaching with one hand tied behind my back (Gilliland 1982:46).

Tom's understanding of Satan's role in his suffering, the reality of spiritual warfare, and the power of prayer, was the result of a spiritual journey across the spectrum of theological viewpoints. Clearly he was heavily influenced by his father's passionate commitment to Christ and to sharing the Gospel with the lost. Tom was rightfully proud of his strong Christian heritage and conservative background. Nevertheless, his spiritual journey underwent some profound changes as God ministered to him in various stages of his life. His ministry and his character are closely tied to the milestones along that journey.

Tom came from a very fundamental, independent Baptist background. It was a Christian environment, but one in which asking questions was not encouraged. Basically the answers were provided for him, and he was not taught how to think biblically or theologically. Tom said that he was taught *what* to think, not *how* to think. All who defined their faith in the same way he did were okay; those who defined their faith differently were not. Those in the latter category included Charismatics, Catholics and "liberals." Both Tom and Betty generally felt that most people who leaned in those directions were misguided and mistaken.

Tom remembered a lot of energy being taken up in one of the churches of his early years to fight against Billy Graham. Apparently Billy Graham would often have "other kinds" of people—people not just like us—on the platform with him, and even if he preached a pretty decent message he was still condemned or guilty by association, so to speak.

Tom also recalled the reaction of our family's pastor when the Revised Standard Translation came out in the 1950s. It was scathingly referred to as the "Reversed Satanic Perversion." from the pulpit. Our churches were of the persuasion "the King James Version was good enough for the Apostle Paul, so it is good enough for me." (In the 1970s, Tom's consulting work for the Living Bibles caused him to be extremely suspect by the pastor of the church his mother attended, which Tom attended whenever he was back in Colorado). In Tom's early churches, a lot of energy was spent in making sure that anyone who ought to be outside did not somehow slip into the fold.

When Tom went off to college, he still had a lot of the same attitudes. He was president of InterVarsity at Memphis State. He and others in InterVarsity often went off to the "Newman Club"—the Catholic club on campus—to argue with the priests and Catholic students there. Tom felt that if they would just give up their Catholicism and their "Catholicness" and worship God his way, then they would have an authentic faith.

Not surprisingly, there were not a lot of Catholic students that agreed with him. In fact, there was quite a *reaction* from the Catholic students and others who received the same treatment, but not a whole lot of *inter*action. There was much legalism in Tom's background and experience, and it manifested itself in Tom's approach to others. Indeed it shaped how he related to God, convinced he must "perform" and "play by the rules."

Tom may have lacked some spiritual maturity and depth in those early years, but no one questioned his spiritual *commitment*. It was readily apparent to Betty Sue and to others when he arrived at the Spanish Language School in Guadalajara in 1966. Both the accident and the divorce were pressure cookers toward spiritual growth and reliance on the Lord. This was one of the first things that attracted Betty to him. That spiritual commitment and his approachability were apparent to others as well, even in the midst of his recovery in those early dark days in Guadalajara. One couple who knew him there wrote:

We met Tom in 1966 at the Spanish Language School in Guadalajara, Mexico. We remember Tom spending time in the small garden
with his Lord. Tom "walked" intimately with God. There was something about his face as he'd wheel himself out onto the patio . . . a
peace that enabled him to look at you with genuine interest as a
person. Each person seemed very important to Tom. He would give
you his total attention when he talked to you. Knowing his intelligence and broad experience usually would make one shy about
approaching him, but his being in that wheelchair seemed to make
him so much more accessible (Frederich 1986).

Tom and Betty's understanding though, of Christians who
viewed theology and worship differently than he did was very limited and largely negative. The Spanish Language School in Guadalajara was their first extended exposures to people who thought
theologically differently. Prior to their time in Guadalajara, neither had met many charismatics whom they respected. There, they
got to respect a lot of them before they knew of their charismatic
leanings, and decided they liked them anyway!

Dryness in the Desert

Nevertheless, Tom and Betty had a spiritual dry spell in 1970
and 1971 when they were going to the University of Arizona. They
had been reading Scripture together and having devotions, but at
one point they both felt it was not doing anything for either of
them. So they quit having devotions together and went back to
having personal devotions. Even that was a bit sporadic and not all
that meaningful. They attended a variety of churches but never
felt that they were being fed.

Finally the Lord ministered to them in the persons of a young
Navigator couple, P.W. and Donna Johnson. P.W. and Donna were
on fire for the Lord and very excited about what the Lord was
teaching them. Tom and Betty Sue hit it off well with them and
started meeting together. It seemed that every time they visited,
P.W. would open the door with his Bible in his hand and begin
sharing with them what he had been reading even as they were
walking in the door. God used this Navigator friend to rekindle

their spiritual flame. Spending time with them over the space of the next few months revitalized their whole spiritual life.

Another of the factors that began to change Tom was a Bill Gothard Seminar on Basic Youth Conflicts in 1971. Bill talked about a lot of things that Tom and Betty Sue wanted to experience but had not taken the time to put into practice or did not know how. They were impressed with Bill's use of Scripture. It re-awakened in them the way that Scriptures deal with every human condition and situation. Tom led a young man to the Lord at the seminar, and it heightened in him a desire to do more personal evangelism. It was one of their most significant spiritual experiences up to that time. In fact, they attended more than once, because they found it so practical, and inspirational.

It was Bill Gothard who also got Tom interested in fasting. Bill pointed out that the Bible does not say *if* you fast, it says *when* you fast. Tom began to make fasting a more or less regular aspect of his spiritual discipline. On one occasion, when he sensed he needed to let up on his system as well as experience spiritual renewal, he fasted nearly forty days, subsisting mostly on water and juices.

Shortly after the Gothard seminar in 1971, Tom suggested that he and Betty Sue set aside a Saturday for fasting, prayer, and Bible study. They studied the book of Malachi together that day, and memorized Malachi 3:7–12. The Lord spoke to them about their finances and led them to want to be even more generous to the Lord and to His people with their money, time, and help.

Tom began to change as he was exposed to different ways of thinking. Fortunately, he had the openness to be able to change. He began to face the fact that his rigidity was not producing life.

Tom's openness came a lot faster than Betty Sue's. While at TIL, they worked closely with Episcopalians, Methodists, and all sorts of other types of Christians. Both Tom and Betty Sue had always assumed that somebody was "liberal" if they belonged to those groups. At first Tom and Betty Sue had reacted negatively to the principal, Don Larson, because he was so open and accepting of these people from other church backgrounds. But Tom began to open up. He began to be able to recognize the reality of others' walk with the Lord, even if their spiritual vocabulary and worship forms were different.

The years at the University of Texas were also a time of growth. They got involved in The Grace Covenant Church which they jokingly referred to as the "Continental Chapel." The name came from the fact that the church service was held in the showroom of Continental Cars, a European car dealership. At first, the staff only had to drive one or two cars out of the showroom, set up the chairs, and roll the piano in on a dolly—and that was all they needed. But the church grew very rapidly, and by the time Tom and Betty Sue left Austin most of the cars had to be taken out of this big showroom before each service to accommodate the growth. Here Tom and Betty Sue found a fresh and alive group of people committed to Christ and to each other in some unconventional ways.

The fact that it was not in a church building was one of the advantages. The regulars could invite people who would come, perhaps out of curiosity, but who would not darken the door of a regular church. The church had a refreshing openness and informality about it, and very caring people who reached out to newcomers and those in need. The pastor or one of the elders led weekly Bible studies attended by Christians and non-Christians alike. One outreach Bible study had a rule that no one could attend unless they brought an unsaved friend with them. Marvelously, those Bible studies were always packed out. There were always requests for more of them because they were led on a very non-threatening way and held in homes all over the city.

It was at that time that Tom and Betty met Dave McClure, who later was very helpful in articulating some of the practical procedures of language learning. Dave and his wife Leilani moved to Austin and lived just a block from Tom and Betty Sue, and became part of the "Continental Chapel."

"Continental Chapel" had what was called "Growth by Groups." Each participant had to make a certain commitment for a certain period of time—say three months—in which he or she agreed to attend all the studies every week unless there was some extreme emergency, and agreed to be prepared and to be in prayer for everybody in the group. The commitment was very specific but for a short enough time, that a lot of people said, "Well I can handle that for three months."

As part of the Bible study program, everyone had to paraphrase the chapter or section the group was studying, and write one or more very specific applications. Dave McClure was a participant who was very direct. If anyone could not tell at the end of the week whether an application was done or not, he would try to pin them down. "How are *you* going to know if you do that? Next week when you report, how are *we* going to know if you actually did it?" He would help people be more specific, getting them to promise, for example, "I'm going to do it so many minutes, so many days, to so many people." It had to be very measurable and specific. They could not get away with a vague, "I'm going to love the Lord this week." "How are you going to know?" he questioned. "What are you going to do as you are loving the Lord?"

One week, Tom experienced a car breakdown. He reported it to his Growth by Groups colleagues, saying that he had been at peace and had sensed God's hand in it. Dave remarked, "If Luke were writing about it, he would say, 'And Tom, being filled with the Holy Spirit, refused to be troubled knowing that God was present even in this. . . .'" That simple lesson meant a lot to Tom. It helped him realize that being filled with the Holy Spirit did not necessarily mean some big earth shaking event, but rather a continual living out what God was teaching them.

It is impossible to work in a variety of ecclesiological and missiological contexts, as Tom and Betty Sue did, without having your preconceived notions threatened and your theology challenged. Working with new missionaries of all different stripes, first at the Spanish Language School in Guadalajara, then at TIL, and in consultation with Living Bible and Campus Crusade translators all over the world eventually had that effect on Tom. His understanding of the distinctions between forms and meanings, and the insights gained from trying to communicate scriptural and doctrinal teachings across cultures in their translation work, made

Tom more and more open to the reality of God working in ways much larger than he had been willing to allow in his youth.

"How Can These Things Be?"

It was on the language acquisition trip to Cochabamba, Bolivia in 1976, however, where Tom began to realize that God was working in and through even Catholics. After finishing *LAMP*, they went to Bolivia for three months to supervise a team of Campus Crusade -Agape language learners. While there Tom was also working on refining his Spanish and Betty Sue was trying to learn a little bit of the Quechua language.

The day they arrived in Cochabamba, they went to the bank to change money and a couple of Mormons came up to Tom. (Betty Sue says Tom was kind of a magnet for Mormons!) Sure enough, they approached Tom and began witnessing to him. But as they did so, he started quoting Scriptures back to them. It was not an antagonistic time, but rather an open time in which each side was presenting his views.

Presently, another gentleman came up and started listening to the conversation. He said to Betty Sue (in Spanish), "I've been to the States and I know English. If you don't mind, I'd just like to listen to this conversation."

As he listened, he began interjecting comments and it became obvious that he was a believer. After the Mormons left, Tom turned to the gentleman and introduced himself. The man was a priest and he invited them to come to his home for lunch that day. When they arrived, they took lunch with two or three other priests living there and had a warm time of fellowship. The priests shared what the Lord was doing in their lives. Their obvious trust in the living Christ was impressive to Tom and Betty, but they could not shake the feeling that the priests had simply mastered the evangelical jargon.

After lunch they went out into the garden, and the priest said to Tom, "I'd like you to lead a Bible study for my people. We need more Bible studies, and I'd like you to lead it in my favorite book— the book of Romans." (Betty Sue said later, "I didn't even think the

Catholics knew that Romans was in their Catholic Bible!") She wondered if he knew the Lord or if he was putting up a front.

The priest was the leader of a charismatic Catholic church. They kept their guards up, but seeing two suspect words, "charismatic" and "Catholic" modifying "church" was intriguing. In their experience, those words did not go together in the same sentence.

Tom was open, but admitted that it "blew all my categories! I didn't have any frame of reference for this. How can these things be? A Catholic man who even knows that the book of Romans is there" (1983:136)?

While their schedules did not permit them to lead the Bible study, they did get more involved in the Catholic community. The priests invited Tom and Betty Sue to the Friday evening prayer and worship time. Wouldn't you know it! The songs they sang were the same ones that Tom and Betty Sue knew as young people. Betty Sue felt, "That's not fair! They're stealing our songs! They don't know the meaning behind it—they're just singing the words." But as they watched their faces, they realized that this was real. They were not just singing the words and they were not faking it. Clearly God was working in this Catholic church and through these dear Catholic priests.

They attended a Mass with the priests but Betty Sue was filled with tension. In a testimony time after the Mass, the lay people related how they were evangelizing their neighbors and what the Lord was teaching them through the Word. Tom and Betty Sue could not believe it. Tom suggested that they go back on Sunday. Betty Sue did not want to, and really did not want to know any more about these people. They did not fit any of her categories either. She wanted nothing to do with it.

Fortunately they did go back and shared in another testimony time before the Mass and another after the Mass. Lay people were leading the service, and it was a genuine worship service. Suddenly Betty Sue was aware of how much Scripture there was in the Mass. Much of it and the worship songs were based on Scripture. Together, she and Tom began to realize that this priest knew exactly what he was doing. They agreed with the priest when he declared, "You can partake of Mass 10,000 times and it won't be worth anything if you don't know Jesus Christ as your personal Savior."

Like Peter's lesson with Cornelius in the Book of Acts, in which he learned not to call what God had prepared unclean, God used that priest to break through to them in a very significant way. They spent the next three months involved in fellowship with the large group of "renewed" Catholic believers who worshipped at the "*Centro Renovación*" in Cochabamba, Bolivia.

During those weeks, Tom and Betty Sue got to know many of the people in the church and, whenever the opportunity presented itself, they would ask them about their spiritual walk, and how they came to know the Lord. Most of the people could not give a specific time when they had trusted Christ. (Uh oh—a red flag!) They would say, "You know months ago I would open my Bible and it said nothing to me so I would put it back on the shelf." Or, "I didn't own a Bible and didn't want one. I would go to a Mass every now and then, and it said nothing to me. I didn't care about having God active in my life, but now in the last few weeks or months the Scriptures have opened up to me and God talks to me through the Scriptures. Now I want to tell my neighbors about Christ. I just love coming to Mass and worshipping the Lord and learning more about God through the worship and Bible studies."

The hunger they saw there was amazing. It became obvious to Tom and Betty Sue that they could no longer say that these people did not know the Lord as their personal Savior. Clearly they had come to know the Lord in a very different style than Tom and Betty Sue did, but there was no question that they were walking with the Lord—and perhaps walking with Him in a deeper way than they were.

Tom's acceptance of these people was not a wholesale acceptance of all Roman Catholic groups or doctrines, nor of Catholicism in general, but rather a realization and understanding that God is at work in the lives of many diverse groups, and has His witnesses in some surprising places. They realized, Betty says, that "God refuses to be confined by our shallow understanding of Him and His work."

(Tom and Betty continued to meet with one of the Mormon gentlemen as well for the next three months, sharing Scripture with him and telling him about Christ. But Tom never did see many useful "bridges" to use in dealing with Mormons.)

Conservative But Open

Soon after the Bolivia trip, Tom and Betty Sue began their teaching positions at Fuller Seminary. The Fuller School of World Mission was and is an innovative environment where much of traditional mission theory and practice was challenged and critiqued. New ideas constantly surfaced and it was not uncommon for a professor to intentionally overstate something new and let everyone take aim to shoot it down or take it in some new direction. Tom was occasionally looked as a little eccentric, but then so was everybody else. Paul Pierson, the former Dean of the School of World Mission described it this way:

> . . . [T]his is a place with a growing group of missionaries and missiological scholars; [Charles] Kraft talking about Christianity and culture, [Paul] Heibert talking about folk religions, and everyone taking a new look at things. To me it seems very natural to have all sorts of things stemming off. I saw the Brewsters' ideas as natural spin-offs of the missiological ferment here. They came up with things that I, or Art Glasser, or [Dean] Gilliland would not have because of their focus and their life-style. We are all coming at missiology from somewhat different perspectives—historical, theological, linguistic, relational (Pierson 1987).

Watching Chuck Kraft grow was always a big influence on Tom. Chuck's freedom was so refreshing and he was so open and transparent. His boyish enthusiasm for his prayer time and walk with the Lord was contagious. Chuck turned off some others, but was a positive influence on Tom. Tom thought it amazing that a man of his stature should be so open and mellow.

A simple diagram (below) from Chuck Kraft, (which Chuck attributes to Paul Heibert, another former professor in the SWM) was revolutionary for Tom. Tom had always assumed that if a person was not conservative—like him—then he must be a liberal and therefore mostly wrong. What other options were there? Chuck's diagram showed him that there could in fact be other positions— that a person could be "open" to all sorts of things, view things quite differently and still be theologically conservative (and more importantly, maybe even be right on some things!).

open

x

conservative ——————— liberal

closed

For the first time Tom had a framework from which to understand what was happening in their own spiritual growth. It was a liberating feeling, for they began to see that they could preserve and value their heritage and experience and at the same time appreciate how God was working in others lives whose spiritual heritage and experience was far different from their own. What Chuck Kraft (and others) call a "paradigm shift" began to take place in both Tom and Betty's life. It did not happen over night, but over time, very significant changes took place in their perspectives.

Signs and Wonders in Africa . . .

The most significant shift however was still to come. That was the beginnings of an understanding of the reality of spiritual warfare and the power of God in this present world and in their own lives. Tom began to see that he and millions of conservative Christians like him had all kinds of *knowledge about* God, but knew little about His power, especially from experience.

One fairly impressive incident in this journey took place during Tom and Betty Sue's time at Kwasizabantu in South Africa in early 1983. This was a mission station run by a German couple, Erlo Stegen and his wife. The Stegens were Germans who grew up in the Republic of South Africa and were involved in planting churches. Stegan was an evangelist in the old sense of the word, but was seeing very little fruit among his mostly white congregation. However, they started a new little fellowship in another town with a group of blacks. The only building they could find to meet in was an old stable, and they had to shovel out the muck before the services. (Stegen said later that that was indicative of what was happening in their own lives at that time. They were going through their lives and throwing out the muck as God showed them the sins in their lives—he and the people who were meeting there with him.)

As the church grew, and because of what God was doing in their lives, they spent a lot of time in prayer. There were various all night prayer sessions, and they read through the book of Acts during one prayer time over a period of weeks. They said, "Lord, either Your Word is true or it is not, but we believe that You are still the God of the book of Acts." They laid the book of Acts open before the Lord and began to "pray through it."

One morning they came out after having spent all night in a prayer meeting. They opened the door and a crowd of people were sitting on the lawn, waiting for them, weeping. A spokesperson stood up and said, "We haven't come here as a group, we came here individually and found one another. But we have all come because God has convinced us that we are sinners. We've got to go to work today, but we can't go in this condition." Many did not get to work that day because they spent the day praying with them and bringing people to the Lord.

That was the beginning of the church. The gifts of the Spirit began to be manifest in their midst—healings, speaking in tongues, prophesies, and all sorts of other things. The church had a rule that anyone who wanted to prophesy or speak in tongues publicly had to be a person who was previously accepted by the eldership as a Christian who had that gift. Until they had been accepted by the eldership, they could only do it in private. Any prophesies were sealed for a number of days during which time the elders prayed over it. At the end of that time, they unsealed it to see if any of it had come true, or if there was any indication that it was from the Lord. If at that time they felt it was a valid prophesy, then it was brought to the attention of the whole church. Safeguards to abuse were important in the things they were doing.

People began coming to the mission in large numbers for healing, deliverance, salvation, and for renewal. The church did not advertise, but the people kept coming. One group, which included three blind people, came by truck. During the evangelistic meeting that night, these three blind people were given back their sight. There was not any laying on of hands, it was just preaching on salvation and repentance. The church even saw at least one resurrection, a young woman named Lydia. Another man, a former witch doctor from Durban, came back to life and then trusted Christ and led his wife to the Lord before he finally died again.

Tom and Betty Sue spent a week with the Stegens, in a very special time of spiritual reflection and refreshment. They were impressed with the care taken by Stegen and his leadership team to avoid excesses and distortions in what was taking place. Most importantly, it was a time of growing openness and sensitivity to the working of the Holy Spirit. Clear manifestations of God's *power* were evident—exactly the component of Tom and Betty's experience that was lacking.

... And Then at Fuller

Meanwhile, back at Fuller, a unique movement was sweeping over the campus. In 1982, the SWM had begun to offer a course in healing and miracles originally called "Signs, Wonders, and Church Growth." The course numbered MC510 quickly became Fuller's most popular and most controversial class. *Christian Life* magazine devoted an entire issue (October 1982) to the phenomenon.

All of the faculty in the SWM had mission backgrounds, and all had noticed their lack of preparation for dealing the issues of healing and the spirit world. Pierson explains that,

> As we shared we found that most of us had similar experiences during our years on the mission field. We were aware of demons

and supernatural powers, but our own ministry had never really touched them. In theory we knew and believed that God was the Lord of the principalities and powers. We taught that the spirit world was real. We had even theorized about the efficacy of the power encounter in missiological situations (Pierson 1982:46).

The power, though, was not there. The faculty was ready then, when John Wimber proposed that he teach a class in Peter Wagner's Church Growth II course on "Signs, Wonders, and Church Growth." Wagner, a professor in the School of World Mission, and John Wimber had worked together in the Fuller Evangelistic Association in the late 1970s until John resigned to start what became the very successful Anaheim Vineyard church, one of the earliest of many "Vineyard" churches across the country. Wagner describes how the class got started:

> I became vaguely aware that throughout 1978 to 1980, John and others in his congregation had begun to pray for the sick and see God heal some people. Curious, I visited the church on Sunday nights now and then. By 1981 John suggested we set aside one of our mornings in [the] Church Growth II [class] for him to lecture on "Signs, Wonders and Church Growth." If the suggestion had come from almost anyone else, I might have hesitated. This was moving into uncharted territory both in the Church Growth Movement and in Fuller Theological Seminary. But I trusted John Wimber; he had displayed such a high degree of integrity and credibility that I gave him the green light. I made a special point of inviting the dean of our Fuller School of World Mission, Paul E. Pierson, to sit in on the class.
>
> Although the lecture was nothing along the lines that Paul Pierson and I had ever heard before, we were both impressed. As we were debriefing over lunch, John mentioned that he had collected much more material on the subject, and we began discussing the possibilities of teaching a whole course on signs and wonders as part of our regular School of World Mission curriculum. . . . I was to be the professor of record, and John Wimber was to do most of the teaching.
>
> When the class began in January 1982, I carefully assumed the role of spectator. I sat quietly in the last row, watching John "doin'

the stuff," as he describes his ministry. I had no intention of doin'
the stuff myself (1988:48, 49).

It was not long though before not only Pete Wagner, but other
professors in the SWM were also "doin' the stuff." Chuck Kraft
attended the class from the beginning, partly out of curiosity, and
with not a little skepticism, but genuinely seeking answers to his
own questions. He was aware that he had gone to the mission field
with a sense of inadequacy and woefully unprepared to answer
questions about the supernatural. He did not want the SWM to
make the same mistake in its preparation of missionaries. "My
experience in Nigeria, was that the people had difficulty understanding preachers who did not heal, and healers who did not
preach. These people perceived the works of healing as coming
from divine power rather than from impersonal medicine" (Kraft
1982a:65).

Chuck felt they desperately needed to develop a theology of
power in the school. "In this day and age," he argued, "we no
longer can maintain our integrity as a School of World Mission and
send out people to minister in the Third World without first
training them how to pray for the sick" (Kraft 1982b:48).

"Signs, Wonders and Church Growth" met that need. Before
long Chuck not only had a lot of answers to his questions, but was
also "doin the stuff." He later said, "Probably no more life-changing
course has been offered at this seminary. The course is not just a
kookie idea. . . . [It] freed me from the constraints of our narrow
western view. . . . My whole life has been changed" (Kraft
1982c:49).

Tom and Betty Sue became curious about the Signs and Wonders class, partly because of their recent experiences in South
Africa, but also because of the waves it was creating throughout
Fuller Seminary. Tom and Betty attended a special intensive version of the course for pastors in August 1982. In the first classes,
they could see that things were happening. Clearly, healings were
taking place. Not the dramatic, quadriplegic walking kind of thing,
but lots of small but significant touches of the Holy Spirit. There

were many restorations, and people confessing sin and getting things cleared up in their own lives. Large numbers of people spoke of how they had heard the Lord's voice and could sense His direction and how their own spiritual life had deepened.

The class became famous across the US. Famous perhaps, but not universally popular even with the Fuller Seminary administration. Throughout the seminary there were feelings of skepticism, criticisms of technique, questions about legitimacy and integrity. Some felt that a seminary was no place for "signs and wonders," or that there was not enough theological and Biblical basis for the course, or that it was more appropriate in a charismatic seminary than for Fuller Seminary. Indeed, feelings about the class got quite strong, to the point that the seminary in 1985 put a moratorium on the class to give a chance for reflection and cooling off. Student reaction though, came quickly. There were demonstrations and petitions. Eventually the students prevailed and the course was offered outside the main course curriculum. So many attended that the seminary relented and reinstated the course the next year.

For many others though, including Tom and Betty, it was a life changing experience. Their paradigm shift was complete. Just as when he had been paralyzed and had to relearn how to do physical things, now he was relearning theology and finding new ways to believe.

Tom wrote to me about one experience in a class for pastors that he attended:

> Interestingly enough, as part of our own personal pilgrimage, the night before we departed for Asia in August, I witnessed the expulsion of a demon at a class meeting taught by John Wimber. . . . It was a special course for pastors, and Wimber taught that one session. These pastors were mostly skeptics, most of whom already had their own "final answers" and were convinced that God is not involved any longer in signs, wonders, and the supernatural. But after the class prayer was requested for one of them. There were no doubters after a two-hour battle in which a demon was expelled from a man and he was also healed of a brain tumor. It became very apparent that we were seeing the very kinds of things the New Tes-

tament writers participated in and described, and that the powers of darkness were very real, yet the Kingdom of God prevails in the authority of Jesus Christ (T. Brewster 1982a).

As Tom experienced more of the power of the Gospel, he became more and more concerned about the fact that most missionaries themselves knew very little about the power of the Gospel they proclaimed.

He wrote of his concern to me:

> One writer [Paul Heibert] has said that missionaries have been the most secularizing force throughout the world. It has seemed ironic to us that western people, who do not experience the reality of the spirit world, are going to people who do experience the spirit world on a daily basis, to give them a message about spiritual things. In our ministry we feel a responsibility to be available to God to equip people to be as effective in their cross cultural outreach as possible. God is causing us to take His power and His Word seriously. Pray for us (T. Brewster 1982a).

A Very Special Relationship

Perhaps as important as anything in Tom's spiritual journey was his relationship with our younger sister, Mona. She was only six when our dad died, and did not benefit from the strict disciplinarian and God-centered training that our father provided the rest of us. In spite of Tom's participation as a "father figure" in Mona's teen years, there followed many years of rebellion and waywardness. Without strong leadership, male or otherwise, in our home, Mona gave our mother quite a bit of grief during her high school years.

The grief deepened to intense sorrow and tragedy when, at only eighteen years of age, she married a strange, very abusive and (we are convinced) demonized individual who made her life miserable for many years. So intense was her husband's hatred for the rest of our family that for over four years he allowed her no contact at all with her immediate family. We found out years later that for years he intercepted all the mail coming from us, and told Mona that her family had turned its back on her.

One turning point for her came in 1979, when I went to Texas specifically to find her and give her the "our permission" to leave her abusive husband. I managed to convince her that we did still love her, that she was still part of the family and that we wanted her to make a break from her desperate situation. It began a process of liberation as she began the separation and eventual divorce but, in the trauma, she lost her faith as well. She relates the story:

> When I called and told her I had left my husband, her immediate response was, "What took you so long?" I was in a phone booth and I couldn't believe what I was hearing. Then she said, "What can I do for you?" I told her I was out of money, so she sent me some. Then I was able to obtain an attorney and go on from there.
>
> But the second most difficult phone call was to Tom. Again I was anticipating the worst. But his response was, "Well, join the club." He meant that he had borne it with Pat, and assured me that there was life after divorce. During that conversation I realized the suffering he had gone through in his own marriage, and I knew that he was soon to be my anchor, which he certainly was over the next two years (Tuma 1994).

Through her agony, Mona got to the point that she did not believe that God existed because He had not answered her prayers. She was by then a mother of two children who were taken away from her by her husband. In her disillusionment she had lost her faith. She did not know what or even if she believed. Tom was very concerned. He sensed that she was at a turning point in her life, perhaps ready to turn her back on God forever.

To reach out to her, Tom paid for airline tickets for Mona and their mother to go to Hawaii to spend Christmas of 1979 with them for a rest with the YWAM folks there. Tom reached out to her and began to draw her back into the family, and back to God. She wrote about the time in Hawaii:

> [Tom] didn't talk to me about God. He didn't shove God down my throat. He didn't chastise me. He didn't tell me I was wrong for the things I was doing. He gave me freedom. He didn't say a word about some of the things I was doing, and I knew he wasn't dumb. When I

wanted to talk, he seemed as though he had all the time in the world (Tuma 1994).

But Mona did not want to talk about what she had been through. She wanted to talk about what Tom had been through. So Tom and Mona would sit by the hour while Mona picked his brain about the things that had happened to him, especially, of course, about his first wife Pat and how he got over the trauma of his divorce. Fortunately for Tom, with God's healing, and the joy of marriage to Betty Sue, the details of his own pain had long since faded. Mona was encouraged, if somewhat skeptical, when he said that someday she too would have to "strain her brain" to remember the details of her own agony.

While she was there, Tom gave her a copy of the book *God's Smuggler* by Brother Andrew. She took that book down to the ocean to read and reflect on. She prayed: "God, if You're not a miraculous, powerful God, a God who does mighty signs and wonders, a Brother Andrew-type of God, then I don't want any part of You. But if You truly are a miraculous God, a God of miracles, then I need You to prove Yourself to me."

When she went back to Tom he was praying—for her. She sat down beside him and asked, "Tom, how is it that with everything you've ever been through, you have never been bitter?" She looked at his hands and said, "You can't move. You can't get out of that chair. You can't go do anything you want. You have to be clothed, have your hair washed, and have others get you out of bed and take you to the bathroom. Why aren't you bitter?"

> He looked at me with love in his eyes, took my hand, and said, "Mona, I've never in my whole life asked God, 'Why me?'" I just stared at him. His response nearly took my breath away, because that's *all* I had been asking for over a year. "Why me? Why does this have to happen to me?"
>
> I asked him then, "If the question in your mind has never been, 'Why me?' what have you asked?" He said the only question he asked, and one he asked every day, was "Why am I still alive?" He looked at me with his penetrating eyes and said, "Mona, why are you still alive?" I admitted that I didn't know. But from that day on,

> I quit asking "Why me?" That was God's first miracle to me. But I
> started asking, "Why am I still alive?" I'm not dead. I've gone
> through a lot, but I'm not dead; so therefore God must have a sig-
> nificant reason for my being alive. Tom always felt that each day
> we have is a gift (Tuma 1994).

That was the turning point for Mona to give her heart back to
the Lord and begin to learn of God's forgiveness, presence and love.
Over the next few years, she faced agonizing verbal abuse, death
threats and costly court battles to win custody of her two children,
finally succeeding only after they too were seriously abused.
Through it all Tom was there. "Tom went to court with me five
times in one year—identifying with me. He taught me the meaning
of identification—he put himself into my shoes. Tom spent his life
identifying with me. He wept with me as though the tears that he
was shedding were for his own children."

But the relationship was not at all one way. God had some special ministry plans for Mona too, and part of that ministry was
back to Tom. After the time in Hawaii, she devoted herself to
prayer and Bible study, for hours a day for several months. The
Lord began to reward her with remarkable spiritual insight and
the gift of intercession. God also drew to Himself another remarkable person, Jerry Tuma, whom Mona met in a bar during the dark
days after her divorce. God made Jerry a new creature as well and
eventually he became Mona's new, loving and deeply spiritual
husband. Before long, Tom's own spiritual journey was being aided
and strengthened by Mona and Jerry's understanding of the power
of God.

Mona began to give back some of what she had received, especially when Tom's health began to fail in 1983. Mona explains:

> God began to knit us together closer than ever before because the
> Lord allowed me to identify with Tom's sickness. I don't have any
> doctrinal theology for this. All I know is that it's reality. When Tom
> began having the kidney failure, he would get very high fevers. And
> even though he was half a world away, I would get high fevers at
> the same time. At one time I had a 106 degree temperature, and
> Jerry had to wrap me up in blankets because I was so chilled. Jerry

took me to the hospital but the staff could find nothing wrong with me. So as I was lying on my hospital bed I asked the Lord, "What is going on?" The Lord told me to begin praying for Tom. Now it was my turn to give back to him. So even though I was racked with fever, I crawled out of bed and started praying for Tom. I prayed for several hours, and the more I prayed the less sick I was. After several hours the whole thing subsided and I felt fine (Tuma 1994).

Later she and Tom talked on the phone, and Mona learned that Tom had had exactly the same symptoms at just the same time. Soon the fevers began coming on a regular basis. Mona began keeping track and Tom began keeping track too.

Mona continues:

It didn't matter where Tom was in the world, every time I got a fever I would start praying for him and after a period of time the fever would break. Later we would compare notes. "Okay Tom, I had this fever on such and such a day. What were you doing?" He would say, "I was fighting a fever." It got to the point after the first year that I began recognizing the symptoms and I knew I should begin praying whenever they came on. At other times, I would get, for example, an excruciating pain and pressure in my lower back and kidneys. I knew I didn't have anything wrong with my kidneys. It was just the Lord reminding me to pray. So whenever I felt the fevers coming on, instead of going to bed I would get on my knees and pray for Tom.

This began a ministry of intercession for Mona. For the next two years she interceded not only for Tom, but for many other people whom God brought to her attention. For some, as for Tom, she had an unusual identification with their symptoms. She learned the difference between prayer and intercession. "I'm not talking just about prayer," she says. "I'm talking about *intercession*. An intercessor identifies with the suffering of the person they are praying for. That is what Tom did for me, and what God enabled me to do for him. Tom, was the 'first-fruits' of my ministry."

Mona's personal growth, and the growth of her ministry of intercession was an important ingredient of Tom's own spiritual development. He wrote to me at the time about what he was learning through Mona:

> As we strive to keep the faith of our fathers and be faithful to Him Who has called us, we find ourselves on a pilgrimage. In our background we've had a lot of head knowledge and our faith was sound, but we haven't experienced much of the power of God. It's been a joy this past year to watch the growth in Ramona and Jerry's lives and they have been transformed by the Holy Spirit's ministry in their own lives during this time of trial concerning the custody of their children. It is also noteworthy that God has recently lengthened Ramona's short leg and healed the curvature of her spine and restored her to physical health. We confess that we are only beginning to inquire, but we acknowledge that we look to God in confidence that He will lead us into the truth" (T. Brewster 1982a).

Cathy Schaller, their friend from the "120" class at the Lake Avenue Congregational Church also had a big influence on Tom's spiritual development, by her example of intimacy with the Lord, her faithfulness as a prayer partner and her extraordinary ability to hear the Lord's voice. Her approach is that prayer is not something you work at—it is rather an intimacy with the Lord.

A particular word of knowledge that God gave Cathy was kind of a watershed in Tom's spiritual understanding. Cathy and her family had gone to Nevada for a short vacation. While staying in a motel, in the middle of the night, God told her to pray for Tom and Betty. She had no idea what the problem was or even if there was a problem, but she obeyed God and went into the bathroom, the only place she could go to use the light and her Bible as she prayed.

That night in Pasadena, Tom and Betty's apartment was being broken into. Tom's wallet and other personal effects were stolen from beside his bed as they slept, but neither he nor Betty nor Jed woke up.

Tom recalled the incident many times after that. He felt so fortunate that they had not awakened, for imagine how helpless and frightened he would have been not being able to defend himself or his family! But just as importantly for Tom was a much deeper understanding that God not only *could* speak to someone on his behalf, but that he *would* and did! Cathy says that this may have been the first time he was aware of someone having a word of knowledge specifically about and for him. Tom himself began to pray with a different kind of faith and expectation (Schaller 1994).

The "Declaration"

Perhaps the most significant aspect of Tom's spiritual journey and paradigm shift was with regard to his own healing. He had always viewed his accident and the resulting paralysis as God's special provision for him to add credibility and inspiration to his message—that God's power could be made perfect in his weakness (2 Corinthians 12:9, NIV). But just before their November 1983 departure for New Zealand and other parts of Asia, a friend, Cecil Pomphrey, got a word of knowledge that by February, Tom would be very much better. Mona also had a dream about Tom's expanding ministry where maybe hundreds of thousands of people were coming to Christ.

Cathy Schaller called too saying, "I think the Lord is wanting to do something. It may be about time for a major change in your health situation." There was a sense of excitement among the people who were praying for him. These events and prophesies were (and still are) puzzling to Betty Sue.

Tom was ambivalent about wanting to be healed. The issue for him was how best to glorify God. He certainly recognized the impact it would have on people's faith if God did choose to heal him, but he was concerned about a possible diminishing of the impact that God had given him *because* he was a quadriplegic. He did, though, begin to have a sense that something unusual was happening. In October 1983 he felt led to write a paper he called a "Declaration of Expectations."

The Declaration was just a statement of why he thought God might do something, and the factors that led to that feeling. It was a kind of step of faith for Tom. It started out as more of a journal, documenting what he and others were saying and experiencing. Then it began to be shared more widely.

Tom did not intend to be demanding that God heal him, though some felt it was worded too strongly and gave that impression. To some, it seemed out of character for Tom. He often prayed for the healing of others, and regularly that he would be healthy enough to carry on his ministry. But Tom had never prayed for his own physical healing—to be able to walk again. His acceptance of his paralysis was so complete, that he often proclaimed that breaking his neck was the "best thing that had ever happened to me."

Ironically, it was on his long trip to Asia over the winter of 1983–84, just after this was written, when Tom became very sick and he and Betty were both fairly sure it would be terminal.

"For the Kingdom of God is not a matter of talk but of power." I Cor. 4:20

DECLARATION OF EXPECTATION
of Tom Brewster October 30, 1983

"The Lord said, 'Write down the vision and make it plain. For the revelation awaits an appointed time.'" Habakkuk 2:2, 3

An accumulation of events has caused me to believe that it is God's will for me to declare that He may soon completely heal me and raise me from my wheelchair. I want this to be a declaration of faith, not presumption, so I am here basically recounting the things I, and others, have been experiencing.

1. Many of our intercessors have been moved of God to be praising Him for my complete physical healing.
2. Dreams have been given and confirmed through the Word concerning my walking.
3. Believing faith and expectancy is being built both in me and in praying friends by the Father.
4. Words of knowledge and prophetic words regarding my healing have been given by the Spirit through anointed intercessors.
5. The witness of mighty works of God in healing and miracles has become an increasingly frequent experience for us.
6. Spiritual warfare has intensified for us and many of our intercessors as Satan seems to be standing against this work of God.
7. God has convicted me of my unbelief which had been rooted in unbiblical limitations of God from my denominational background. This

unbelief resulted in rejection of spiritual gifts and the quenching of His Spirit.

8. God has convinced me that He is preparing me to minister to missionaries in the authority of Jesus and in the power of His Holy Spirit. The timing seems ripe to give Him maximum glory.

9. Preliminary healings have already begun, and though "small as a man's hand," He seems to be confirming that the "heavy rain is coming."

10. He has revealed that persevering, holiness and feeding on the Word are to occupy my attention until the promise has been received.

"Arise . . . in its time I will do this swiftly" (Isaiah 60, beginning and end). "I will strengthen them in the Lord and in His name they will walk,' declares the Lord" (Zechariah 10:12).

13
IDENTIFICATION WITH THE POOR

> The deeper Tom got into God, the deeper he got into missions. And the deeper he got into missions, the deeper he got into ministry to the poor (Glasser 1987).

> I remember Tom going down Guatemalan streets leading a parade of kids in his wake, and then wheeling around and telling them about Jesus. I can remember almost wanting to be disabled and having his soapbox for ministry (Wes Collins 1993).

In the last years of Tom's life he devoted much of his energy and prayer life to the needs of the world's poor. But Tom's concern for the poor was not something he came to late in life. From Tom's earliest days, he knew poverty. Indeed, Tom was known for his involvement with the poor throughout his public ministry. But his love for the poor and burning desire to see them come to Christ in fact grew out of his youth.

Both Tom and Betty Sue grew up knowing poverty—both by exposure and experience. Not many people, even in the depressed times of Tom's youth, lived in a shack with a boxcar attached. Betty Sue grew up as a missionary's kid, and also lived among the rural poor while she was growing up and saw the needs of people. Her own adopted sister Juanita was starving to death when her folks took her in.

Where Are Your Treasures?

Our dad never progressed very far financially beyond those impoverished roots, and neither, in fact, did Tom. But there were other factors that brought Tom eventually to an almost all consuming concern for and identification with the poor. Tom's income for most of his life was a subsistence allowance provided for him by his insurance company. He did manage to accumulate some money, and early on in his ministry he made some investments to try to preserve it. Invariably, it seemed, his investments went bad.

Tom became convinced that the Lord was trying to tell him something, and decided that he would spend his life storing up treasure in heaven rather than on earth. For Christmas in 1979, I gave them a copy of *Rich Christians in an Age of Hunger* by Ron Sider, which was an important book for Alice and myself. Tom and Betty Sue began thinking more about investing whatever money they had in people and in justice issues. If they were not giving money away, they were investing in things like the Dwelling House Savings and Loan where there was less return but the investment was given to help people who would not otherwise be able to afford their own housing or own their own homes. For the rest of his life, Tom gave away virtually everything above what he and Betty and Jed needed to meet their minimal needs.

Some very special friends were also a profound influence on Tom and Betty Sue in their pilgrimage toward addressing the needs of the poor. Betty Sue describes the influence of Mica Lugenbeel on her thinking about the poor:

> She had such a caring stance towards the poor. At the language school [in Guadalajara] we were told that if a beggar ever comes around, you just say "no" otherwise they'll keep coming around. But she gave and gave to anybody that came by, for almost any reason. She didn't give them money. She gave them food and clothing and produce from the garden. She gave them a drink of cold water. Even the garbage men when they came around, she was ready with a drink of cold water for them. And if little kids came around she would send them home with eggs for their parents. She was constantly giving of herself to people.
>
> Her explanation? "I grew up knowing how it felt to be poor and not knowing where my next meal was coming from and I can't let other people stay that way. I might get ripped off once or twice, but I'm not giving something that's going to hurt me. I can give food without taking it out of my own mouth. I can give used clothing because I have enough clothes to wear." That attitude was a real blessing to me because it had bothered me not to give to people. I felt within myself that it was unfair and I didn't have any other

models. To have her as a model was really encouraging (E. Brewster 1993).

To an extent, both Tom and Betty knew *about* the poor, but it was their traveling around the world, increasingly in areas of the unreached peoples, that the extent of the world's poverty, and God's concern for the poor, began to be the motivating factor of their ministry. To a certain extent, Tom and Betty Sue's lifestyle demanded that they live frugally. For over ten years, Tom and Betty Sue traveled to more than seventy countries around the world, often being gone for many months at a time. There was the necessity, if not the choice, to live simply. Betty Sue could not carry a lot of suitcases, look after Tom's electric wheelchair and battery, a young son, and toss Tom in and out of cars, boats, planes, and trains at the same time. So Tom basically carried with him one suit and some changes of shirts. Betty Sue traveled with a three-piece suit—a skirt, jacket and slacks—and some changes of blouses and underwear. That was nearly it as far as clothing. The rest of their luggage was books and supplies for Tom.

Even while they were "at home" in Pasadena, Tom said they always felt like they were camping out. It was not necessarily their choice but they both felt it was good for them. It freed them up to travel and gave them that much more empathy with the many, many others in various situations around the world for whom camping out is also not their choice, but, sadly, is their lot. (Betty notes that it was a struggle for Tom to keep to as simple a lifestyle as he would have liked, since she, his wife, though relatively frugal, had a "missionary pack rat" tendency, wanting to save bits of string, plastic bags, plastic yogurt containers, and so on since "they might come in handy later on.")

As they traveled, however, the necessity and reality of living simply, traveling light, and identifying with the poor became a value and a ministry objective. The more they traveled to the poorest parts of the world, the more they sensed a calling to be Good News to the poor.

The 1974 trip to Calcutta had been the catalyst. The vastness, immensity and depth of the poverty was a shock to them as it is to anyone who visits the ghastly slums of that city. James Cameron describes Calcutta well:

> Experienced travelers argue and contend over their images of what is best remembered, of beauty or pleasure or tranquillity or fun, but among them is rarely any difference of opinion about what is worst, the most irredeemably horrible, vile, and despairing city in the world; few who know it will dispute that this place is Calcutta. The urban awfulness of Calcutta has become a cliché of such dimensions that one flinches from even trying to say more about it. . . .
>
> The inhuman cruelty of Calcutta defies the normal language of odium; its total wrongness has become base measure of injustice, and its paradoxes are a platitude. It is immensely rich, and its poverty is of such an inescapable, all-pervadingly intrusive kind that generations of sociologists, reformers, planners, do-gooders and destroyers have, in the end, thrown up their hands and hopelessly retreated, loudly proclaiming that Calcutta's wretchedness has gone not only past redemption but beyond description (1987:178).

The Lost Are Poor and the Poor Are Lost

The Calcutta visit, along with the visit to the refugee camp in Hong Kong in 1982, dramatically impacted their lives. You do not see the worst of the horrors of the human condition without it changing your life.

Tom and Betty's lives and ministry was already firmly committed to see people come to Christ. But along with this was a growing concern for the poor. Tom began to realize that, as Bryant Myers has reminded us, "the lost are poor and the poor are lost" (1989). As they focused more on the lost, they began to also focus more on the poor.

"Our primary commitment," Tom wrote, "is to the Great Commission. We would not be interested in language learning if it weren't for our Lord's command to go into all the world and communicate the Good News of Jesus Christ" (YWAM pg. 82).

For Tom, this commitment was more and more a commitment to the *unreached peoples* of the world, and he had begun to identify more closely with groups such as YWAM who were thinking creatively and boldly about ministry where the Gospel had not yet penetrated. These were areas where Christians typically could not go as "normal" missionaries, and where "normal" missionary language schools did not exist. Clearly, their teaching of language learning through relationships then, and their insistence that communication *is* ministry, were all the more appropriate and useful in such areas. Tom felt that God has challenged us to reach the unreached peoples of the world, and felt that in order to meet that challenge, people would have to be willing to learn the languages of unreached peoples.

> I view the unreached peoples of the world as being, for the most part, out of the reach of our language school mentality. And so we have trusted the Lord for a strategy to prepare people so that they can go out into the languages where there never will be language schools. I don't make any apologies for orienting and identifying with unreached peoples, and our goal will be that people will be challenged to go to people groups who speak languages where there are not language schools, where there are no materials (T. Brewster 1983:25).

Tom and Betty's high-involvement language learning exposures also had already regularly drawn them to the poor. They had always insisted on what was virtually a vow of simplicity for the language learners whom they took on field learning experiences in various parts of the world. On the Bolivia trip they allowed the learners to take only twenty kilos with them to ensure that their lifestyle would not get in the way of ministry. The students also were not allowed to have a vehicle. They were to take public transportation wherever they went.

Invariably when they sent the learners out into the communities, those who did their language practice in the middle and upper middle class sections of town came back discouraged. They did not find many people out on the streets, and those few were closed to them. However, those who visited the poorer areas always found plenty of people to talk to.

With the receptiveness of the poor not only to language learners, but also to the Gospel, Tom and Betty began to encourage new language learners, wherever they were in the world, to go into the poorest sections of town when practicing the "use what you learn" phase of the learning cycle. Not surprisingly, at times they met with resistance: "I have nothing in common with those people," some said, or "No way am I going to expose myself to that risk!" Naturally, Tom and Betty Sue were concerned about the safety of the learners, but they always walked through those same areas with the learners without sensing any great danger. They led by example, and invariably proved that the "learner" role dissipated whatever suspicion or hostility might be present. "Didn't Christ die for the poor? Don't we have a responsibility?" he pleaded.

Tom's work was often with new missionaries, and he wondered if the hesitance new missionaries had toward ministry among the poor was shared by more experienced missionaries. To his disappointment, he found that it was. When he asked experienced missionaries, "Who is working among the really poor?" he found very few who could honestly say they were. Some said, "I live in the middle class area but I go down there once a month for services."

Tom felt that often new missionaries were so well trained by the model of middle-class missionaries, they were not willing to live among the poor either. If they did have a ministry to the poor, it was often what Tom called a "foray" ministry—"just go down and hop back out as quickly as you can." Tom's expectations were high and he had little sympathy for such cautious approaches, especially by those whose ministries should have drawn them to live among the poor.

Tom also led from Scripture. He understood that God is not neutral with respect to the poor. God is on the side of the poor! Tom knew that, as Sider says,

> The Bible clearly and repeatedly teaches that God is at work in history casting down the rich and exalting the poor because frequently the rich are wealthy precisely because they have oppressed the poor or have neglected to aid the needy. God also sides with the poor because of their special vulnerability (Sider 1990:61).

Tom began incorporating in the classes some of the scores of passages and hundreds of verses showing God's concern or His "preferential option" for the poor.

Sadly, just in reading these verses, sometimes the reaction of the class was electric. "You have no right to be reading those verses to us," one man objected. Another complained, "Your mandate is to teach about language learning—skip the meddling!" Some students even objected to reading Scriptures about the poor in pre-class devotionals!

The worst instance happened on an occasion when Tom was talking about the car being an "isolation capsule" which separates us from the people. "Even our houses," he said, "if too different from those of the local people, can isolate us from people. If we really want to bond with the people and become one with them and if we've chosen to minister to poor people, then we ought to choose to be one with them in lifestyle to the extent that we can. If we can't go all the way, at least simplify our own lifestyles so that our appearance of wealth is not a stumbling block" (E. Brewster 1993).

At that, one of the young missionaries in training stood up and literally yelled at Tom. "Only Communists talk about simplifying lifestyles!" he shouted. Betty Sue recalls,

> I was so proud of Tom. He just sat there and waited. When the guy finally finished his harangue, Tom said, "I'm really sorry that you feel that way but I sense that was what the Lord would have me say this morning and I've said it and I've said as much as I've planned to say on the subject" (1993).

The next day the man came back to class and someone else raised the subject of simple lifestyles. They wanted him to go a little bit deeper into what he meant and how far one could go. Tom replied, "How far one person goes does not necessarily affect how far another one goes. Some may choose to go almost all the way and live a life of poverty, especially those who don't have children."

He had not gotten very far into the subject when the first man got so angry that he got up, grabbed his wife, and walked out.

At the beginning of class the next day he came to announce that he and his wife were leaving. Tom had the mandate to teach about language and culture learning, he fumed, and he was not doing that. He made a public invitation for others to leave with them that day and go back home. A few couples did. One couple, from the same mission group as those who left, stood up and apologized then for those who had left.

(Not too surprisingly, perhaps, Tom found out later that the group had arrived in the country very shortly prior to the course. Finding the exchange rate so favorable, several had purchased not one but *two* cars as investments.)

While Tom had said all he wanted to say about ministry to the poor in that particular class, he certainly had not said all he was going to say on the subject. Such conversations however, made Tom realize the lack of teaching that evangelicals have in this area in their Bible and missionary training. It made Tom want to find non-threatening ways to talk about these issues. In subsequent courses he found ways to raise the issues less abrasively, sometimes just by talking about his own pilgrimage toward a commitment to the poor.

That commitment continued to grow, and he was pleased when he saw doors opening up in areas where the Gospel had not penetrated. He followed closely the moving of the Holy Spirit among the "frontier" peoples and rejoiced at any news of Christ becoming known among the unreached. "We are especially enthusiastic about the potential of what God will do in the countries of Nepal and Pakistan," he wrote to his friend Johann Louw in South Africa in March of 1982.

> The Gospels describe the concern that Jesus had for the multitudes, and His compassion for the poor and His incarnation among them. Maybe the critical issue of the church in missions in the next decade is the accelerating gap between those who have the world's riches while continuing to exploit the quarter of the world's people who are starving. When one asks "for whom does the heart of God cry out for justice?" it seems reasonable to believe God for an outpouring of His love and grace to these multitudes of the world's poorest (1982b).

As Tom and Betty became more and more aware of the poor and God's call on their lives to minister to them, they began reading biographies of missionaries who ministered selflessly to the poor. Tom was moved by the example of Francis of Assisi, a son of a wealthy cloth merchant who exchanged his fine clothes for those of a beggar and sat on the cathedral steps to beg and experience for himself the life of these outcasts. From this beginning, God raised up the mighty Franciscan movement of men and women who give their lives in service and ministry among the poor.

Another impressive example was that of Toyohiko Kagawa of Japan. Kagawa was the son of a wealthy headman of nineteen towns who, touched by the plight of the poor, brought a sick beggar into his dorm room in a Christian seminary. This was unacceptable to the school officials, who informed him that his charities would have to be on the outside of the school. So Kagawa moved into a 6x9 foot shack in the slums where he lived for *fifteen years*, always sharing it with the needy. For Tom, Kagawa was a missionary prototype who met the poor at their own level—the kind of identification he envisioned for more effective ministry to the poor.

Missionary "Tourists"

Tom was concerned about the *tourist mentality* of so many missionaries he had seen.

> I think this *tourist mentality* explains why 80% of the missionaries have gone to only 17% of the people. That's where the "tour guides" are. That's where they can go and get somebody to take them by the hand and introduce them into the language or the culture. But the unfinished task today demands at least an *adventurer mentality*, if not an *explorer mentality* on the frontiers. I trust that new missionaries today will be willing to throw off that tourist mentality and become adventurers and explorers, participating in the task that remains to be done. It can't be done using the tourist approach. It's going to require a whole different kind of mentality in order to get close to the people and to see the job accomplished (T. Brewster 1983:28).

Tom continued:

> We have had the privilege of seeing mission activity in many places throughout the world. And too often we see missionaries who are simply involved with keeping the machinery of their mission in operation. They don't have the flexibility that permits them to even

ask the questions about making sense and whether their ministry is meaningful from the perspective of the local people. They don't live in ways that give them enough flexibility to change their approach even it they wanted to (T. Brewster 1983:30).

Tom felt that missionaries today were not much different from the original disciples. Jesus told the disciples to go and make disciples. But those disciples did not go. They did not go for a long time. All of a sudden, in chapter 10 of Acts, Peter finds out what God was talking about—that He was not just talking about food.

> Peter traveled a great distance. I'm not talking about distance geographically. I'm talking about the distance inside his heart and mind. Cornelius was a godly man. And Peter came to some very deep insights—God showed him in a vision that he should not think of anyone as inferior. In Acts 15 we have the council of Jerusalem— a meeting to talk about all these issues. That meeting took place 16 years after Jesus told the disciples to go. And there they were, still hanging around with other Jews (T. Brewster 1983:62).

"The Word became flesh and dwelt among us . . ."

In "As Poor Among the Poor," Tom wrote: "'The Word became flesh and dwelt among us.' This is the incarnation. As a model and strategy for ministry, incarnation suggests that the messenger becomes one with the people, enters into their experience, lives with them and shares life from their perspective" (1985d:22).

Tom was certainly not the first to talk of Christ's incarnation as a model for ministry and for mission. Chuck Kraft has written much about it in *Communicating the Gospel God's Way*, and in *Christianity in Culture*. Many others have also explored the awesome truth of Jesus:

> Who, being in very nature God, did not consider equality with God something to be grasped, but made himself nothing, taking the very nature of a servant, being made in human likeness (Phil. 2:6, 7).

But Tom left no doubt about what he felt were the harsh implications of the incarnational model. "As a lifestyle among today's poor, it means living wherever there are people like the one billion who make less than $300 a year. It may increasingly mean living in the slums" (1985d).

Tom felt there was a great need for incarnational ministries among the poor people of the world. "Where are those who are willing to give their lives to the poorest of the world's poor?" he asked. "We don't find very many in established missions today."

> If our Lord would have delayed His coming by 2000 years and were to have come today rather than yesteryear, it seems to me consistent with all we know about Him that He would have still come and incarnated Himself among the poor. He would have been born into a poor family and would have lived His life among poor people. It's reasonable to expect that He still would have inaugurated His ministry as we read in Luke 4, by quoting from Isaiah, saying that He had come to bring the gospel—the Good News—to the poor (T. Brewster 1983:124, 125).

In Tom's mind, this is the challenge for missions today. He agonized that so many missions and mission activities were so ineffective, and was convinced that part of the reason was that western missionaries did not know how to live close to the people. "Unless we do something about it," he warned,

> the wheels of our missionary machinery may continue with greater and greater speed but with greater and greater ineffectiveness. The wheels are turning, but we have to ask the question, "Are the wheels on the ground?" "Are the ministries really making sense when viewed through the eyes of local people?" Unless we're willing to get close to people, we may miss completely what God is doing in their midst. We need to live incarnational lives—the Word became flesh and dwelt among us. The message became a real live Person and lived on our terms, in ways that we could understand and relate to. Only when we live in this way will we really be good news to the people we minister to (T. Brewster 1983:58, 59).

There were (and are) however signs of hope. To many new missionaries and to some with lots of experience, Tom's encouragement toward an incarnational ministry among the poor was a new and exciting challenge that opened the door to much more effective ministry possibilities.

One new missionary learning the Thai language, Rona Tingsmore, was at first offended that Tom would advocate such a "dangerous" strategy of actually going to live among the poor: "He [Tom] had the audacity to imply that my hesitation to live among some poverty stricken people, in total disregard for the hygiene I have come to know and love, was a reflection on my relationship to Christ. Fortunately, the sensible students in my class agreed with me that [Tom] had gone too far." But then she had an experience which changed her outlook:

> [Noticing a waitress] I asked her, in English where she was from. Quite defensively and without eye contact she asked why I wanted to know. Persistently I again inquired. She lifted her head just enough for me to hear the word Thailand, then she scurried to the other end of the shop. Boldly I called out to her in Thai. Immediately she stopped working and rushed back to me, a huge smile spreading across her face. Her dark eyes were filled with expression as she assailed me with a Thai soliloquy. At that moment the Holy Spirit showed me what Brewster spent his life trying to put into words. As long as I sat in that shop as an American, the Thai woman never knew I was there. But when I spoke Thai, I had stepped out of my world into hers. Once in her world she could see me and hear me (Tingsmore 1988).

Adele Chaney Fulton was another such new missionary. She wrote:

> Tom's ideas have helped me to recognize the value of humility, of not being afraid to "get dirty," of rolling up my sleeves and being "one" with the people I want to help. Also, I realize that such people have a lot to teach me, and that bonding can be accomplished through a teachable spirit. Many people, Christians and non-Christians alike, try to help others from afar. Money is easy to give. It's far more sacrificial and Christ-like to walk in the shoes of others, and it's a far more effective evangelism method (Fulton 1993).

". . . Contented to Be Poor and Little Known . . ."

Tom was moved by and meditated on the examples and models of incarnational ministry that he read about in missionary biographies and other writings. He reflected deeply on the poem "William Burns" by H. Grattan Guiness, which he often recited at the end of his courses. Tom viewed Burns as an example of one who adopted an incarnational approach to ministry. William Burns went to China prior to Hudson Taylor and at some point he and Hudson Taylor joined forces. Hudson Taylor by then had already adopted Chinese dress, one of the early missionaries to do so. He was severely looked down on by other missionaries for having done something so terribly heathen. But Burns saw how important the identification with the Chinese people was and followed Taylor's lead. As a result, he found he was much less of a curiosity, and many more doors for relationships and ministry were opened to him.

Burns had a passion for teaching the Chinese people about Christ, and having them accept Christ as their Savior. His zeal resulted in imprisonment. When he was released he went into Manchuria where he died after some years of fruitful ministry.

H. Gratin Guiness, himself a trainer of young people to be missionaries, though not able to go personally, wrote a poem about William Burns when he heard of his death in China. The poem moved and motivated Tom, for it revealed a man, like himself, passionately concerned about the lost, and willing to go to the poorest and live among them:

> . . . Choosing to toil in distant fields, unsown,
> Contented to be poor and little known,
> *Faithful to death*: Oh, man of God, well done!
> Thy fight is ended and thy crown is won. . . .

> . . . Oh, William Burns, we will not call thee dead!
> Though lies thy body in its narrow bed
> In far-off China. Though Manchuria keeps
> Thy dust, which in the Lord securely sleeps,
> Thy spirit lives with Jesus; and where He
> Thy Master dwells, 'tis meet that thou shouldst be.
> There is no death in His divine embrace
> There is no life but where they see His face.

And now, Lord,
Let Thy servant's mantle fall upon another.
Since Thy solemn call
To preach the Truth in China has been heard,
Grant that a double portion be conferred
Of the same spirit on the gentler head
Of some Elisha—who may raise the dead
and fill the widow's cruse, and heal the spring,
And make the desolate of heart to sing;
And stand, though feeble, fearless, since he knows
Thy hosts angelic guard him from his foes;

Whose life and image fairer still may be
Of Christ of Nazareth and Galilee,
Of Thine, oh, spotless Lamb of Calvary!
China [and unreached peoples],[1] I breathe for thee
A brother's prayer.
Unnumbered are thy millions.
Father, hear their groans which we cannot.
Thine arm make bare,
And reap the Harvest of salvation there.
The fullness of the Gentiles, like the sea
Immense, Oh, God, be gathered unto thee,
Then Israel save, and with His saintly train,
Send us Immanuel over all to reign (Guiness 1962:384).

---

[1] Added by Tom when he recited the poem in his classes

14
SERVANTS AMONG THE POOR

This was the capstone. It was a natural growth of Tom's ministry, so fundamental theologically and so missiologically relevant (Glasser 1987).

In mid January 1984, after more than a month of rest and some recovery in Canberra, Tom was well enough to travel again, and they began what was to be almost two more years of intensive travel and consultations.

Almost all of February and March were spent in remote parts of Indonesia, Irian Jaya, and New Guinea, much of it bouncing around in small planes. For anyone, this schedule would have been immensely grueling. For a quadriplegic and his wife and four year old son, it was all the more so. Considering the fact that Tom was not fully recovered from the serious health problems faced just days earlier in New Zealand and Australia, it is almost unbelievable. In those two months they conducted more than a dozen language and culture learning workshops for Wycliffe Bible Translators and other missionaries serving in one of the most remote and linguistically diverse areas of the world.

On March 22, 1984 they began their long trip homeward after traveling over four months, being extremely sick for a good part of that time and even near death for days. They overnighted in Fiji and Honolulu, and got to Los Angeles in time for just a few days rest before starting to teach Spring Quarter courses at SWM on April 3. The following weekend they attended a Weekend Marriage Encounter—a very positive experience for both of them. Not surprisingly, they were feeling quite depleted after such an intense trip. The Encounter was a healing and refreshing time both spiritually and physically.

The Mexico Challenge
Tom and Betty Sue's hearts were broken for the poor, and they longed to see new missionaries called to live among them. He knew

well from having seen much of it that the poverty of our world is almost overwhelming. Three quarters of the world's people survive on less than $2 a day per person, and one-third of these live on less than $200 per year. Most cities throughout the world are being flooded with squatters, and the growing masses of these poor now number in the hundreds of millions. Tom believed that the poor are the harvest fields that God is preparing.

He and Betty began to think through more what it would mean, and how they could facilitate and motivate missionaries to actually live with the poor as they ministered to them. Mission boards at that time did not think having missionaries live with the poor with income at or near the levels of the poor was wise or a viable mission strategy. But Tom began to think otherwise. He dis cussed it at length with Viv Grigg, who had come to Pasadena for gradu ate work at Fuller Seminary. Viv had written an important book on ministry to the poor, *Companion to the Poor,* which provided some useful models and they began to see how it might be possible.

That summer Tom asked Paul Pierson, the Dean of the School of World Mission, for permission to teach a class on "Incarnational Ministry," with the idea that it would include a significant field learning experience of actually living among the poor. Permission was granted. The class studied the Scriptures reflecting God's con cern for the poor, and read biographies of missionaries whose ministries focused on the poor. "The life and incarnation of Jesus is accepted as the model for our ministry," he told the students, "and He who had all privilege chose to leave that behind, to empty Him self, and to come and dwell among us. He did this for our sake, so that through His poverty we might become rich. And He says to us, 'Follow Me. Follow My example and live with Me among the poor.' Jesus is moved with compassion for these harassed and helpless crowds. Are we similarly moved? Are we moved enough to leave our own wealth and privilege behind and follow Christ's example to minister to the poor? Jesus says to His followers, 'This harvest is plentiful, but the workers are few.'"

Tom threw out the challenge to the students to live among the poor, and some began to take up the challenge. During the course, a number of students wrote to mission boards, asking if through those missions, they could be involved in ministry to the poor, living directly with them on a salary commensurate with what the poor themselves earned. Without exception, the mission boards said "No—it would be too risky. Insurance won't allow it. Our policy doesn't allow it. That is not 'our' ministry. It can't be done."

Some students began to feel that if no one else would let them do it, they would have to do something themselves. There was a feeling of solidarity in that first Incarnational Ministry class, and they discussed regularly their frustration at not being able to find a mission board which would allow them to follow up on what they felt was a call of God. A strong feeling developed: "Tom, you got us into this; help us find a channel to live out this vision."

Viv Grigg also felt that Tom was creating an obligation for himself. He felt that Tom could not talk about God's desire for missionaries to live and work among the poor on the salaries of the poor without providing some kind of a channel for them to do so.

Viv was convinced God was leading them to link up a new organization with the New Zealand Servants to the Poor. He wrote:

> [God was speaking] to myself and to Tom and Betty Sue. We'd compare notes and discover the same God saying the same things. Is this what it means to have unity of spirit? A mission thrust, mission structure and a mission strategy began to emerge. An American *Servants* movement linked to the embryo New Zealand *Servants* movement and others as God raised them up in time from other countries (Grigg 1984).

Tom was not sure he agreed. He felt his role was to share the vision, and he was not convinced that he should be involved in founding and administering a new mission sending board. "God started it, not me," he argued, "and I am not sure that directing it is part of his mandate for me." Moreover, he and Betty were concerned that they might have less credibility with other mission boards if they started a mission board of their own. Some mission boards might feel that they were now competing.

Betty Sue was often the devil's advocate: "What if we *don't* get involved in this?" she asked. "Will anyone else pick it up? Or if we do, are we willing to compete with mission boards for recruits and devote a lot of our time to administration?" Tom never resented her questioning. He felt that God may have put her into his life for just that purpose. Tom never forced anything through that she was uncomfortable with. He was willing to wait, talk it through, and to come to some kind of consensus. He knew he had to take into account her feelings and intuition. "I was sometimes initially reluctant to follow his ideas," Betty says, "and sometimes tried to help sort out the do-able from the too visionary. But I appreciated and admired his visionary spirit and tried not to stifle it. It is one of the things I miss very much now" (E. Brewster 1993).

But was the implementation not part of the call? Tom reluctantly agreed with Viv and with his students and began the paperwork process to incorporate a new mission called Servants Among the Poor.

The Incarnational Ministry class at Fuller was very much a part of the birthing process. The "significant field learning experience" that Tom put together for the Incarnational Ministry class was a trip to the urban slums of Mexico City. Not all of the class was able to go, but a core group of committed young people began to make preparations. People like John Macy, John Shorack, John and Gwen Elmer, Pat and Bud Kenick, Derrick Ketchum, David Ling, Susanne Primer, and Tyler Zabrinski were among the early Servants prepared to minister to some of the poorest people in the world by living with them at or near their own standard of living.

As Viv Grigg was still in Pasadena, Tom thought it would be great if such an experienced urban missionary could participate with them, and he invited Viv to go along.

The invitation was in fact an answer to prayer, and Viv quickly rearranged his travel plans to include the trip to Mexico. Viv said he had been praying and fasting for days concerning the spiritual warfare in the huge urban areas of Asia and the rest the world. He wrote:

> Over these cities he showed the principalities and their nature. As his power would come it would take over my body and bring me against them in power. In some places he showed the crowds, in

some the weeping of the poor, in others the demons over squatter areas. This continued over several weeks.

[That night after the invitation to Mexico] as my head hit the pillow, the Holy Spirit came in such power that my whole body began to shake. It is something I have learned to respond to quickly. I got up and the Lord showed me twenty or so people walking through the slums of Mexico City; a band of wandering preachers who would intercede amongst the poor, coming against the spiritual powers that dwell above the city, healing the sick, preaching the good news of the Kingdom (Grigg 1984).

A day or so later, Tom was talking to Gordon Aeschliman, the editor of *World Christian Magazine,* about an article they had asked him to write on "Missionary Preparation from Jesus' Point of View," based on Matthew 10. Tom mentioned that he was going to spend a week in Mexico City with Viv Grigg. Gordon felt it would be a great learning experience for himself and some of his *World Christian* colleagues, so he asked if they could accompany Tom.

"Sure, come along!" Tom responded.

During the next couple of weeks several other individuals felt God leading them to join the group. In all, eighteen people joined the first outreach of what became Servants Among the Poor.

Viv Grigg was pleased to have the additional people along:

[These people] have commitments to justice, to simplicity, to evangelism, to community. . . . It seemed we should go up, spy out the land and come back to the leaders of the churches as Caleb and Joshua did saying, "Let us go up at once and occupy these poor areas; for we are well able to establish movements of disciples amongst the poor of this mega-city" (1984).

In the six weeks before departure, these individuals were knit together through various times of worship, intercession and information. At the same time, God was raising up a number of intercessors who would not be able to go, but who would stand with them in prayer while they were gone. Some made resources available so that others could go.

The Mexico trip was a spiritual mountain top for all. Most of the participants kept journals of their thoughts and experiences, including Tom and Betty.

They had planned to stay in a very modest or "slum" hotel and two participants were sent a day ahead to find such a place. They really had not found anything suitable and were feeling the pressure of meeting the expectations of the group. The only promising one was the hotel Ecatepec. But that seemed to be too nice. In reality it was God's provision:

> Feeling like they had failed us in their reason for coming early—getting us a slum hotel, [the two advance team members] went to meet our arriving flight. They let us know that they had failed to find a slum hotel, so they would have to stay in something a bit more upscale. We all piled into a bus and went to the hotel where we were stunned two times in succession. First, it was only $6.00 a room and two could share a room—$3.00 each. Yet the rooms are incredible! Seldom have any of us stayed in such beautiful rooms—king size beds, big European bathrooms and enough open space at the foot of the bed in our room for all eighteen of us to sit comfortably in a circle on the floor. God's sense of humor was striking. We had all come with our sheets and blankets tied with a rope, ready to spend the grungiest night of our lives (with rats and fleas and roaches) and God put us here. God who owns the cattle on a thousand hills had intervened (T. Brewster 1984a).

The rest of the group arrived on Friday and immediately began exploring the neighborhood. They found a small Catholic church and attended some services there. The service was led by a lay leader, with worship and praise choruses, interspersed with little sermonettes. They were pleased that the spontaneous sermonettes indicated that the lay leader had experienced personal salvation and a walk with the Lord. One was about the Catholic attention to the saints. "Saints are saints not because of special merit," the leader said, " but because they followed the Lord so closely. It is their walk with the Lord, that we should emulate and imitate." The leader also emphasized the resurrection. "Christ died on the cross, and the cross is therefore beautiful to us, but the truly glorious part is that he didn't stay dead. He is alive!"

Scouting in the neighborhood that evening led them to a friendly family restaurant where they all piled in and watched as tortillas were made and various special foods prepared. The group all sang to the family (in English), and Betty Sue prayed in Spanish and blessed them. Before they opened their eyes, the Señora began praying for them—blessing them and praying that God would pour out His Spirit on them wherever they went around the world. How did she know to pray for their ministry around the world? Was she praying prophetically, they wondered?

With full stomachs at the end of the day they walked back under the stars through the streets to their hotel on Avenida Central to get a good night's sleep and to savor those great king size beds. They piled into bed and rejoiced in God's blessing on the day.

But then came the mosquitoes. Not in hordes, but one at a time constantly throughout the night. Various times Betty Sue got up to try to swat them. She counted seventeen bites on Jed. "Could it be," Tom wondered, "that these little creatures, only a quarter inch long could be instruments in Satan's hands to bring discouragement and failure to those that God would seek to send to minister among the very poor?"

Tom began to think about the sufferings of Christ, the price He paid because He loved so much. "He who was rich became poor and suffered so cruelly just because He loved me so much because he wanted to make me an heir to the abounding riches of His own home." Tom observed:

> God is beginning to raise up a movement of people to live and serve among the squatters and the very poor of the urban cities throughout the world. People whose primary goal is to gain intimacy with God and serve the poor and intercede for them, standing in the gap for them. So that these, the poor, the ones that Jesus first said He came to reach might also become so very rich in Christ (1984a).

A few mosquitoes caused Tom to begin to reflect on entering into the sufferings of Christ. *By His stripes we are healed.* Perhaps by their experience of a few mosquito bites and sleepless nights, he thought, some of the exploited, hungry, and poor might be healed.

Tom prayed,

> Thank you Lord, for this gentle reminder of Your great love to me. Thank you even for the mosquitoes. Thank you especially for the

mosquitoes. Thank you also for a wife who could have slept through this last early morning hour, mosquitoes and all, but who instead sat beside me and helped me write down my reflections on our first night in Mexico. And thank you that already my main purpose in coming is beginning to be accomplished—the beginning of a new intimacy with Jesus (1984a).

On Saturday morning they began to look for a poorer area. There, they met some young people and Tom explained to them that various ones from their group would like to stay with them in their homes. Several said they would like that. So some of the Servants group were able to move in with poor families right away.

On a mud soaked and pot-holed street, they noticed a small yellow-front building that said "Iglesia Pentecostal Getsemani." Betty told the pastor's wife there that they wanted to find out what God was doing among the poor. She invited them into a very small church with some benches, a platform across the front with a wooden pulpit and a table. She told them that her husband was on the highway selling *gorditos*—a kind of pastry. He could have had a full-time job with somewhat better pay, she explained, but felt that God was calling him to shepherd this flock as a lay leader.

They fellowshipped through the afternoon in the pastor's home, learning about the needs of the families in the neighborhood. In the evening, the pastor Leoncio came home and he and his wife set up some tables in the church and began serving the delicious *pozole* that the church members had prepared during the day. After the meal they sang together, and Tom presented a short message.

Several of the group then went to the homes of some poor families for the night while Tom, Betty and Jed remained with the pastor's family. Betty tells about the night:

> They discovered it would be too awkward to try to get the wheelchair in and out of the narrow doors of their two-room house, so they had decided we should sleep in the church. We put some benches together, planning to sleep in our sleeping bags on them. But the family brought in the one family mattress from their bedroom and put it on the benches. We tried to argue with them about

it but they insisted we use it. So we let them use our sleeping bags and we used their mattress. We had brought sheets and blankets which we put on the bed, (and gave them to the pastor's family in the morning) (1984).

The Wounded Healer

One day, the group went to visit the home of a community worker named Margarita. She'd been asked by the community to be their community leader and within a few months the Lord had promoted her five times. At that time, she was responsible for half a million people including nine squatter areas. As they talked, the nine year old blind son of another community leader was brought to them. He had been blind since birth.

Lacking faith, they hesitated to pray for the boy. But they knew not to pray for him would have shown their disbelief. Viv thought:

> To pray would probably lead to another one of a multitude of prayers for the sick without answer. Yet God could do it. We prayed three times with no effect, Tom, Betty Sue, Jim, Adele and others— the folk from the community standing around watching. Then Tom noticed the skull around the neck of the father. He refused to take it off. It would be three days later that we learned its significance" (1984).

Another member of the team, Paul Peterson, wrote about the incident with the blind boy:

> Tom was speaking to the child's parents, and Viv crouched down with his hands on the boy's shoulders. I realized they were going to pray for healing. I moved closer and placed my hand on Tom's back as Tom put his hand on the boy's shoulder. Here was Tom in his wheelchair with every excuse in the world not to be in Mexico City and among the poorest of the poor, yet he was freely giving of himself at a cost none of us could imagine (1985:3, 4).

On Thursday they met for worship and intercession for Mexico City. All of them sensed spiritual warfare throughout the city, and they remembered the skull around the neck of the blind boy's father. Surely it was indicative of the spiritual battles being fought over the boy—and the city. Viv prayed against the demonic spiritual powers that rule over the city. Another prayed against the spirit of death that he sensed over the city. Then Adelle mentioned a dream she had in which she was aware of the blood of the sacrifice victims crying out to God. The group remembered that thousands of people were sacrificed in the Aztec temples as offerings to their gods in the very spot they were standing.

Then Betty recalled an experience she had a few nights earlier:

> Jed had been sleeping restlessly, perhaps because of the mosquitoes, and began having nightmares. He crawled in bed with us, but continued having bad dreams every 20 minutes or so. I was very tired and didn't fully awaken, nor did he. At the same time, I was having a real heaviness of spirit. I felt that I was being told that Jed would die in order that Mexicans could come to the Lord. I gave Jed up to the Lord, reminding Him and myself that we had dedicated him to the Lord even before he was born, and that we recognized that he was only on loan for us to train and raise. But each time Jed stirred, I still sensed a heaviness in myself, a feeling of impending death. Finally I awakened enough to pray with Jed to ask the Lord to take away the nightmares and to give him more appropriate dreams. Jed then went to sleep more peacefully and I began to realize that my heaviness was also not of the Lord. I prayed asking the Lord to take away that heaviness and give me His peace, as Christ had already died to save the people of Mexico. Now, as we were praying against the spirit of death and human sacrifice, I sensed that it was *that* spirit which had been troubling me the other night (1984).

With this as background they began to spend more time in specific prayer to battle against these spiritual powers, to bind them, and to loose the power of the Holy Spirit at work in the city.

On Listening to Christ

Ministering in Mexico had a profound impact on all the participants including Tom. Tom had expected and planned for the week to be a contemplative time for all participants. Their daily times of praise, worship, singing and prayer had indeed drawn them into the heart of God. They had come to learn all they could about the poor and exploited of the city, to live with the poor and to intercede for them. And, through the process, to gain intimacy with Christ. They certainly accomplished those goals.

But Tom and the others learned other lessons about intimacy with Christ. He wrote:

> Experiencing intimacy with Christ came in unexpected ways. Maybe what surprised me most was the joy and blessing that our presence brought to those we ministered to. The lay pastor, Leoncio, with the little flock he shepherds, were deeply touched by our presence. Our staying with them was an affirmation of their ministry and an indication of God's faithful love for them. We didn't do anything particularly, except take the initiative to come and be with them. And God used that to bless them and also to touch us. I'd always thought intimacy with Christ came from studying the Word and praying and meditating and contemplating. Is intimacy, rather, also gained by being an instrument in God's hands that He uses to touch another? In that touching of another, Jesus meets us and draws us into His own heart.
>
> An incarnational life and ministry among poor people produces days that are filled with opportunity for ministering and reaching out in Jesus' name. And the people are so receptive. Our presence was always welcomed enthusiastically. Seldom, if ever, have these poor people experienced middle class people choosing to leave behind their privileges and coming to live with them. Our fears of rejection were all unfounded. Of course they didn't have room, but they made room for us. We knew their food only comes a day at a time, yet they treated us to special meals—even feasts and banquets. Seldom have we been loved so quickly and so deeply by new acquaintances. We discovered that one way to experience intimacy with Christ is through deep sharing within the body and we discovered the opportunities for his kind of sharing can be almost a way of life among the very poor (1984b).

A Dream

Tom's concern for the poor even manifested itself in a dream which he wrote about after returning from Mexico:

> We were in another country with a number of missionaries. We were walking and we arrived at a destination ahead of others.

About 20 homeless and poor, poor people met us and asked for just a small corner of land where they could have some cardboard and other supplies and put up shacks to live in. The land was not ours and therefore not our privilege to give, so we could offer no encouragement. Soon others arrived who might have given permission, but the request was denied. I thought, "If only Viv were here, he would at least go and stay with the people, living with them until their situation was resolved somewhere." Were there not any of the missionaries who would be willing to do that with these people? The people were in such desperate need and their hearts and eyes cried out for help. If only someone would go with them! Surely their lives could easily be directed to joy and fullness in Jesus. But no one would go. How many similar people around the world would be ready to be led to the Savior if only someone would go and live with the people and share their plight with them.

Lord, send forth incarnational laborers into these harvest fields of the world (1984c).

Tom and Viv Grigg wrote about the emerging strategy of Servants Among the Poor:

Servants Among the Poor challenges its members to walk in the footsteps of the Master (and of His disciples) by following His instructions and example in ministry. We seek to know our Lord more intimately through a life of obedience and devotion, and through following the model of the incarnation for our service and ministry to the poor of the world's slums and squatter settlements. Our strategy is to establish multiplying movements of disciples who are congregated into indigenous fellowships and churches, and ministering according to the gifting and empowering of the Holy Spirit.

We recognize that this kind of ministry requires a special grace and gifting from God. But we are also seeing many who want to live their lives to account for God, who are willing to pay the required price of discipleship. To many of these, our Lord has granted the gift of voluntary poverty. With proper training and Biblical perspective, these obedient and gifted ones can minister effectively among the poor (Brewster and Grigg 1985).

A Sense of Urgency

There was a sense of urgency in Tom's life, especially those last two years. The Kingdom of God became a very important concept to Tom because it tied together a lot of the things that he was trying to say. Moreover, Tom truly believed that the Lord's second coming was soon.

Clearly, too, there was a sense of personal urgency because of his own frailty. Tom always knew there was a good possibility that he would die young because of the complications of quadriplegia. But after his sickness in Australia and New Zealand, he had a heightened sense that he might have only a short time left.

Realizing that for all of us, the time is short, Tom began reciting the following poem in almost all of his classes:

The Judgment Seat of Christ

When I come to the judgment seat of Christ, and He shows me his plan for me.
His plan for my life as it might have been, had he had His way
And I see how I blocked Him here and checked Him there and would not yield my will
Will there be grief in my Savior's eyes, grief though He loves me still?
He would have me rich but I stand there poor, stripped of all but His grace,
While memory runs like a hunted thing, down paths I cannot retrace.
Then my heart will well nigh break with tears I cannot shed.
I'll cover my face with my empty hands and bow my uncrowned head.
Lord, of the years that are left to me, I yield them to your hand.
Take me, break me, mold me into the pattern Thou hast planned
(Nicholson).

15
THE LAST LAP

The years that Tom and you [Betty Sue] traveled and made your services available worldwide will continue to be used for God's glory in the years ahead. I doubt that there exists a segment of the western missions community that has not been helped by Tom. Few Christians could hope to attain that breadth of service (Kyle 1986).

After the week in Mexico City, Tom and Betty went on to San Jose, Costa Rica for a seminar with teachers and with students at the Instituto de Lengua Espanola (ILE). Then, for the rest of the year they ministered at various places in the US. They spent Christmas 1984, in Greensboro, North Carolina with Betty Sue's folks, and then did a language learning seminar at the Urbana conference in Champaign, Illinois just before the new year.

Tom liked to get out of the US for the winters. He really disliked the snow and cold weather, and preferred to be available for ministry outside of the US during the colder months. He tried to schedule classes during the warmer months in Pasadena, and then be ready to move south at any hint of cold weather. Winter of 1984–85 was no exception: They had arranged yet another extended trip to Africa, Australia and New Zealand for that winter and flew directly from the Urbana conference to Europe, and from there on to Kenya on January 3, 1985.

In the Kenyan coastal city of Mombasa, they conducted a language learning course for African Inland Mission (AIM). Most of the thirty-seven participants were from AIM but there was also a sprinkling from other missions.

Language Learning
for Experienced Missionaries

There they met with the language committee of Africa Inland Mission. Some of the older, conservative missionaries were not convinced of the necessity of language learning for new missionaries. Many were especially unconvinced of the necessity or wisdom of an "incarnational" approach to ministry—identifying with the people at or near their own lifestyle level. To help them examine their position on language and culture learning, Tom asked them the same questions he often asked of mission leaders. "What was the vision of the founder of your mission and of your early missionaries? How would they fit in your mission now? How happy would they be with what is happening in your mission now?" For some missionaries, an honest answer would provoke concern at the present focus, the loss of commitment to "being the Good News" in the language and life-styles of the people.

That was Tom's concern as well for the traditional mission boards. He knew the history of many missions, and was disturbed at the loss of vision, and the amount of energy expended by some of the missionaries in some missions today in "looking after their own needs, making themselves indispensable, and building their own empires" (E. Brewster 1993). For Tom, one evidence of that tendency was the concentration of missionaries in the "comfortable" urban centers, like Nairobi, Quito, and Manila. Another indicator was the lack of attention to learning the local languages, especially in areas where missionaries can get by in English.

This was the first time Tom and Betty had ever had such a large percentage of experienced missionaries as participants— some had as many as forty years missionary experience, and the average was ten-plus years. Only five had been there less than one year. The first few days Tom felt that some were there to just to look but not to develop skills or participate in fieldwork. Overall, though, they were thankful that almost all became real learners and involved with people in the community. They worked in the Gujurati, Luo, Swahili, Arabic, Somali, Kikamba, Luhya, and Giriama communities.

An Incarnational Example

Tom and Betty were privileged to have three teaching assistants at the AIM conference: Margaret Dawn with AIM, Gail Seebeck, and Linda Severns. Gail and her husband and Linda and her husband took the language learning course a year earlier at Fuller. Linda and her husband had been living in Maasai huts with the people and she and the Maasai ladies built their own house. Their experience was a powerful example to those who felt that living with the people was impractical and unrealistic. In a letter after his visit to Mombasa Tom remarked:

> It was very special having Linda particularly as a TA because when we talked about incarnational living or following a model of incarnational living there was no room for anybody to say, "yeah but that can't be done" or "that's too idealistic." Their monthly expenses for rent are about 150 shillings, (just under $10). . . . They have no vehicle, their transportation expenses are about 200 shillings per person per month, or less that $20 per person. Their food expenses are more than that, but still modest and they are completely happy with that, learning a lot and having a tremendous ministry at the same time (T. Brewster 1985a).

On the final day they had quite a few helpers attend the "text" session—various Digo people they had met, some Kikamba, and an Arab girl helper. The learners said their texts well and it was obvious they had really worked hard and spent time in community. Betty wrote that Tom was glad to see that you *can* teach old dogs new tricks, "because most of these weren't puppies." Many of them even surprised themselves that they had been able to learn. One lady was coming home from field work at the end of the first week when it suddenly dawned on her "Hey, even I can learn!"

A Digo Feast . . .

While with the language learners in Mombasa, they also took the time to participate in a goat feast with some of the Muslim language helpers from the Digo tribe. Art Davis, Keith and Florena Gustafson, and other learners were working within the Digo community for their fieldwork in the Mombasa course. The Digo people became curious about this teacher-*bwana* who used a wheelchair and gave people an assignment to spend time with the Digo people. They were so intrigued they planned a feast for the learners and some community elders. They killed a goat, cooked plantain in coconut milk, and prepared fresh pineapple slices.

When the group arrived they had put out large woven straw mats on the ground in the yard inside their little compound. The women and smaller children sat on two mats on one side and the men and older boys on mats on the other side. Betty and Jed sat on a mat with the women and tried out the little bit of Digo they had learned.

> After all were seated, a Digo woman came around with a wash basin and pitcher of water so they could rinse our hands in preparation for the meal. Then they brought around two bowls of meat cooked in a tasty sauce and two bowls of plantain. They ate with their fingers out of the common bowls—all done politely and with evident manners. Eat with right hand only, and use just the tips of the fingers, don't lick fingers, make sure all get a fair share. (Tom got his own bowl and spoon as he could not sit down on the mat to reach the bowl, and also to honor him as the *Mzee*—the Swahili term for respect for an "honored old man") (E. Brewster 1993).

At the end of the meal, a Digo woman came round again with the basin and pitcher of water and also with soap, to get the grease and food off the hands. They sat around under the stars with a bit of light from the flame in the kitchen nearby. Tom shared a little, through an interpreter, about his accident, about language learning, and about his belief in God. An old mama—the chief cook— came and blessed him. At the end, Tom prayed for them. Then one of them, a Muslim, prayed also, showing the group how to raise their hands and say "amen" when he said a phrase various times in prayer.

Then quite a number of the men walked the group back to their place under a mile away. It is the common, gracious way of the Digo to walk the visitor at least half the way home after he has visited you. The hearts of the group were warmed by the Digo hospitality and their graciousness. They were not believers, but Tom was impressed with their "God-consciousness." It was the sort of "bridge" he always looked for into the heart of those who needed Christ.

. . . and an Indian Wedding . . .

January 19, they returned from Mombasa to Nairobi and again had the opportunity to demonstrate the love of Christ through their openness and love to non-Christians. With the Hensleys, who had participated with them in the Mombasa workshop, they had the privilege of attending an Indian Hindu wedding.

There were about 500 guests—mostly Indians. The ladies dressed in bright jewel-tone saris, many with gold or silver embroidery. There were also some Muslims, Africans, and Europeans. The bridal couple and priest/official were under a canopy which was brightly decorated with ribbons, crepe paper, balloons and fruit. An official sat at the front edge of the canopy facing bride and groom. Between the couple and the official was a brazier with fire. At various points the bride and groom walked around the fire—sometimes the groom walked first, sometimes bride first. At other times the bride and groom and relatives threw handfuls of rice into the fire. The bride was in a beautiful red sari with gold threads, and also wore much gold jewelry. Relatives sat behind and around the canopy on chairs and mats.

Tom and Betty were surprised to note that this particular sect of Hindus did not have visible idols. The only representation in the hall was a picture of their founder. Archie said that when other sects of Hindus used the hall, they would bring in many idols and ring the whole front of the hall with them.

Near the end of the ceremony the official tied the end of the bride's sari to part of the groom's clothing. Then the bride bowed before her new parents-in-law to receive their blessing. All the relatives threw flower petals on the new couple. The bride and groom then embraced the relatives.

After the wedding a table was set up near the front for the bridal party to sit at for the feast. The guests then filed by tables to enjoy a rice dish, a spicy bean curry, a pea-lentil curry, a vegetarian patty in yogurt, and some delicious flat round bread (nan).

It was good to see the warm relationships that Archie had developed among the Asians. Tom and Betty met the father of the groom who greeted Archie warmly as a good friend. It was encouraging to see Archie and a few other believers participating so caringly with these Hindus in ways that showed the love of Christ without compromising their own Christian faith. Again there was the hint of an openness and a missionary with a "bonding" approach which Tom was sure could create a bridge.

. . . and a Kikuyu Welcome

Once again while in Nairobi, they stayed with their YWAM friends, and had morning seminars for their new learners there. They were also able to visit Mathare Valley, one of Nairobi's worst slums and one of the worst urban slums in the world, and think again of incarnational ways to minister Christ's love to the poorest of the poor. Tom wrote that their purpose was "just to talk with them about how they would feel about people coming, people who would not come with a big budget, a big agenda, . . . just come to live right with the people to be available to pray with the people and to experience life from the people's perspective" (T. Brewster 1985a).

They visited a place where the people are employed in a cooperative—carding and spinning wool, and using large efficient looms to make cotton or wool cloth. They then visited a little church building and met with the pastor, an elder, and an assistant to the chief. Tom asked them questions about the hopes of people in the Valley. Their response echoed the response of the poorest all over the world: "survival, work, and enough money to not worry where the next meal comes from."

Tom questioned them further: " What would you think if there were missionaries willing to live in the Valley at the same income level as local people?" At first they were skeptical that such people would exist—but then were enthusiastic about the prospects.

"You mean white people would live that way?"

"Yeah, I think they would."

"Well if they would, wow, that would be exciting! The people would be ready for them."

They were not sure if any families would have room to take in a couple but perhaps they could accommodate a single person. "But," they decided, "a couple could get a room in one of the longer row houses where rooms are rented individually." They felt that such a ministry could "give opportunity to see what God can do." They felt $200 a month would be more than adequate for living expenses.

Another Christian lady welcomed them into her house. A tarpaper and frame structure, but cloth curtains in the window and hand-made crocheted doilies on the table, a verse poster on the wall, were indications of an appreciation of beauty. She sent one of her children off to get them a drink from the corner shop. Her family was clean and well-behaved and very respectful. She had an evident love for the Lord, not the stereotype many would have of a slum family and dwelling. The home seemed to radiate the joy and peace of Christ, and was an encouraging sign of what the Spirit of God could accomplish in the midst of that bleak setting if there were laborers willing to live and share the good news.

In each place they visited, Tom relished learning about the customs and cultures of the people, and the privilege of being able to share with them. And he was constantly watching for the "bridges" or "redemptive analogies" which might help to open their heart's door to the message of Christ.

Keeping Commitments

From Nairobi, they traveled once again to South Africa where they visited with Nico Smith, and spent a couple nights with the Morobi family in the Black township of Mamelodi. Unfortunately, Tom got sick so they had to cut the visit short. After a few days of rest Tom was again able to continue. They conducted a two week seminar at Emerentia Geldenhuis, Warmbath, South Africa, once again hosted by their friend Johann Luow.

Sadly, as elsewhere, some of the American missionaries reacted angrily to portions of this seminar because they felt that Tom had gone beyond strictly language learning in talking of bonding and simple life-style and developing deep relationships with Africans, and had moved to meddling. Later the Afrikaner missionaries apologized for the others and expressed their appreciation for his dealing with those sensitive but, in that context, crucial topics.

On February 15, they made the trip from Africa to Australia, this time via Mauritius and Perth. They went to Melbourne where they conducted a one week workshop for SIL. They followed this with a special trip to Hobart, Tasmania. Betty tells about the trip:

> We flew on the "Douglas Mawson" DC-9. Normally we don't notice the name, but this time we did. Asked stewardess who he was, she asked captain who informed us that he was an Antarctic Explorer. That day we were driving around outside of Hobart and saw a museum of Australia's Antarctic explorations and sure enough there were photos and descriptions of Mawson and his explorations (1991:38, 39).

There they also visited the Shot Tower built in 1870 to make shot. They poured the hot molten lead through a sieve at the top of the sixty-one meter tower—large holes for large shot, small holes for smaller shot. It free fell and landed in a large tub of water at the bottom. By the time it hit the water it had formed perfect spheres from the free fall and had cooled and hardened sufficiently so that its impact with the water did not flatten it. Just the sort of technology that held a fascination for Tom.

From Hobart they flew to Christchurch, New Zealand where they spent the month of March. They had a seminar at Living Springs Conference Center, but spent part of the month enjoying the sights and closely watching Tom's frail health. For once again, just as had been the case the previous year in New Zealand, Tom experienced serious kidney and ureter problems. At times they shut down altogether. Once again, Betty stayed up many nights massaging his kidneys, "irrigating" his catheter, and keeping him warm in his feverish chills. And once again they weathered the health storm, kept most of their commitments and enjoyed the southern summer before making their way back to the US.

They wrapped up their visit to Asia in late March 1985, and resumed their teaching schedule at Fuller. Again, Tom's focus was on the poor, and how to reach them. Tom wrote to me in May:

> This quarter I'm teaching both language learning and incarnation in mission among the world's urban poor. People are going to Tijuana and staying with families who live on the rubbish dumps

and in the squatter settlements on the ravines outside of town. We are excited about the way people are being challenged for ministry in the course. We expect to see a new mission formed in the next few months to sponsor people to live as poor among the poor. There will be over a billion squatters in cities of the world by the year 2000. James 2:5—"Has not God chosen those who are poor in the eyes of the world to be rich in faith and to inherit the Kingdom He has promised to those who love Him?" (T. Brewster 1985b).

In July, Tom led a second Servants exposure trip to Mexico to follow up on the time of intercession and learning and living with the poor squatter families. Mona and her husband Jerry, as well as some other intercessors accompanied them in order to know better how to pray. Tom was encouraged by what he saw as a growing understanding and acceptance of the incarnational model for mission. He wrote to me in August:

> We have long been convinced that the life and incarnation of Jesus was intended to provide a model for mission activity. Now we see a groundswell of people who are questioning the American cultural norms of materialism and comfort and who want their lives to count for God. Furthermore, people are coming to us who have counted the cost and are willing to pay the price to make sure their lives *do* count. We feel God is privileging us with the opportunity of being a part of something quite special (T. Brewster 1985e).

Tom was more and more aware, however, that his role in what God was allowing them to be a part of might not be long term, for he knew his health was fragile. Tom was forty-five years old. He reflected much of the fact that his father had died at the age of forty-four. Tom suspected that he also would die young, if not due to complications of his quadriplegia, then because it was in his genes. He wrote to me in a round-robin letter that same August. As always, he was noting little personal anniversaries and thinking about others:

> July and August are big celebration months around our house. On July 24 I had been paralyzed for 27 years. Three days ago, August 1, marked 33 years since I trusted Christ at about 9:00 o'clock P.M. at Covenant Heights Bible Camp near Estes Park, CO. (In those

days in our circles if one couldn't say when and where he was saved then he no doubt wasn't!) On August 20 I wonder if I will get a computer chess program like Dan has to celebrate my 46th birthday (I have dropped a hint or two. If I get any extras I'll see if I can't find some way to give them to the poor! (1985f).

In the Summer and Fall of 1985, Tom and Betty worked on editing *Community is My Language Classroom!* This book is a marvelous collection of stories from successful language learners around the world who learned in the context of cross-cultural relationships. The book had two purposes. The first was to replace the typical pessimism that language learners face with optimism by highlighting firsthand accounts of people who proved that it could be done. The second purpose was to accent "the ministry payoff that comes as a fringe benefit for those who learn the new language through these relationships in their new community" (T. and E. Brewster 1986:2).

Tom and Betty wanted to show that, as one learner put it, she could then view the people among whom she learned the language as friends to share their hearts with, rather than simply targets for evangelism. The stories provide ample and exciting proof that languages can be learned directly from the people, and that missionaries can bond with the people to whom they minister by adapting to living at their own level. Most importantly, they demonstrate the power of an incarnational lifestyle in communicating successfully the claims and teachings of Christ. (The book came out in January 1986, one month after Tom's death. That was painful for Betty, to have worked so hard on it together, and not be able to share the gratification.)

GRASP

Tom began to rethink and restate his overall approach to ministry, setting it in the context of the work he and Betty had done up to that point. His intended to incorporate the thinking into a new book to be called *GRASP*. *GRASP* was an acrostic representing the progression of issues on which the Lord had led them to focus in the course of their ministry. Tom saw that progression as:

God, His Kingdom
Relationships, and "incarnational" ministry in the new community
Approach, becoming a learner
Strategy, the learning cycle
Procedures, techniques for learning

Tom explained that the emphases of their ministry had actually progressed from the bottom up of these five levels. When they were training missionaries to be language learners at the Spanish Language School in Guadalajara, language learning *Procedures* and techniques were for the most part in focus. The eleven years that they taught at the Toronto Institute of Linguistics each summer, beginning in 1968, had caused them to refine their procedures and look into the areas of language learning techniques and phonetics.

Donald Larson and other colleagues there were key players in their development of the "G.L.U.E." learning cycle," which characterized the *Strategy* stage of their ministries, and with the publication of *LAMP,* was their focus during the mid and late seventies.

The *Approach* was the next level to come into focus. In this, they had turned their attention to the learner himself. They began to develop new attitudes and learning approaches by raising the question, "How can the individual best fulfill his/her potential?

Many people felt that while *LAMP* was packed full of great ideas, it would be better if they could use it under supervision. Tom and Betty saw that the *student* attitude of the typical teacher-centered approach often created a dependency on the teacher and sometimes became counter-productive. Tom wanted to develop *learners* who were prepared to develop their own language learning programs and study where there were no language schools. This, they felt, was essential, especially for missionaries who would be equipped to go into "unreached people" areas where there are no language schools.

In *Bonding and the Missionary Task,* they began to challenge people to lay aside that self-sufficiency and independence and develop deep relationships with local people. They encouraged newcomers to enter their country of service without any structured help being provided by expatriates. They found that when learners did get out into the community and use the local people as their language helpers, many reported that this resulted in a far greater dependency on God as well as the privilege of seeing His faithfulness in significant ways.

Relationships, the next level, was something that Tom and Betty had always emphasized. They had always stressed the importance of building, with speakers of the target languages, and learning from the friends and friendships that were built among the native speakers. Much of their ministry had been to help people learn how to build those relationships in cross-cultural environments. Key to the deepest level of relationships, Tom said, was an incarnational ministry approach which required that people be able to live among the people to whom they ministered.

The last level of emphasis, though in reality fundamental to all, was the emphasis on *God and His Kingdom.* Tom felt that the missionary, as a representative of Christ, was entering Satan's turf. He believed that Satan and his powers of darkness had usurped God's rightful place in the world. It was not an empty offer when Satan tempted Jesus by offering Him the nations of the world. Tom wrote:

> We have looked at the nature of the cosmic battle in which the powers of darkness have confronted the Kingdom of God and we're recognizing that the missionary is by definition moving into Satan's turf. The nations of the world are into Satan's hand. (It was not an empty offer when Satan tempted Jesus by offering to give the nations to Him—it was within his power to do so). But God is in the business of winning them back from the usurper. And the Abrahamic Covenant promise is that all the nations would be blessed, and the Great Commission is to go into all the nations of the world and make disciples. The fulfillment of the covenant and the commission is the work of God and is being accomplished in His own way (T. and E. Brewster n.d.).

Incorporating Servants among the Poor

While Tom and Betty were conceptualizing *GRASP*, with its ultimate emphasis on God and His Kingdom, in the Fall of 1985, they also worked, somewhat reluctantly, on the incorporation of

Servants Among the Poor. Viv and others had continued to press to have it incorporated and for Tom to be the director. For various reasons, however, the incorporation process had been held up for over a year. Tom felt this might have been a confirmation that he was not supposed to be the director. For him, the value of Servants Among the Poor was in the process, not in the results—the exploring of what was possible in terms of identification, incarnation, and actual living among the poor.

Moreover Betty still was not sure Tom was the person for the job. She felt that his strength was in encouraging people and strengthening people but not necessarily leadership over people. She was not sure that Tom had what it took for the long-term, long haul leadership of people.

Perhaps most importantly, Betty was not sure that Servants *ought* to become an independent mission. They were drawing from so many mission boards in their work and stimulating many people from different mission boards, she was bothered by the possibility that in starting a new mission board, they might cut themselves off from all the others. She feared that it would jeopardize what was still their broader ministry. Tom was convinced that he was not to be the long-term administrator. He did not know how prophetic that was, as he continued to battle with urinary tract malfunctions. These and the related problems were discouraging, debilitating and, more and more, life-threatening.

In September they thought it might be good to rest and relax with their friends Buzz and Mica who had now moved to Tucson.

Buzz was in poor health himself but still worked on projects whenever he could. On an earlier visit, he had helped Tom cast a bronze Bible, and now, enjoying the rest and the warmth of friendship with Buzz, Tom spent several days polishing it between chess games. It was quite rough when they started, so they used a grinding wheel to get the worst off, and then a lot of sandpapering by hand to finally get a nearly mirror smooth surface. Buzz entertained Jed by giving him a slingshot, encouraging him to try to hit some of the wild rabbits that hopped by. (The rabbits were perfectly safe!)

They drove through northern Mexico on their way back from Tucson, through a new subdivision in Mexicali that had recently been built for low income families. They were nice little houses, very unpretentious. Just the kind of house they felt they would like to rent while they continued to rest and guard Tom's fragile health. They made arrangements to rent one, thinking they could stay there while working on *GRASP*.

Tom and Betty thought of making the little house in Mexicali their headquarters and only live at Fuller when they were actually teaching courses there. But they never stayed there at all, because shortly after they returned to Pasadena, Tom began feeling much worse and was not up to traveling even that far.

The problems with the actual incorporation of Servants had, however, continued. The papers came back needing more signatures, not once but three times.

In October they went to Palm Desert to seek God's direction. They did not know where they were going to stay, so they asked the Lord for a place. In fact, they decided to make the time a prayer challenge and each of them asked for something specific for that time. Jed asked the Lord for a swimming pool, and Tom asked the Lord for a sunny place where he could sit outdoors and get lots of sun. Betty was hungry for some flowers and so asked the Lord for beauty.

They found a place with not one swimming pool but several swimming pools: hot pools and cool pools, big pools and little pools. The room and grounds were exploding with beautiful flowers, and it was sunny enough for even Tom. Answers to their prayers for physical things gave them more faith for the Servants ministry. When they returned from that weekend Tom told Viv that he was willing to work toward setting up the Servants mission board, and Tom would direct the mission until someone else could be recruited to take it over. Finally, in November of 1985, Servants Among the Poor was officially incorporated .

That Thanksgiving Tom was feeling very poorly again. They had a young Iranian woman living with them for a short time who was a new believer and needing a place to stay. Tom had Bible studies with her, answered questions, and helped her in her early growth—from his bed.

Tom ate his Thanksgiving dinner in bed even though they had guests. They kept a "Thanksgiving log" that year—before each meal each person had to state one thing they were thankful for. That morning Tom was thankful he was still alive to celebrate Thanksgiving.

16
"OPERATION HOMEGOING"

For me personally, adjusting to life with Tom was the fun part. Adjusting to life without him has been by far the more difficult and painful experience (E. Brewster c1987:7).

Tom was a man of vision, one not afraid of going against the trends in mission or education. Most recently his search produced a ministry to the poorest of the poor in the large cities of the two-thirds world. He has touched hundreds, maybe thousands of lives with the challenge to follow the model Christ set for us in an incarnational way. In a sense the torch has now been passed to those of us who most richly benefited from Tom's search (Glasser 1985).

The Spirit Is Willing But the Flesh Is Weak

Over the years Tom got to know his own body very well—better than most doctors. Even though technically he did not have feeling below his shoulders, Tom could sense what was going on in his body, probably much more accurately than most people. He attributed his knowledge about and jealousy for his own body to the influence of John Young, his main doctor at the Craig Rehabilitation Center. He planted the idea that Tom should know how to care for himself, how to prevent problems, and how to deal with them when they came up. He encouraged Tom to understand his own body, to understand his own feelings, and to evaluate the feelings to know whether they were appropriate or inappropriate.

Young was also one of the people who stimulated Tom to a real "can do" attitude. He felt that even handicapped people were limited only by their attitude, creativity, and their dreams. It was Young who planted the idea and inspiration for Tom that "it is far better to be paralyzed from the neck down than from the neck up."

Tom learned to sense what was going on in his own body in remarkable ways. He was fairly accurate in his self-diagnosis, even when the doctors did not believe him. He could, for example, feel that something was going on in his kidneys, even though he had no feeling of pain there. At first when he would give Betty Sue internal status reports, she thought he was imagining things. But it was confirmed enough times by outside evidence that Betty Sue began to realize that he really did know what was going on.

Tom's excellent attitude notwithstanding, he could not reverse the downward trend of his health problems in the last three years of his life. But while he could not reverse the trend, he still wanted to be in control of his own body. Naturally, given his condition, he needed the care and advice of doctors more than most people. But, except for Young, doctors were always a decidedly mixed blessing for Tom. Unfortunately, Tom had extraordinarily bad luck with some doctors. Once when he went to Colorado for a week-long checkup, a doctor began to be concerned that some little polyps in Tom's bladder might be pre-cancerous, and so had them taken out.

Later on, in a follow up checkup, a doctor who was not at all sensitive to the particular problems of a quadriplegic bladder, did not recognize what he saw under examination and told Tom that he was covered with cancer cells. Tom tried to tell the doctor that what he was seeing was typical of a quadriplegic bladder which atrophies and simply looks different. Nevertheless, the doctor cauterized most of the inside of his bladder. Tom felt that from then on, his bladder never stretched like it should have, and that this was the beginning of more serious problems.

It incensed Tom when doctors would not listen to him. He would describe some conditions and suggest what was going on, and the doctors would say, in effect, "We've been in medicine a lot longer than you have, and we know what we're doing."

In Tom's biased view, almost everything doctors and nurses did seemed to be done for their own convenience rather than for the overall welfare of the patient. Tom's attitude was that, "by and large doctors are not health oriented—they are disease oriented."

The unfortunate effect of Tom's battle was a strong distrust of doctors, shared at least in part by Betty Sue, for she had her own share of bad experiences. It may be that the deterioration of Tom's kidneys, ureters, and bladder could not have been arrested, and that there simply was nothing that could have been done with all the problems that he had. On the other hand, the right doctors might have been able to treat him properly and extend his life somewhat.

Whatever the causes, as noted earlier, Tom had serious bouts with sickness, especially in the winter of 1983–84 and in 1985. At times, his urine was almost completely blocked. His skin began to take over the functions of his urinary system, and he perspired profusely. Betty would wrap him in towels and change them several times throughout the day. Yet he persevered, continuing to conduct workshops if he could be upright at all, some of them in Africa and in very remote areas of Indonesia. His endurance astounded all who knew what was going on. One missionary there wrote of Tom's perseverance in carrying on even though very sick while teaching at Boyolali in central Java:

> The incarnational ministry strategy was then and continues to be one of the greatest challenges of my life. I feel that this is a critical issue in missions today—an often neglected one, and I might also say an unpopular one. Their emphasis in this needs special note as they not only taught it but modeled it. The day Tom and Betty Sue taught the one day seminar at Boyolali, Tom had a fever (fairly high) yet continued to give himself. He would have had every reason to cancel and rest, but he didn't. The incredible perseverance, courage, and mental and spiritual strength that took him to travel around the world ministering is almost without equal. Having lived and traveled in Asia for 15 years, being usually in good health yet knowing the physical and mental drain it takes, it is hard to believe that anyone in his condition could do it year in and year out (Truax 1986).

Get Out Here in a Hurry!

In November of 1985, I was winding up my time as Development Specialist for Compassion International in Ecuador. I and my family began to make plans to visit with Tom for a while when I passed through the States en route back to Africa. Just before leaving Ecuador I received a letter from him dated November 17th.

Our lives have been complicated by our health, Jed has had bad earaches for a few days and I have had lots of complications with my deteriorated urinary system. Between the two of us Betty Sue hasn't gotten much sleep either. My bladder, kidneys and the urethra tubes that run from the kidneys to the bladder are all doing their intended purposes in very marginal ways. I am in the process of getting tests done these days. So far it looks like that they have confirmed that I don't have any stones. I think I knew that! Options are to get things running satisfactorily, or else to surgically bypass or to surgically sever nerves to bladder. Both these procedures are irreversible with little expectation for much success. Added kidney degeneration could lead to dialysis (1985g).

He knew it was serious then, but he was ever mindful of the people that were praying for him. Clearly, kidney dialysis was a very unattractive option for someone used to being as active as Tom. His letter continued with remarkable detachment, yet optimism, "It has been special to see the Lord raise up the community in my behalf. People are praying and we know that God is able. It is also possible that it might not turn out to be as serious as the present concerns suggest."

Tom went on to talk about their plans:

Because of the health complications we have a degree of ambiguity in our schedule for the next few months. We have greatly lessened our writing commitments, and if we don't have to spend much time in hospitalization routine, it is our desire to go to Mexico for a few months. We might get down towards the south where it would be warmer (1985g).

This was the first that I had heard about his most recent sickness, and the tone of the letter alerted me to something more serious than I had been aware of before. I continued my plans for my visit in the States, and wrote to him confirming that I would try to pass through California after my meetings in Colorado.

By the time I had gotten to Colorado, Tom realized that his hopes of spending more leisurely days in Mexico were not to be realized. His condition continued to deteriorate and the doctor advanced the surgery up to emergency status. As I arrived in Colorado Springs on December 7, I learned that surgery had been scheduled for the following Thursday, the 12th.

I called Tom to ask about the situation and he expressed an unusual confidence in the doctor who was to be his surgeon. For nearly the first time in my life I heard Tom talk positively about his doctor, Dr. Raz, who had proposed a surgical procedure that had made sense to Tom. They intended to reconstruct the top part of his bladder which had become fibrous and stiffened. They would do this with a piece of his colon. This was a procedure that Dr. Raz had already performed many times and he communicated his confidence in it to Tom. I could tell on the telephone that Tom was feeling very poorly, and it was clear that he knew that he had no choice. But I could also tell that he had God's peace about the surgery, the procedure, and the doctor who was going to do them.

On Wednesday, December 11, Tom got ready to go to the hospital. Before leaving his apartment he wheeled over to the table to check the new lay-out on a brochure they were preparing to advertise some of the Lingua House language-learning materials they were making available. As they went out the door he rolled over to admire the Bird of Paradise blossoms that graced his apartment garden, and made a special trip around to see if there was yet any snow on the mountains. Pepper Grimes, a long time close friend, hugged him and said "I'll see you soon, 'old man,'" reminding him that he had been calling himself an old man throughout the recent difficult weeks (Grimes: 1986).

That same day, I called my sister Martha and discussed whether one of us should go to California to be with Tom. Martha's fear was that Tom's heart would not be able to take the surgery. "After so many bouts of extremely high pressure," she worried, "his heart might not be able to take the stresses." I got a disturbing call from Paul Pierson of Fuller Seminary. With great concern in his voice he told me that he thought that I should get out to see Tom before he went into surgery. Obviously, he thought the situation was very serious.

"Are you suggesting that if I don't get out to see Tom before the surgery, I may never get to see him alive again?" I asked.

"Dan," said Pierson, "I believe that is what I'm saying."

After I hung up the phone I decided to call Dr. Raz who was going to perform the surgery. Dr. Raz was still full of confidence. He said that he had performed this surgery many times and he did not expect any unusual complications in Tom's case.

"Should I come out to see him before the surgery? " I asked, "or should I wait and come after as I had planned"

"Why don't you wait," he said. "He'll be coming out of it by the weekend and you should be able to have a good visit."

I was torn then as to what to do. The surgery was scheduled for 2 p.m. the following day. My week was full of meetings with people whose schedules I did not want to alter. Meanwhile outside the weather was deteriorating. Snow was falling and the roads were getting icy. A secretary told me that there were no flights out of Colorado Springs, but I would be able to get one out of Denver at about 9 p.m.

I made the decision to leave the meetings and drive the seventy treacherous miles to Denver in order to catch this flight. Just before midnight the vast array of sparkling lights that make up the greater LA area came into view. I rented a car and headed towards UCLA. I found a motel room on busy Wilshire Boulevard and checked in for a short night of rest.

Early the next morning I watched the news. A tragedy was unfolding in Newfoundland where a plane bringing back soldiers from somewhere had crashed and claimed some 250 US soldiers' lives. I pulled on a jacket and had a bite to eat before going over to the hospital, and found my way directly into his room. At 8:30 in the morning I walked into his room and said, "Hi, Tom." He was very surprised to see me but obviously relieved.

I had a wonderful time with Tom and Betty Sue that morning. Surprisingly, given his distaste for doctors and hospitals, Tom was very pleased with the care that this particular hospital staff was giving him. They had made arrangements for Betty Sue to stay in the room with him and allowed her to care for him in whatever way was necessary. The staff, at least in Tom's mind, were far more sensitive than other medical professionals that he had been around. He talked in glowing terms about their professionalism and their genuine concern for his needs.

One of the necessary things that morning was to make sure that his bowel was completely cleaned out so that they could use a portion of the bowel for the bladder reconstruction. A nurse came in for the second or third time to do an enema and Tom in his usual way joked to her about the necessity of "fooling around" with him back there. She was a delightful Christian, whose sense of humor did much to ease the tension of the morning.

This Is It!

For a good part of the morning Tom talked about the directions their ministry was going, the blessing of all the people praying for him, and the miracles they were seeing in people's lives. He talked at length about the book that he had reread recently on the missionary, Toyohiko Kagawa of Japan. The nurses told us that surgery would be about 2 o'clock and so we had a relaxed and enjoyable morning talking together.

We were surprised then when around 1 o'clock a nurse came in and said, "Let's go." With a surprised look Tom said, "Let's go where?"

"This is it," she said, "we're going down to surgery." A look of fear crossed his face and he characteristically stuck out his lower lip and made a face. Betty Sue and I helped transfer him to the trolley to take him to the surgery. Then we had a final word of prayer together. As Tom was wheeled out of the room he said, "Give me a verse, Dan." I quoted Jeremiah 29:11 to him. *"For I know the plans I have for you. Plans for good and not for evil. To give you a hope and a future."* We walked down the hallway to the doors to the surgery. I gave Tom one last hug and told him I would see him in a few hours. Betty had a few quiet words with him and told him to "behave himself," as they wheeled him away.

Betty Sue and I went back to the room and settled down to wait. The surprising thing to me was that I was the only one waiting with her there. Tom and Betty Sue had many, many friends praying for them. The Fuller faculty devoted their entire Faculty luncheon time to praying for Tom. But nobody was able to be there with Betty Sue. I was immensely glad I had come.

We waited for another hour or two together. The time came and went when the doctor said the surgery would be over. Betty Sue went down to make inquiries, but was politely informed that when they knew anything, they would let us know. Still we waited. We had expected Tom to be into recovery by 3 or 3:30 p.m. Now it was nearly 4:30. Our anxiety grew. Finally, at about 4:45, Dr. Raz walked into the room. He was a changed man. He looked totally exhausted. His hair was ruffled and his eyes creased with fatigue.

"We've had a problem," he began. Betty Sue and I rose to greet him and I held her in my arms. "We've had a problem," he began again. "Surgery was going very fine. We opened him up. Everything looked good for the surgery and we were just about to take a section from his colon and then his heart stopped. Quickly we did a heart massage and then we opened up his chest to massage and shock the heart."

The doctor explained several other procedures that they did and as I stood there anxiously listening to him, I was thinking, "Get to the point, Dr. Raz. Get to the point. What happened?"

Betty Sue was thinking the opposite. "Please don't tell me! Please don't tell me!"

"We tried for about two hours to get his heart going," the doctor continued, "but nothing would work. And so he died."

Betty Sue crumpled into my arms in tears. We cried together and then sat down while Dr. Raz explained in even more detail the heroic measures they had taken to restart his heart. The first person I called was Chuck Kraft who took the call sitting on his front room floor. "I am afraid we have lost Tom," I said. "Would you call the others for prayer?"

Then, while Betty Sue began to gather up their things from the room, I called other members of the family.

Den Besten, who had just been appointed as the new provost of Fuller Seminary while finishing up his tenure at UCLA as head of surgery at the UCLA medical school, and a personal friend of Betty, came in and prayed with us, and assured us that he would take care of everything on the hospital side. "Obviously," he said, "an autopsy won't be necessary." While we waited to sign the release forms, Betty Sue and I found ourselves alone looking at a beautiful orange sunset over the ocean beyond. Betty Sue cried silently as we realized that that sunset was Tom's first sunrise in heaven. From Betty's Diary:

Dec. 13, 1985— I said to Jed, "Well, last night was Daddy's first night in heaven." Jed's response, "No, Daddy will never have another night—it's always light in heaven."

Dec. 16— Tom's funeral. Jed wept at the beginning of the service and said, "I was just remembering the good times we had when Daddy used to read the Bible to me" (E. Brewster 1985).

Fighting for "No Frills"

Tom's concern for a simple lifestyle extended to his planning for a simple funeral and burial. It was so important to Tom that he made arrangements well ahead of time with a funeral parlor which pledged to keep the funeral as inexpensive and simple as possible. As it turned out, however, the people with whom those arrangements had been made had gone out of business, so Betty was left to deal with some new people who supposedly had the same objectives. Their pressure on Betty to increase the cost, though, was intense and very distasteful.

Tom had said all along that he wanted a pine box and they had even corresponded with a company that made pine boxes. He had called around in the Pasadena area, and found that no one there would sell him a pine box or guarantee that he could get one at the time of his death. So he called back east to a company that made pine boxes. Tom had seriously considered having them ship one out so they could use it as a book shelf and then would have it when they needed it. He had finally decided against it, but he was that serious.

When the time came, Betty Sue got the names of some places which promised a funeral with "no frills." Betty Sue told them that her husband had written in his will specifying that she was not allowed to get a fancy coffin—she had to get a simple one. But she had given their representative their business card, and when they found out that Tom was a professor at Fuller and had a Ph.D., he turned on the pressure. "But what about your husband's standing in the community? Think of Fuller Seminary. He's a professor and he shouldn't have to be buried like this! Your husband's friends won't like it. Your husband wouldn't like it!"

Betty Sue said that her friends would say that he died exactly the way that he lived. He lived a simple life and he wanted to be buried simply. She showed her contract for a "simple funeral" with the guarantee that such would be provided. She demanded to see a simple casket. "But it's ugly. It has plastic handles" (as if that was the worst thing he could think of!). Betty Sue said, "I don't care if it has plastic handles, I want to see it." Finally he huffed out of the room and said, "There is one out there in the hall. You can go back there and look at it." He would not even go with her. The hall was dark and cold, and she could barely see the casket in the dark. He would not even turn on the lights. But Betty Sue could see that it was a casket and it did not look like it was falling apart so she agreed to buy it. She did not know until she got to the church that it looked fairly good.

Betty then had to argue over all the other details for a simple funeral which she thought had been worked out in advance. Space in the funeral parlor, the police escort, the hearse. Betty said, "I have a station wagon. Why don't I just drive my station wagon. You can put the body in my station wagon. I'll drive it out to the cemetery." "No," he said, "that's against the law. But if you insist on a station wagon, I have one." Then there was an exorbitant fee to have the body dressed. Betty Sue was tired of fighting with him.

"I've dressed this man every day of our married life for almost twenty years," Betty fumed, "and if you wish, I'll come out and dress him. I don't mind at all."

"Okay," he said grudgingly, "it's a lot of work, but I'll do it."

Astonishingly, the funeral director even wanted to cancel the funeral at the last minute! Everyone was dressed and almost ready to walk out the door when the funeral director called. When Betty Sue heard his voice on the phone, her heart sank. He said, "I'm sorry, ma'am, but we're going to have to have an autopsy, so we can't go through with the funeral."

"Why do they have to have an autopsy?" Betty asked, her anger barely controlled. "I have already been assured that one isn't needed."

"Well," he said, "Right here on the death certificate it says that he died of "paraplague," (his misreading of the notation that Tom was a "paraplegic"), and that's obviously something for an autopsy." Betty Sue felt like laughing right in his face. (Tom would have loved that one!) The man himself had failed to get the death certificate, so at the last minute thought paraplegia was a horrible disease that Tom had died from!

Betty had to fight very hard for the simplicity Tom had requested. But her effort was not lost on her friend, John Perkins:

> I won't ever forget the morning in Lake Avenue Congregational Church when it was time for Tom's body to be brought into the sanctuary for the funeral. We were standing up and looking, and they were bringing Tom's body down the aisle of the church in a plain, wooden box casket. I almost stood up and said, "Go, Tom, go!" . . . Tom lived with conviction, and he was buried with a conviction. Thank God that Betty Sue had the courage to carry out Tom's wishes (Perkins 1986).

Finally Betty was able to carry out Tom's wishes for a simple funeral, one that fit his style and his beliefs. Chuck Kraft read a series of Scriptures, which marvelously traced an overview of a life committed to God, taken largely from the Living Bible which Tom loved. In the middle of the list of verses was Psalms 100 which Jed boldly recited from memory in front of the 400 or so gathered for Tom's "coronation" celebration.

Beside that simple coffin was Tom's empty wheelchair, never to be needed again. By then Tom was walking and leaping and praising God—in His very presence!

PART III
THE MAKING OF A MAN—LESSONS OF A LIFE

17
A WHEELCHAIR WITH AN ATTITUDE

There are a lot of models in Tom's life that can be models for every-body even though a person doesn't have a physical handicap or have the unique kind of ministry that Tom had. But in a sense we all need that feistiness—confidence that God has called us to a task, the willingness to do it, to go out on a limb for it (Pierson 1987).

You know when I saw that wheelchair coming, I felt like a truck was coming (Gilliland 1987).

One of the things that made Tom's life remarkable, was how he coped and how he adapted. His creativity, endurance, attitude, perseverance, and, yes, his suffering, was a constant source of amazement to almost all who met him. Tom's attitude was always to make do with what he had. Just as he taught language learners to "learn a little and use it a lot," Tom always utilized whatever he had to the maximum extent. He always felt there was a way, and he was not going to "let a little quadriplegia" stand in the way.

Tom's muscle recovery never improved after those first months of rehabilitation at the Craig Rehabilitation Center in Denver. But he learned to use what he had so that it often looked like he had more physical dexterity. He had fairly good flexing, though no extension ability in the fingers in his right hand. This was enough to give him a firm handshake, the ability to hold a pen, spoon, and to grip things for balance and support. He had the ability to lift his shoulders and arms which allowed him to get his hands to his face and lift lightweight objects as high as his chest. His arm and shoulder movement also aided his balance, enabling him to shift his weight somewhat in his chair, and to hook his arms over the handle on the back of his wheelchair for support.

My wife and I remember fondly his curious way of scratching his head. He could get his hand to his head, but with no triceps, could not hold his arm up when he turned his hands toward the top of his head. Nor could he extend his fingers to "scratch." So he was forced to lightly "pound" his head with his fingers, by lifting his hand to his head and letting gravity pull it down. Tom had no feeling below his chest, but could sense pressure and so was aware, to some extent, of his body position. He was especially sensitive to the danger of pressure sores from sitting or sleeping too long in one position, or even such things as having his feet or ankles resting on one another for too long. He could not "feel" hot or cold, but at the same time was bothered a lot by being cold or chilled. His temperature comfort level was much higher than most able-bodied persons, partly because his relative inactivity kept his body from generating much heat. For Tom, it meant that he was almost always cold. He remedied this by keeping the house temperature about 10–15 degrees higher than the rest of us were comfortable with. And at night, even in the summer time, he would often make good use of an electric blanket.

(On one trip, they were staying with Tom's Uncle Joe in San Francisco. Their first night it was rather cool, and they were sleeping on a king size bed in his uncle's room. Tom was cold, so she turned up the blanket on his side of the bed. Betty Sue was warm, so she turned her own side down. But every little while Tom kept asking to have his side of the blanket turned up because he was too cold. At the same time, Betty Sue was too hot and kept turning her side down. Finally, she helped him scoot over to her side of the bed where it was warmer. Of course in the morning, they found that the blanket controls had been reversed by mistake when the bed had been made up for them!)

Finding a Way

Sometimes Tom's coping involved finding a new way to do something he wanted to do. Soon after his injury, when the extent of his eventual recovery was still uncertain, he was anxious to try the artificial muscles and artificial lifts. I remember Dad working in our garage until late at night many nights, experimenting with pulley systems, lifts, and braces to work out ways to get Tom in and out of bed and in and out of vehicles.

What turned out to work best and what he used most through all of his life was a simple sliding board. This was a stiff board about three feet long with a very smooth surface. To transfer from his chair to bed, or to a car seat, Tom would have his helper, (usually Betty Sue) first put his legs onto the bed or into the car. Betty would then slip the board a few inches under his backside, and get a hold of him from behind, slipping her arms under his and gripping his wrists. With a lift and a swing, Betty could slide him across into the car or onto the bed with the board carrying most of his weight. With the proper technique, it worked well and Betty could usually do it without a problem even though she was small. That method was his primary means of transfer from one place to another for the rest of his life. A small sliding board which fit into their suitcase was part of their baggage wherever they traveled.

Early on Tom and his rehabilitation team also experimented with various artificial muscles. Since he was able to lift his shoulders, the trigger for various of the muscle contraptions was that movement of his shoulders. Some versions of it allowed him more mobility with his arms, and some attempted to simulate and reconstruct hand and finger movement. Tom eventually gave up on the artificial muscles and learned to live with the little movement that he had. Nevertheless, therapists and doctors learned a lot from Tom's willingness to experiment with them, to let them try different possibilities and different contraptions. His attitude was that even if he could not benefit from the experiments himself, perhaps others in similar situations could. Indeed, many have.

Getting into and out of showers and using the bathroom presented other difficulties. Particularly with their traveling lifestyle, and untold numbers of variations worldwide on the basic bathroom theme, Tom needed a convenient way to shower and use bathroom facilities. Virtually everything available for persons in his condition was heavy and bulky, and certainly not designed with a frequent traveler in mind. Tom and Betty Sue thought much about the problem, and eventually designed a portable, lightweight, folding shower chair that fit into a briefcase and enabled Tom to get into small showers and use small bathroom facilities. Everest and Jennings, the wheelchair manufacturers, made one to Tom's specifications which became part of their travel gear. Everest and Jennings used Tom's as a prototype with a view to selling them to a potential broader market, but the idea was eventually dropped since the company did not think many quadriplegics would be as interested in travel as Tom was.

The Project Manager

What Tom could not do for himself, he was always happy to supervise someone else doing for him. He was, as he said, "only paralyzed from the neck down," and he was very good at thinking through problems and organizing others to get projects done. An early project that sticks in my mind was the building of a "boardwalk" at the house where I grew up in Colorado Springs. The house had a long pathway from the driveway to the steps to the entry way on the back porch. There must have been some pavement on the pathway years before, but when Tom was able to come to live at home with us, soon after Dad's death, the path was rugged, pot-holed and often muddy.

Neither Mom nor Tom liked tracking in mud and water on Tom's wheelchair wheels. So as a thirteen year old, I was nominated to build a boardwalk. I aware that I knew nothing about construction. Not to worry though, Tom could "manage" it, and sure enough he did. Under Tom's watchful eye and following his instructions for every detail, I built a long boardwalk over that path, using mostly scrap lumber, with smooth cement approaches and a very respectable curve around to the porch steps that survived for many years after we moved from that house.

When Mom moved to a new house in Colorado Springs, I had to start over in modifications to accommodate Tom on his frequent visits. Tom was always quite a bit more enthusiastic about the improvement projects than I was, since I did not have the skills, confidence or patience to build up to Tom's standards. Nevertheless, with his encouragement, I got a number of projects done with a degree of precision that never would have been possible without Tom's supervision. When I tiled Mom's basement floor and paneled her basement walls and ceilings, Tom had me stop and think about each cut and each placement. He was able to visualize the angles and fit and offer precise instructions from his wheelchair "perch." At times I resented his attention to detail and almost overbearing oversight. I also did not have nearly the stamina to do the work that he had to supervise it! But I never failed to take pride in the finished product.

The "Bulldozer"

Class was to start in just a few minutes. Tom had asked that the chairs in the classroom be moved against the walls so that the floor space was free and the students could sit on the steps or on cushions or pillows in a very informal kind of setting. But the chairs were all over the room in neat rows. No problem! With Tom's electric wheelchair and his joystick, he did a very respectable imitation of a bulldozer, moving chairs out of the way and creating the kind of space and environment he wanted.

That "bulldozer" approach to classroom arrangement characterized much of the way Tom lived. He had a kind of bulldozer approach to many aspects of life.

Tom was a bulldozer at times in his relationships with others. Some of my earliest memories of Tom were when he was still a healthy young teenager, arguing or fussing with Dad. Dad, of course, brooked very little open rebellion, but Tom was just bull-headed enough, brave enough, or stupid enough to buck the rules from time to time. One incident stands out in my mind. Tom did not like to drink milk. Dad wanted him to drink milk. After one confrontation, Tom forced down a glass, but cast a distinctly unfriendly glance at Dad as he was doing so. I think Dad won the ensuing battle, but it seems blows were struck by both parties.

In fact there was kind of a rebelliousness throughout our family. Perhaps we took the lead from Tom. As noted earlier, our father was something of a fanatic about various things and we reacted to some of them, though not very openly. There was not any middle of the road for my father. Everything was always very definitive, very black and white. I believe Tom inherited that from him.

I believe also that God used Tom's impatience and independence to guide him along in several phases of his ministry. At the Spanish Language School, in Guadalajara, Tom could have been a passive administrator, following the rules and pursuing the methods of traditional language school study. But Tom saw a better way, and pushed hard for changes. Perhaps he could have accomplished as much at the school with more patience and tact, but that was not his style. "Tact" was not yet in his vocabulary.

Anyway, he was on the move. And it was the same when he was Translation Director for Campus Crusade. Clearly, there were serious problems with both the approach and the results of the translation policies in place when Tom took over. Perhaps the needed changes would have been made eventually at Crusade. Almost certainly, Tom could have pushed for changes with more patience and tact. But Tom was a bulldozer. He did not do remodeling. His method was to tear down the old and clear out the rubble. Sadly, but not surprisingly, relationships were frayed in the process.

Even at Fuller Seminary, where Tom had his longest and most satisfying ministry relationships, he often came on so strongly that his colleagues were sometimes wary and concerned. Betty Sue admits that "when Tom went in to any of the offices at Fuller, he would often go in with an adversarial stance."

Tom did not usually say, "I think such and such." He would say, "I'm *convinced* of it." Tom knew what he believed and was very intolerant at times with people who did not feel as strongly as he did about things.

Dean Gilliland, who joined the Fuller faculty shortly after Tom and Betty, remembers well Tom's aggressive style:

> I came here as a new faculty member just on the heels of Tom and Betty Sue, and I can remember getting ourselves ready for Tom. His reputation preceded him. Sure enough, while he was here he would argue strongly about what he wanted in his program. We weren't always comfortable with that. That is not to say that what he was doing was not good for him or for the school. But it was very much Tom's style to be aggressive and abrasive (1987).

While Tom was aggressive and abrasive, the Fuller School of World Mission was a big enough tent to accommodate even his style. Paul Pierson believes that Tom was there in the providence of God and needed to be there. Speaking of Fuller's ability to absorb and benefit from even non-conformists, he observes that

> there's a high enough level of security among our faculty and a high enough level of commitment so that first of all, everyone recognized that our hearts beat together in our basic commitment, cause, and goals. We were all coming from quite different paths in our life-long pilgrimages to this place. We are enough missiologists and missionaries to recognize that God, more often than not, has used the mavericks for new breakthroughs. And Tom was a maverick. So he fit. And if we didn't always understand some of his ideas, we could always respect and love him (Pierson 1987).

Tom's students also often commented about Tom's bulldozer style. Wes Collins, who was in Tom and Betty's Guatemala training with the Summer Institute of Linguistics, speaks for many:

> I often think of Tom and quote him—especially when teaching missionary candidates. He had a great grasp of the issues of cross-cultural outreach. He was very bold, and of course outspoken. I found this endearing and challenging—never intimidating . . . I know that he wanted only for people to think. He never wanted to bad mouth anyone, but man, could he generate sparks! (Collins 1993).

Tom's attitude showed through in his writing. "Language Learning Midwifery" seemed to some to have been an "angry" article. I mentioned this to Betty Sue, and she responded:

> Much of Tom's writing and lectures sounded very strong, sometimes almost without tact. He used hyperbole and overstatement in order to get people's attention. Even he acknowledged that he sometimes came across stronger than he meant to or sounding more angry than he was. When you heard him in person you could see the twinkle in his eye. I often tried to tone down the presentation a bit, but couldn't often transfer the twinkle to paper (1994).

Occasionally, Tom *really* angered people. The fact that Tom was in a wheelchair, though, usually tempered the anger. "It would be very hard for us to receive some of the things you are saying if you were standing up," griped one learner whom Tom had managed to thoroughly infuriate.

Tom was so committed to what he was doing that he had very little tolerance for nonsense. He sometimes provoked anger on the part of learners or those with whom he related. That did not bother Tom too much, but it often bothered Betty. One of the most frustrating things for her was getting him to tone it down a bit. Now, though, she feels that Tom's style forced people to confront the issues, and not sit on the fence (E. Brewster 1993).

Given Tom's bulldozer style, it is striking how warmly he treated his students and learners. With few exceptions, around the world the participants in his classes and workshops commented not on his abrasiveness but rather on his humility and sensitivity. Nico Smith, of Stellenbosch University in South Africa was one of many who felt that

> Tom was such a gentle and humble person. He never gave the impression that he was a "know-it-all" person, that he was an authority in a new field, or that his method was the best and only. He always wanted to learn from others. He could make a person feel that he or she was unique and someone who had an important contribution to make towards making the lives of others meaningful (Smith 1993).

It is also surprising, given his reputation, that he was known among his students for his personal warmth. "Tom was the only professor I knew who wanted me to call him by his first name. Despite his physical difficulties, he was also the only professor who I saw freely hug his students. He taught me more by his love than by his lectures" (Ford n.d.).

Breaking Down the Physical Barriers . . .

Obviously for a person confined to a wheelchair, even small physical barriers presented problems. During all the time Tom taught at Fuller Seminary, he lived in apartments rented from the seminary. These were conveniently located only three blocks or so from the campus, and Tom was able to drive his electric wheelchair, sometimes even alone, to get to the classes he taught. The problem was the one or two inch lips left on the curbs at the side-walk intersections, when the ramps for the handicapped and wheelchairs were installed. Those little barriers would be unno-ticeable to an able bodied person, but since Tom's electric wheel-chair had small wheels—only six inches in diameter—those two inch curbs were real obstacles.

Sometimes Tom could negotiate with some maneuvering, but at times he was almost thrown from his chair as he made short runs up to get his front wheels over one. Tom went to the Pasadena City Hall to complain about them, but was told that the lip was left to give the brushes on the street sweeper trucks something against which to catch and gather the dirt. Tom was not impressed. The bulldozer in Tom did not take too kindly to nearly being thrown out of his chair, or to the reasoning of the City Council.

His first response was to offer a city official a spare wheelchair to let him see if he could negotiate the curb—an offer that the dumbfounded official politely declined. Next he got me and Betty Sue out at night with hammers to break off enough cement to let his wheels roll up onto the sidewalk. He "managed" the project, making sure that we did enough to solve the problem. It was hard work, and I felt like a vandal, but Tom was adamant that some-thing had to be done. Tom wrote a note to City Hall saying, "I had those lips chipped down on purpose because I couldn't get up those curbs. If you'd like to have some more chips, let me know."

Tom finally won that battle when one day he and Betty saw a bicycle curb that was completely flush. Tom went back to City Hall and asked an official for ten minutes of his time to go see that curb. The official went along and Tom pointed out that the curb for the bicycle, which had a radius much larger than that of the wheelchairs, had no lip at all. The official could see that the lip presented real difficulties for Tom, and that if a bicycle curb had no lip, ramps built for wheelchair access should not have one either. The official realized that the problem and the unfairness were genuine. He agreed that from then on any curb change would be truly wheelchair accessible. (Today every new curb in Pasadena is flush with the street.)

If lips on curbs were a problem, stairs were even more so. While Tom was not an activist for handicapped persons rights, he did frequently fuss with institutions and businesses about their lack of wheelchair accessibility. During his years at the University of Michigan and the University of Arizona, he complained more than once about all the stairs and the lack of ramps. He regularly prodded the administration at Fuller Seminary to improve accessibility there as well. He taught there for nine years, but most ramps were only installed after Tom's death.(A feasibility study at Fuller done at Tom's request indicated that ramps could not be installed in the building where Tom did much of his teaching. It is now ramped and fully accessible to handicapped students.)

. . . and the Spiritual Barriers

With few exceptions, Tom did not fight against physical kinds of injustices, though he did let people know how he felt. He was a fighter and a crusader, but not frequently about physical barriers. He was much more concerned about other kinds of barriers, such as a lack of Scripture in other languages, barriers that keep the poor from knowing the Lord and being all that God wants them to be, barriers facing new missionaries who want to learn a language and culture. Tom challenged people's ideas. He challenged doctrines, and challenged nonsense.

Tom's anger was not meant to tear down, but always to open pathways for others to follow. Tom got frustrated when people with creative ideas were hampered or not allowed to put them into practice. He did not like the roadblocks put in the way of learners. He had little patience with rules that got in the way of effective ministry—rules that keep people separate, rules about lifestyles, rules about how much money missionaries have to raise, or how much "junk" they have to take with them. His disgust with missionary endeavors in which most energy is devoted to self-maintenance, was never very well disguised.

Betty says that Tom saw himself as a bulldozer for other people, breaking down some of the barriers that other people faced. He usually was not an advocate for himself. He was asked by The

Center for Independent Living (for handicapped assistance and advocacy in Pasadena) to get involved more as an advocate, but Tom declined. Most of his bulldozing was not done for his own benefit. He was fairly tolerant of his own limitations and the barriers that he faced, but not of barriers that other people faced.

More commonly, however, Tom was bucking institutions and rules and policies that did not make sense, and programs not moving fast enough to suit him or things not getting done. Tom was always warm and open to students and learners, but often came across abrasively to the gatekeepers and "authorities." Wes Collins, one of Tom's students notes, "Tom was hard on self-acclaimed experts and the academically secure," he says, "but he was a staunch defender of his disciples."

> I can picture Tom as clearly today as 15 years ago. I enjoyed his confrontive style which was "just for discussion's sake." Then when people would get riled, he would say, "Why get so upset, I'm just a gimp." Yah, right (Collins 1993).

Tom also was very intolerant of people not living up to their potential, making excuses, or unwilling to make sacrifices. It showed up early on with his relationship with Mona.

Mona was the last to leave home and during Tom's rehabilitation he came home from time to time to live for various periods of time with Mom. When Mona was young, Tom even physically disciplined her. While he had very little movement of his arms and hands, by moving his shoulders about just so, he could bring his arm down with considerable force. When he did that on top of someone's head, it usually got their attention. When she was just small enough for Tom to be able to whack her on the head from time to time, it provided the only physical discipline she got.

At other times Tom's discipline was less physical, but just as effective. She remembers him backing her into a corner with his chair and scolding her for mouthing off to Mom or other infractions. Once when Mona was doing the dishes, she went into a typical teenage griping and complaining routine. Tom ordered Mona to sit down. He laid his paralyzed hands open on his lap. He looked at his hands and up over his glasses. "Mona," he said, "I would love to be able to do the dishes. But I can't. You can, and I'm not going to let you *not* appreciate that fact."

Mona may not have appreciated Tom's discipline at that stage in her life, but she certainly looks positively on it now. And she sees Tom's bulldozer qualities as part of his own heritage, and something he passed on to her and to others:

> Tom was bold and daring. Nothing stood in his way, and he felt nothing should stand in anyone else's way. He saw a task to do and did it. Whatever it took, it was done. That's a part of my inheritance from Tom because I also walk that way. Whatever it takes, there is a way. That would ring in my ears during whatever situation we were plowing through. There is a way. There is a way.
>
> And that was Tom. If it meant getting Betty Sue to get out a sledge hammer to beat down the pavement to where he could get his chair up onto the sidewalk, there was a way. There was always a way. It may take some effort. It may take some dying to self. It may mean that you lay down your life, but if there is a task before you, there is a way. There is a way (Tuma 1994).

Mellowing Out

Some of Tom's closest colleagues suggest that around the fall of 1983, Tom began to mellow in his attitudes and abrasiveness. He spent a lot more time in the Word in his spare time. He was hungry for the Word and seemed to be hearing the Lord's voice a lot more. Perhaps as his health began to slip, he began to be more patient and to walk more in mercy and kindness. He seemed to be able to express himself a lot less abrasively and aggressively. Betty says that he did not feel things any less strongly, but was able to express them with more love and sensitivity. He began to take himself less seriously, and tempered some of his impatience.

Dean Gilliland observes that:

> . . . somewhere around 1983 there was a definite warming up in Tom's person, more of an openness. He was not anybody you would greet with a hug in his wheel chair in my earlier experience. He became much more outgoing and I always wanted to talk with Betty about what it was that warmed up in Tom's heart. Was it the continuing disappointment and recognition that God owns his body?

What was it? My enjoyable years with Tom started about 1983. It was not just a warmth but almost a reaching out to people which didn't characterize the earlier period in his life (Gilliland 1987).

Betty Sue saw the mellowing too:

I'm not sure what all was happening but there was a real renewal in his life. Dean [Gilliland] was absolutely right. Tom would go in [to faculty meetings] with his proposals and they were absolutely right. He would fight you tooth and nail. But he went through a time of real renewal and mellowing . . . he became much more willing to compromise on the small things and push things through a little more gently (1993).

Tom's mellowing was evident too in his more willing acceptance of criticism late in his life. In his urgency to get things done, Tom was sometimes impatient in his relationships with people. There was a time when several of the secretaries in the School of World Mission office felt Tom's brusqueness and harshness had gone too far and they went to Chuck Kraft to complain. They felt that Chuck was close enough to Tom to speak to him effectively.

Chuck was dismayed. He certainly recognized the problem in Tom, for he had seen it often himself, but was not sure how Tom would take the counsel. He desperately wanted to say something direct but sensitive that would not offend. Chuck prayed about it and carefully worked out what he would say. When the opportunity to mention it arose, however, he forgot his speech and blurted out, "Tom, be nice to people." Chuck cringed inside, thinking that Tom would take offense. Instead, Tom softly said, "Have people talked to you?" Chuck admitted that they had. Tom's response was sincere contrition, and grief. He thanked Chuck, and then rolled off to apologize to the ladies he had hurt (Kraft 1994).

18
THE EXPLORER

So many times I've heard of missionaries who have to have all the pleasures of home. Tom didn't need that. He slept in the huts and ate their food. He loved people where they were. Tom was for real (Kalsbeek 1993).

Although life in another country will always be full of surprises, through cultural differences Tom and Betty Sue taught us to be part of the human family and to find joy in the encounter between human beings seeking to serve God and find meaning in life (Overduin 1986).

Perhaps it could seen from the time Tom could walk—he was always an explorer and a wanderer. He carried that quality with him into adolescence and adulthood. In his lectures, he frequently spoke of spelunking in Huckey Cove as a teenager. Huckey Cove was part of the labyrinth of caves that is no doubt connected to the maze of underground passages known as the Cave of the Winds in the mountains west of Colorado Springs. the Cave of the Winds, of course, is a small but beautiful cave which has been amply exploited commercially, and treats visitors to an enjoyable but well controlled and sterile exposure to the underground.

Tom much preferred nearby Huckey Cove which had not been commercialized at all. In fact, the authorities regularly closed the entrance, but enterprising young people like Tom just as regularly found new ways to get into it. Tom loved exploring the cave and participated in giving descriptive names to the various features in the cave: the Nutcracker Suite, the Chimney, the Stovepipe. Tom was much more at home charting his own way in such an environment than following the crowds and the tour guides.

We have seen too that Pikes Peak and Tom had a very special relationship. We've noted in earlier chapters his success in the grueling Pikes Peak marathon. But Tom also attacked the mountain on his own, even in winter time. There is a group of people who regularly climb Pikes Peak just before New Years Eve in order to set off the fireworks that mark the beginning of the new year. (They call themselves the "AdAmAn" club, because they "add a man" each year to make the climb with them.) The trip can be dangerous. Climbing to 14,000 feet in the middle of winter can present extremes in weather conditions. That did not deter seventeen year old Tom from tagging along behind the AdAmAn Club during their trek one year, and he actually reached the top ahead of the club members.

Tom loved exploring. He always said he liked to enjoy God's creation "to the hilt." Obviously, Tom had to love visiting new places. How else could he have tolerated the rigors of travel for nearly twenty years, visiting over eighty countries? Tom did much more than just go from point to point when he traveled. He took every opportunity he could to visit out of the way places, experience new cultures and peoples, and make the absolute most out of every opportunity. And that, in fact, is the way he lived all of life. No one could ever doubt that that he knew "this world was not his home," but at the same time, he was not going to miss out on anything while he was passing through.

Mini-Vacations

One of the characteristics of his travel was his willingness to free himself up for the mini-vacations. Tom also liked to "follow the sun." He had a real aversion to cold weather, and it was really no accident that in many winter months in the northern hemisphere his schedule found him in South America, Africa or the South Pacific. He also valued his "modular" lifestyle. It allowed them to work hard during training sessions or writing projects, and then have the freedom to take time off. He liked working intensely for days (sometimes night and day) or even weeks, and then having a complete change of pace.

It's true that most were working vacations of one sort or another, since he always had one or two projects that he carried with him to complete along the way. But he was never adverse to taking days off, and in fact he built time into his schedule to go out of the way for the unusual or simply the relaxing vacation time. The list of the "world class" out of the way places that he and his wheelchair managed to visit "because it was in the vicinity" is astounding—Machu Picchu, Victoria Falls, The Great China Wall, Petra (in Jordan), The Maasai Mara, Borobudur (the ancient Buddhist temple), the Taj Mahal, and many, many more.

It was during their visit to Peru in 1973, that they visited the ancient Incan ruins of Machu Picchu. To get there, one must go by train from the town of Cuzco to the base of the mountain, then by jeep to the top, then walk by narrow trail from the way station around the side of the mountain. When they got near on the trail, they still could not see anything, and the trail became too narrow for the wheelchair.

Tom was disappointed, but suggested he would stay behind and Betty Sue should go on ahead and take pictures. But some of the other tourists objected to having him miss out and volunteered to carry Tom around the bend to where he could see the whole panorama. Betty Sue was *very* hesitant about this because of the steep drop-off at the edge of the trail, but a couple of the men grabbed Tom and a couple more carried the chair (Betty Sue closed her eyes) and sure enough, just around the bend was a great place for him to see most of the view.

Tom thought he was probably the only person in a wheelchair to ever visit there, but a few years later in a wheelchair magazine was an article by a woman in a wheelchair who claimed to have been the only chair up there—so there have been at least two!

Another time, in 1974, when I was working in what used to be Rhodesia (now Zimbabwe), Tom and Betty Sue came to visit and they found time to take a memorable visit with my wife and me up to Victoria Falls. Again, not to be denied "experiencing it to the hilt," he rented a small plane for us. We "tossed him in" and enjoyed the Falls' magnificence, doing figure eights over the zigzag chasm that characterizes the "smoke that roars." One of the most memorable pictures that I have of Tom is taken on the rocks on the shores of the Zambezi River above Victoria Falls, with Tom sunning himself and all of us enjoying the leisurely pace that Tom was always ready to take time for.

This was not the first time that we flew over a spectacular falls. On an earlier occasion in the US, after a reunion of the Brewster clan at my sister Mary's home in upstate New York, we once again piled into a small aircraft and flew across New York, heading for Toronto and another month at the Toronto Institute of Linguistics. This time, we flew over the Attica State Prison and of course we took a side trip that gave us spectacular views of Niagara Falls. That's the way Tom did things.

Tom would always take diversions on his travel schedule if it would create an opportunity to visit with one of his siblings or relatives. Since my family and I lived in Africa for most of sixteen years during the 1970s and 1980s, he arranged to stop over in Africa many times. We always made time to have vacations together or have other enjoyable outings. Once we hired a car and drove down through the Tsavo Game Park between Nairobi and the coast. We stopped at the famous Mzima Springs, where the underwater observation post gave us great views of hippos feeding. As we watched, a large bird dove into the water in front of us and snatched a fish.

As we drove on through the park, we counted well over 100 elephants. Unfortunately, we also came on the rotting carcass of an elephant which had been poached—killed for its tusks. A sad commentary on what is happening to elephants there. (We read that when we first went to Africa in the mid-1970s, there were something like 120,000 elephants in Africa. By the time we left in 1990, the numbers had dwindled to less than 20,000.)

Later on in that same trip, we rented a house in a remote area on the north coast at Mombasa and enjoyed several days of sunning ourselves and exploring the coastal reef that makes that beach so beautiful and popular.

On another visit to Kenya, in 1975, Tom and Betty Sue decided to see what they could see at Kilimanjaro. They hired a light aircraft, thinking that they would fly down and circle Kilimanjaro.

Obviously, they had no idea how big that mountain was. They did fly down and got close to it, and came away awestruck by its size and grandeur. Tom and Betty had invited their friend, Carolyn Mullenix, to go along. On the return, they flew low over the Amboseli Game Park and after buzzing the strip to frighten off the zebra, landed at the Amboseli airstrip for a quick drink before returning on to Nairobi.

Tom did not even want to miss out on the thrills of white-water rafting. That adventure was one of the very few, however, which was denied him. The year they had an opportunity to do so in British Columbia was one of especially high run-off, and the proprietor of the rafting company would not let Tom on board for insurance reasons. Betty Sue admitted that she was quite relieved about not being able to experience that one "to the hilt."

There were other times when Tom's wild ideas really did defy good sense. A small glider port north of Colorado Springs presented a strong temptation to him. One Sunday afternoon, he and Betty Sue drove out to see what the possibilities were of taking a ride in the glider. The pilots there were delighted to have him give it a try. Tom was loaded into the back seat of the glider and taken up for a ride. He always bragged later that he even got to fly it for a while.

(There was a time when Tom thought he might be able to pilot a small aircraft and use that as a means for getting around. He even had some special hooks put onto the braces that he wore to keep his shoes on and ankles straight. The hooks were designed to help him get in and out of small aircraft and function while he was aboard. This idea, however, never quite "took flight," and he wound up doing all of his flying commercially. The hooks on the braces were a feature of his footwear for many years. He never wore out the bottom of his shoes, so he rarely changed the braces!)

Exploring with Buzz

Tom's quadriplegic friend Buzz Lugenbeel was very influential in helping Tom learn to relax and try things he might not have otherwise tried. It was Buzz who got Tom interested in fishing.

But casting a line into the water presented very serious challenges for a person with such limited muscular control. Together they designed a pole with a crook at the end which wrapped around his elbow. The crook kept the pole in place, and worked like an extension of his arm. After lots of practice, and using only the muscles to lift his shoulders and his biceps, Tom was able to do a reasonable cast as long as he hooked his left arm around the back of his wheelchair and made sure he was balanced adequately.

For a time in the 1960s and 1970s, Tom and the fishing pole were regular companions. Tom fished the trout streams of Colorado, some Canadian lakes and even the deep seas off the coast of Mazatlan, where he caught several fish and proudly brought them back on ice. Whether catching or not, there was virtually nothing that he enjoyed more than sitting at the shore of a warm lake under a broad-brimmed cap, and practicing casting that line into the water and slowly reeling it back.

I was privileged to be with Tom and Betty on some of their remarkable stopovers. One was the trip in 1969, after teaching at TIL, when I joined Tom and Betty Sue in the little cabin in the woods above the incredible Lake Temiscaming in Quebec. We spent the month listening to French tapes (yes, listening to language tapes is a legitimate supplement to the *LAMP* method!) and going into the village to practice the French that we were learning. (Learn a little—use it a lot!)

Many mornings during that marvelous July we got up very early in the morning, drove to the lake, and rented a small boat. In order for him to be able to sit securely, we let the air out of his tires and he had his "perch" like the captain of a ship on the front of our small outboard. We would get there early enough to be out while the lake was still smooth as glass, and nothing disturbed the morning stillness of either the mirror-like lake or the peacefulness of the mornings except the haunting cries of the loons.

Then, we would go island hopping, sometimes going ashore. One particular island that we dubbed "Victoria Island" had a fine black sand beach that provided an excellent resting place for us before we continued fishing for the two-foot long trout later on in the day.

After leaving Quebec, we traveled around the north shores of Lake Superior, proudly sporting on the front of my little Volkswagen, a large set of moose horns we had found.

On another memorable occasion, we took a pup tent and camped overnight in the mountains of Colorado. In the warm afternoon while fishing, a mini-tornado formed at the far side of the lake. We watched it become a water spout as it came across the 500 yards or so of the lake. Just as though it had some kind of internal guidance system, it came straight for Tom. The rest of us were far enough away that we could only watch as it moved his way. Strangely, it came right over the top of him, whipping his hat off, pulling at his clothes, and very nearly throwing him out of his chair. Fortunately, his chair did not tip over and by hooking his arm over the back of his wheelchair, he held on until I was able to get over to him to pull him upright and get him sorted out again.

It was Buzz who got Tom interested in camping. Buzz could do it with the help of his petite wife Mica, so why couldn't Tom? They went together a number of times in Mexico. I was with them on one camping/fishing trip that took us to a remote lake down a very dusty road, near the volcano that had grown out of a corn field, Mount Paracutin. That night we stayed in a little cabin where the air got quite chilly. The cold though, was no problem for Tom—he simply had me warm the sheets up by the fireplace before he let me "toss him in!"

Buzz also got Tom involved in making little wax sculptures and making molds to cast them in bronze. Then it was wood working. Naturally any such project presented special challenges for a quadriplegic. Buzz's creative genius helped them both adapt and find ways of holding or fixing the work piece so they could fashion it with their limited muscle usage.

Tom worked hard to carve out time for side-trips and mini vacations. In fact, Betty Sue says that while most of their bigger decisions in their lives came relatively easily, Tom sometimes pored over smaller decisions—like how to spend vacation time.

At times he would go over and over possible itineraries and possible things to do. Betty Sue was never quite sure whether it was something they were *really* going to do or just something they were day-dreaming about. Sometimes the dreams were larger than reality would permit.

> We would plan these really big itineraries and the next thing I knew reality set in and our plans were cut in a half. For example, we were going to take a trip to Europe on a ship and we ended up going through the Great Lakes on a ship. But it was great fun. There were various times when it looked like something big was coming up and then it got cut very small (E. Brewster 1993).

Small by some people's standards, but almost always unusual and creative.

Tom loved to get out into the open spaces. The California desert had a special attraction for him, and he tried to get out to the Salton Sea as often as his schedule would permit. On one occasion, Howard Raik of Center for Human Potential (CHP) in Chicago flew out to spend a couple of days with Tom and Betty Sue at the Salton Sea. They were on a brief vacation there and Howard agreed to meet them. The CHP had a contract for training US Peace Corps personnel for Costa Rica. They had learned about *LAMP* and were using it to some extent and wanted some help. (He later invited them to go to Costa Rica to teach a couple of workshops.)

While at the Salton Sea they went for a walk together. Tom loved the wide open spaces there and the hot weather. But Howard is a city boy and said that he found "all that open space and sky oppressive" and almost claustrophobic. That was really hard for Tom to fathom.

Exploring "Inner" Worlds

Tom devoted much of his spare time to creative pursuits that stretched and taught him. At one point, Tom got very interested in genealogy of the Brewster and Green families. Tom asked his uncle about the spelling of the Brewster name because he had seen it spelled two different ways by his grandfather. It seems that in the early days, some spelled it with a "u" out of convenience, but his grandfather changed it back from "u" to "ew" because "that was the proper way to spell the Brewster name, and a family name should never have its spelling changed."

Tom and Betty Sue spent quite a bit of time in genealogical records while at the University of Arizona and the University of Texas. They wrote letters to various older relatives to learn what they could, and were able to unearth a great deal of information about their families' origins.

Also while in Austin they became amateur radio hams. Tom met a man who was legally blind who was teaching a class on ham radios. They attended faithfully and passed the first level tests for Morse code and for radio laws. They bought a sender and receiver and Tom practiced sending and receiving Morse code over the air.

Later on, Tom also became very interested in astronomy and, as always, he attacked the new learning with enthusiasm. Shortly after he and Betty became part of the Fuller Seminary faculty, they bought a telescope and a star-finder chart and began to spend evenings when they could out in the desert, studying the stars. The astronomy was part of Jedidiah's home schooling, and from the time he was very young, he was able to recognize many constellations. My wife Alice and I joined them on a weekend mini vacation in the desert and spent most of the night with them learning about the stars. We never had the appreciation or expertise for it that Tom did, but we did marvel at their willingness to give up sleep to spend time in the cold night air, and at the energy that he (and Betty) were willing to invest in this and other new learning opportunities.

Later on it was computers. Around Fuller Seminary, Tom and Betty were the first to see the possibilities of office computers and then portable computers, especially given their busy, traveling lifestyle. At first they were considered somewhat "avant-garde," perhaps a little radical, but their enthusiasm for using computers for word processing eventually rubbed off on most of their colleagues. Tom was the first to purchase an Osborne computer—a little one with a tiny orange screen and two 360 k floppy drives. Right away that became part of their luggage (as if they needed more!) as they continued to travel around the world.

When they switched computers, it was first to a rogue Northstar machine which they grieved to learn had no compatibility with anything, and then to a Kaypro, and finally to a Macintosh. Tom loved the Macintosh because of its pioneering icon and mouse-driven operating scheme which was easier for him to use with his limited muscular ability. Reluctantly, he did leave it behind when he traveled. There are limits, you know.

Tom was also very much a game enthusiast, and among my most precious memories of my brother are the many hours that we spent playing chess. Tom enjoyed nothing more than sitting in the warm sun, enjoying a chess game while "forcing fluids" to keep his kidneys functioning. I remember so many afternoons, when I had a nagging feeling that I probably should have been doing something more constructive, but indulged myself with the pleasure of one of those long chess matches. (Occasionally, Tom and I even played chess games by mail, a move per letter, but I do not think we actually ever finished one!)

Tom was always interested in games, especially those that would stretch his mind. For a while they enjoyed a very difficult game called "Equations," which called on participants to solve complicated equations. Tom always had time for Scrabble, but liked to liven it up with a modification he called "Scramble" in which the letters were turned over rapidly and players shouted any words that could be formed from the letters turned over.

Tom and I also developed interesting variations on other games. One was three dimensional tick-tack-toe, sometimes with four by four grids which we played in our minds. We mentally lettered the "layers," and called out the layer and intersecting squares, remembering all of the previous moves in our heads. It was something we could do as we walked together, while pushing Tom's wheelchair or after he got an electric one, walking along together.

Tom's "mind stretching" also involved memorizing long Scripture portions and poetry. He memorized a compilation of verses from the four Gospels of the trial and crucifixion and often quoted it in churches and seminars. His poetry repertoire was not extensive, but he memorized several pieces and found frequent occasions to share. An example of the secular and humorous variety was "The Cremation of Sam McGee" which he quoted to brothers, sisters, nieces and nephews who frequently requested it. Tom identified well with the hapless Sam McGee who insisted that his friend cremate his remains when he succumbed to the arctic cold, but was revived by the warmth of his own cremation:

> . . . Some planks I tore from the cabin floor, and I lit the boiler fire;
> Some coal I found that was lying around, and I heaped the fuel
>   higher;
> The flames just soared, and the furnace roared—such a blaze you
>   seldom see;
> And I burrowed a hole in the glowing coal, and I stuffed in Sam
>   McGee.
>
> Then I made a hike, for I didn't like to hear him sizzle so;
> And the heavens scowled, and the huskies howled, and the wind
>   began to blow.
> It was icy cold, but the hot sweat rolled down my cheeks, and I don't
>   know why;
> And the greasy smoke in an inky cloak went streaking down the sky.
>
> I do not know how long in the snow I wrestled with grisly fear;
> But the stars came out and they danced about ere again I ventured
>   near;
> I was sick with dread, but I bravely said: "I'll just take a peep inside.
> I guess he's cooked and it's time I looked;" . . . then the door I opened
>   wide.
>
> And there sat Sam, looking cold and calm, in the heart of the fur-
>   nace roar;
> And he wore a smile you could see a mile, and he said: "Please close
>   that door!
> It's fine in here, but I greatly fear you'll let in the cold and storm—
> Since I left Plumtree, down in Tennessee, it's the first time I've been
>   warm" (Service 1987).

Language Learning with the "Right" Brain

Another area of exploration for Tom was how, in fact, people normally learn languages—what are the mental processes and functions? In the early 1980s he began to study some of the relevant research and draw important inferences for language learning. He learned that the two halves of the brain can function quite independently, but that they learn in very different ways. "Each side specializes in thinking in its own unique way."

The left side is more analytical, logical and academic. It is the side that controls speech, keeps track of time, handles symbols, and does logical functions.

The right side is creative, imaginative, experiential and intuitive. It is the side that handles perception, recognition and many spontaneous responses.

Tom learned that

> [a]pparently the two sides learn so well but so differently that one or the other needs to establish dominance over the other, and therefore becomes sort of the commanding officer of the two. This process of establishing dominance is called "lateralization." It usually happens by the time the individual is about twelve years of age. For most of us in the academically oriented West the left side becomes the dominant hemisphere. Often the dominant hemisphere has little or no patience with the learning and thinking styles of the subordinate side. To spend time in certain creative ways may, for example, be viewed by the left brain as wasting time (1983).

Tom realized that this may be precisely what often makes it so difficult for academically oriented westerners to learn a new language in adulthood. Tom had taught for years that language learning was a social activity—not an academic one. He realized that when children learn a language, they do so with the right side of their brains as a social activity. But most westerners, after their brains have lateralized, usually to the left side, and after they have become academically oriented, try to learn a new language with the left, or academic side of their brains. Tom began to share these ideas with his learners. Understanding the processes, he hoped, would help left brain people relax left hemisphere dominance so that language learning could more spontaneously occur in the relaxed relational experiences that allow the right brain to fulfill its learning potential.

Theological /Missiological Exploration

Tom was always very open to theological exploring. He was convinced that westerners did not have a monopoly on theological understanding, and, in his later years, was always learning from other faiths. He wanted to learn from other religions, not for "accommodation," but rather to search for the bridges and "redemptive analogies" that might open the door for effective evangelism so that they too could have the opportunity to know God through Jesus Christ.

We have seen that Tom was very concerned about the unreached peoples of the world. He recognized that many of those unreached were poor. He also recognized that a very large segment of the unreached and the poor were Muslims, Hindus and Buddhists. He thought deeply about their plight. He studied Islam. Tom constantly questioned how much even Christians really understand their theologies. He felt very strongly about the need for salvation of Muslims but wanted the message expressed in ways that did not place stumbling blocks to their being able to listen to the message. He observed that a fairly small part of worldwide evangelism was directed towards Muslims, and much of the what was done was from a western cultural standpoint that was not very open to God working in ways outside of our cultural understanding. He wrote:

> I'm a little troubled that we in the West have all our theologies perfectly refined for ourselves. We call it systematic theology. In fact, it's called dogmatics in seminaries; but it's so systematically organized that we can even be dogmatic about it. And people who are highly trained in their systematic theology find it easy to [impose] that on people in other cultures. We fail to realize that all the ground is covered from within our own cultural perspective, but very often when related to another culture, it just doesn't fit. Yet we have the power and prestige and the money and authority that allow us to impose our own will on people, regardless of whether or not it's good news when viewed through their perspective (T. Brewster 1983:120).

Bridges to the Heart of Muslims . . .

Tom longed for the day when "every knee shall bow" to Christ the Savior. He constantly explored what we *mean* by our jargon. How is what we say *perceived,* for example, in the hearts and minds of Muslim hearers? He recognized that for Muslims, the idea of a "triune God" was a stumbling block. Tom questioned just how well we Christians really understand the concept, and how important it is, especially in the context of Muslim evangelism:

> I don't want to minimize the importance of the Father and Son rela-tionship—"God so loved the world that He gave His only Son." But I'm not so convinced that we really understand the Godhead. I think it would be presumptuous for us to pretend that we do. I believe that the term 'Father' and the term 'son' enable us to under-stand more of the Godhead than we could understand without that, because it gives us something from our human relationships to relate to. But I don't pretend that it really helps me understand the fullness of God (T. Brewster 1983:148).

Certainly salvation is only through Christ. "But," he asked, "how much of our Christian doctrine do Muslims have to know to become a Christian? And to what extent does their perception or understanding of the Christian fundamentals have to be identical to our own?" Following Chuck Kraft (1979a) and others, Tom wanted missionaries to explore how supracultural truths (i.e., those absolutes in the mind and heart of God) were understood and could be expressed more meaningfully in cultural (i.e., non-abso-lute) forms.

Tom was convinced that, for many Muslims, their God was the same as our God. He called Muslims the "Corneliuses"—the God-fearers. Tom wanted to approach them in a manner that said, "Yes, you do already know God—you just need to know more about Him."

He knew that while Muslims believe that Jesus was a great prophet, they react strongly against the idea that Jesus is the "Son of God." Tom of course believed that Jesus was and is the Son of God. But in what sense? What does it really mean to say that Jesus is the "Son of God?" As Chuck Kraft had written, "to the

Hebrews, a firstborn son is at least as important as the father in the household. When Jesus called himself Son of God, his original hearers understood him to be claiming equality with, not subservience to, God (1979:304). But to a Muslim, it could be understood as being different from and separate from God. "God the Father, God the Son, and God the Holy Spirit" can mean, to a Muslim, three different gods. And, since even Christians cannot truthfully say that they understand precisely what the phrase means, how necessary is it for Muslims to acknowledge or believe it before salvation?

> I don't know if it's absolutely essential that people have to believe that Jesus is the Son of God in order to be won into the Kingdom of God. It's very interesting that Jesus passed up all those opportunities to say that He was the Son of God. Instead, He said that He was the Son of *Man*. Why didn't He say He was the Son of God? It wasn't until 300 years later when they were trying to work out the creeds that they were struggling with this issue of how much He was God and how much He was man. Do we really understand? We use the term "Son of God," but does this really help us understand the nature of God? (T. Brewster 1983:143).

Tom felt that to insist on an understanding by Muslims of terminology like "Son of God" and some other elements of Christian jargon as a prior condition to salvation created a stumbling block. Rather, it might be more productive in witness to Muslims to find other points of agreement and other bridges to their hearts.

Tom was concerned about the lack of fruitfulness in missions to Muslims. Not that success should be measured in numbers, but it troubled him that much of the problem might have been that traditional missions have often taken such a confrontational approach to Muslims, failing to respect them and their faith, failing to look for the "bridges of God" and "redemptive analogies" which might touch the heart of Muslims. He was convinced that the single greatest failure of typical missions to Muslims was a failure to truly listen. "We can look back at decades of ministry among Muslim people today," he said, "and many ministries will go back 100 years—and have very little fruit to show for it. Have we listened to what we are saying and how it is being understood? Have we stopped talking long enough to notice what God may be doing in and through their lives, and how we might further it along? Have we really listened to what they are saying and respected it" (1983:144)?

An effective ministry to Muslims, Tom felt, would be a ministry which respected the Islamic faith and culture, and one which preserved much of the outward forms of Islamic religious and cultural practice to express the Gospel. He realized that, while there are very important differences between Christianity and Islam, still a good deal of Islamic teaching agrees with Christian teaching. Clearly there are crucial differences, but still there are bridges within Islamic teaching on which a Christian can build.

Tom argued that traditional Christians might not recognize God's salvation in the lives of some Muslims unless they stepped out of their strictly western understandings of how God works:

> I can't help but wonder if the Great Commission might be fulfilled in the Islamic world and western Christians not even know about it, because I believe they would still pray five times a day. I don't see any reason why the places where they worship couldn't become places where Christ is worshipped (T. Brewster 1983:155).

... And to Hindus

Tom was equally open to learning about other religions and looking for bridges that might provide openings for effective witness in their cultures as well. While in Mombasa in January of 1985, Tom and Betty had an opportunity to visit the home of a Gujarati language helper. Paul and Alice Ryan, who had been in a language learning course with Tom and Betty at Fuller and were now learning the Gujarati language, invited them to meet with Mr. Mehta.

Mr. Mehta and his wife warmly welcomed them into their home. He had heard that Betty was good at phonetics so one of the first things he wanted to do was to read her some Gujurati and have her write it down phonetically and read it back to him. It was a tongue twister poem about the sounds of animals at dawn. They had a lot of fun with it.

Mrs. Mehta served them a rice dish with spices and parsley, jelly sandwiches, chutney sandwiches and sweet pound-cake bread, plus spiced sweet Indian tea, with oranges for desert. As they were eating, Tom noticed a painting of a deity on the wall and asked about it. Mr. Mehta, a Brahmin, explained: "We believe that God is one—the Supreme Being. But he has three manifestations, and then there are nine representations of his power. We do not worship these paintings or these representations—they just help us think of God. The Muslims here laugh at us and say we are idol worshippers and have many gods—but actually we only worship one god."

Tom felt that this was perhaps a Brahmin viewpoint, but probably not the understanding of the average person in India. Nevertheless, it was the first time they had ever heard anything approaching monotheism in Hinduism, and wondered if there may not be some significant bridges here that could be used to lead to a true knowledge of God.

19
A GIVING LIFESTYLE

I think it shows how deeply bonded we were to Tom. It was not only the excellent material that he so capably prepared, but it was also his sacrificial concentration on serving others in spite of his physical limitations (Stevens 1987).

One of the things that stands out vividly in most people's recollections about Tom was his giving lifestyle. The fact is, Tom was incredibly generous and caring when it came to the needs of others.

Giving of Finances

Tom's generosity was not something that developed late in life. It was something that characterized even his early years. His sister Martha notes that even during his distress after his divorce, he still thought of others when it came to money matters. When he and Martha got their income tax returns, they pooled their money and "had a great time deciding who to give it to." They decided on the Peterson family, who had taken Tom in and given him comfort from time to time during his distress. Fern Peterson writes,

> In 1965, we were transferred to Michigan. Martha was helping Tom during a very troubled time in his life. [Tom and Martha] came to see us several times, and I do think Tom found our home to be a haven during his anguish. Our income was minimal, and with five children to feed, the dentist bill was often hard to handle. I'm not sure how Tom found out about this need, but he did on one occasion—and he paid it in full (1986)!

Learning to Give

It is also true that God provided some special learning opportunities in finances early on in their marriage. Tom and Betty Sue tried their hand at various investments. While in Mexico, Tom had most of their savings invested there. Just when it was about to mature, the peso was devalued by 300 percent or more and they lost much of the investment. In the mid-1970s, Tom followed me in investing a fair chunk of his savings in a "sure thing" oil field investment in West Texas. That "sure thing" turned out to be a bust, and in spite of the efforts of the Christians who coordinated the investments, we both lost virtually everything we had put up.

As noted earlier, Tom and Betty finally decided that God must be trying to tell them something. Storing up of treasures here on earth was not paying off, so perhaps they should be storing up treasures in heaven. From that time on, Tom and Betty Sue covenanted to give away anything they did not need for their modest lifestyle. Tom explained that "The Lord has given us a real sense of freedom from the bondage of possessions, and we realize that our belonging is with people and not with things" (T. Brewster 1983:17).

Tom loved to give to his family. He fed and housed me for nearly six months in Mexico when I was trying to get my life sorted out after giving my heart to Christ. He paid for my tuition and expenses when I studied at the Summer Institute of Linguistics, and later on used his influence to enable me to use that training by becoming a teacher at the Toronto Institute of Linguistics. On many other occasions, Tom paid the bill for training or some other opportunity that he felt might be useful in my development or spiritual walk, such as paying for Alice and me to go to Basic Youth Conflicts early in our marriage, since he felt that was so important an input for newlyweds.

In general, however, Tom was not much interested in giving Christmas or birthday gifts. He hated shopping, and he felt that the Christmas scene was far too materialistic. Instead, he and Betty often gave what they called the "Gift of Giving." They gave checks to their relatives as Christmas presents with the instructions that they were to fill them out to give to the ministry of their choice. Tom's grandmother was especially pleased with one such gift. She had been wanting to give something to a particular ministry and had not had anything to give. This met her need precisely.

But their generosity was not limited to members of his and Betty's families. They both loved to give anonymous gifts to people. They gave numerous partial scholarships to Fuller Seminary students. And they were generous in their giving to small, obscure missions and those whose ministry was especially caring or on the cutting edge of frontier missions.

Waldron Scott was one recipient when he founded a new ministry himself. He wrote, "A couple of years ago, when I resigned the presidency of American Leprosy Missions to begin a new ministry, Tom and Betty Sue were among the first half dozen friends to pledge regular monthly support" (Scott 1986).

Tom and Betty gave a generous gift to YWAM in Australia for a building acquisition. Tom Hallas of YWAM in Australia remarked:

> Tom was a man who was trusting God to get him through life and who gave so much everywhere and who no doubt had an awareness of the pressing needs of people throughout the globe—he also ministered affirmation to us demonstrating confidence in our ministry by sending a large gift to help us in the initial payment of our training facility. He was a giving friend all the way (Hallas 1993).

Tom's generosity extended to fellow faculty members as well. Dean Gilliland relates an experience that changed his relationship with Tom:

> Increasingly Tom was saying, "What can I do for you?" One day I said I needed $2000 because my kids were stuck in West Africa. I would never have told that to anybody if he hadn't asked. And Tom said, "I have $2000." That was the biggest joy Tom had to write that check out and give it to a friend. [What amazed me was] the openness with which Tom gave . . . I have never borrowed money from friends or enemies. But [Tom] made it impossible to refuse. . . . That was the other side of Tom and that changed our relationship. [He made it possible for me] to say, "sure you can help me," and I just didn't feel that way with very many people (1987).

Giving became second nature to Tom and Betty Sue. In fact, it was so predictable that when they were invited to participate in a "newly-wed game" in Malawi in February of 1981, they were each asked independently what they would do if they were given $1,000.

Both of them responded, independently and without hesitation, that they would give it away.

John Perkins, founder of Mendenhall Ministries in Mississippi and who later began a very significant "3Rs" (Reconciliation, Restoration, Relocation) ministry in the high crime area of northwest Pasadena, wrote of Tom's ministry to him and his son Derrick:

> I met Tom Brewster when I first returned to California in 1982. I moved into northwest Pasadena, a highly drug-ridden community, to begin a ministry. Before I had done anything, Tom, Betty Sue, and Jed came to visit me. What a glorious experience it was for me to meet a handicapped person who never looked upon his handicap as a deficiency, but who concerned himself with the needs of others. He lived . . . with a complete concern for the down-trodden, for the poor, and for furthering the Gospel in the world. . . .
>
> Shortly after we moved into northwest Pasadena, my son, Derrick, was going to Azusa Pacific College which is about 12–15 miles from Pasadena. Derrick did not have a car. Derrick and I and Tom's family all attended Sunday school class in a group of about 200 people. . . . Derrick shared in the class about his need for transportation to Azusa. The next week, Tom and Betty Sue were leaving on another of their trips around the world to teach for three months. They let Derrick have their station wagon to drive during those three months. Tom was responding to a young man whom he barely knew, but he recognized the fact that this young man was committed to Jesus Christ and the furthering of the Gospel. Tom wanted to be involved in that ministry. That was Tom and Betty Sue's life. . . . (Perkins 1986).

Tom and Betty also used their giving as a means to combat Satan's activities. In a remarkably generous gesture, they matched Mona and Jerry's giving to thwart what Satan was apparently doing in their lives. He wrote to me about it in October of 1982:

> We have been blessed by Ramona and Jerry's response to the trials that they have been going through to regain the custody of the children. If Texas would only recognize the judgments of the California courts then the children would be Ramona's and the case would be settled. That not being the case, they have had to reinitiate proceedings in Texas courts. . . . We were blessed when we learned that

they matched the five thousand dollars they had to deposit with a lawyer on the very same day by also giving five thousand dollars to missions. Upon learning that, we decided to join with them and also make five thousand dollars available to a mission project.

We have a suspicion that once Satan understands that at least two dollars (maybe more, if others join us) will go for the Lord's work for every one dollar that must be spent in the custody case, that maybe he will call off his attack (T. Brewster 1982).

Giving of Himself

One contradiction about Tom is the difference in how he related to "authorities," and the way he related to his learners and the missionaries with whom he consulted. Tom was known for his abrasiveness in relating to the "establishment," but that is certainly not how he was viewed by his students and nationals. An overwhelming impression from testimonials of learners and missionaries around the world is of a patient, caring individual who loved to spend time with them and was concerned about details of their personal lives. Aretta Loving, a participant in one of Tom's workshops in New Guinea, says that "Tom's gentleness was always there for the 'underdogs,' but not for the 'topdogs'" (1986).

Tom had a special appreciation for the YWAM missionaries, and it was certainly mutual for most of them. One of them speaks for many:

> The moment I met this couple and their son, I felt they possessed something special. As soon as we started talking, I discovered what it was—they had a genuine compassion for mankind, especially for the poor and needy. Whenever I talked with them, all I could ever think about was "Jesus."
>
> I have lived for many years among different nationalities and languages, and even the missionaries seem to have their time-tables. If anyone shows up outside of their time-table, he simply has to come back another time. With the Brewsters, Christian philosophy goes beyond the time-tables as people are their first priority.
>
> Ever since I met the Brewsters, I have found for myself as well that people have become a priority in my life, and as a result of that experience I now believe I have grown deeper in God's love

> extended to others. . . . One cannot have more love for God unless
> love for people, and vice versa. In the past I often prayed, asking
> God to increase my love for Himself, but through the Brewsters the
> Lord has taught me how I can grow in loving Him. . . .
>
> This appreciation of learning others' culture, language, etc.,
> takes time to develop, time to listen, time to sit and bond. I don't
> mean just head knowledge, but one needs to live among the people
> and make their culture his culture, their language his language,
> etc. Isn't that just what it means when the Bible says, "The Word
> became flesh and dwelt among us"? Or to put it in the Brewsters'
> language, "bonding." The Brewsters have taught me this—not just
> verbally, but by the example of their lives (Zemdekun 1986).

Tom was known for his willingness to take time with nationals
whom he met, especially the poor, during his travels. Wes Collins,
of Wycliffe and a learner in one of Tom and Betty's workshops in
Guatemala, said that "Tom *always* had time for people. He was
well known, but reached out to the world vicariously through those
in his world—his disciples, and Betty Sue and Jed. This has been a
great model for me" (1993).

Tom knew that the people of many cultures are much more
reserved than are Americans, and never will "get to the point" if
we do not have patience enough to first listen and build trust. Tom
explained the intense concern he had for being patient with people
from other cultures by relating an incident in which an African
man came to their door in Africa. He and Betty Sue were in their
room and had laid down to rest that afternoon. The man knocked
at their door, and was invited to come in. He sat down in Tom's
wheelchair beside the bed and they talked for the next two and a
half hours. He wanted to share about his inability to communicate
with the missionaries:

> "Whenever I go to the missionary's house with something I need to
> talk about, he comes to the door and leans against the door post and
> asks me, 'What do you want?' But we can never talk about what we
> want, standing there like that.'" When he told us this, Betty Sue
> and I were resting and we've always been thankful that we didn't
> say, "We're resting; what do you want?" or "Why not come back
> another time?"

After about two and a half hours, it became apparent why he came. He reached into his coat pocket and pulled out a newspaper-wrapped package and gave it to me. In it was a lovely Katanga-print shirt that he had brought for me. I wonder how many gifts have never been given (T. Brewster 1983:31, 32).

"Some things just can't be done leaning against the door post," Tom said. " If we don't take the time to gain an insider's perspective, we may be very busily doing the Lord's work but not making sense, or being Good News to people."

Lots of Time for Learners

Tom and Betty Sue made a habit of spending a lot of time with their students. They hardly ever taught a course without inviting all of the students into their home in small groups. Usually everybody would be invited over within the first week in order for Tom and Betty Sue to get to know them and for the students to get to know one another.

One very important ingredient to the loyalty and affection Tom received was his attention to learning their names. It was an idea he got from TIL. The first time he and Betty arrived at TIL, they were handed a fat book of pictures and told to learn the names before the people came. It was called the "Rogue's Gallery." Tom realized how important it was and he practiced memorizing people's names as soon as they met.

Spending time with them, listening, praying, learning about their spiritual pilgrimage, and getting to know them as individuals, was central to Tom's style. Frequently, even in class, Tom would ask for prayer requests and pray specifically for people's needs. Just as frequent were prayer times with students during the breaks and before and after class.

One of Tom's students wrote:

My foremost impression of Tom's class was "honoring God." We were there to honor and glorify God. We were learning to learn a language for the purpose of honoring and glorifying God. We began each session with a chorus, *"My total reason for being here is to glorify God by my life; to grow to be more like Him and to see Him pro-*

duce remaining fruit." I didn't know Tom or Betty Sue well, but that chorus sums up my impression of his and their ministry. . . . No other class that I have ever taken was as honoring to God and as centered on Him as the two-week class that I had with Tom and Betty Sue (Severns 1986).

Tom's colleague at Fuller, Dean Gilliland agreed:

There's no question that Tom had a real identification with the poor and vulnerable. He had an overriding concern—a passion—for the spiritual and physical condition of the poor and the unreached peoples. This passionate caring also extended to people in his classes. And the people in his classes sensed that he cared and returned his caring with an intense loyalty. His students would feel that they had a cause. There was massive approval on the part of the students for what Tom and Betty Sue were doing. . . .

Tom got such a loyalty from his students. . . . They felt like they had a cause. I didn't feel like I had a cause. [There was] massive approval of what Tom and Betty Sue were doing. I'm speaking of bonding. I'm speaking of the way in which they developed a relationship with their students. Sitting on big pillows. Taking off your shoes. I had no opportunity to do this, but I admired it so much. I used to think how good it would be to have students who would think so well of me and support me wherever they go. I didn't have that kind of loyalty in those days (1987).

Tom was not above teasing students, which sometimes would put them on guard but eventually disarmed them. Once while teaching a group of students to hear and mimic tones in a phonetics class, one young lady had a particularly difficult time. She was nervous and frustrated about not being able to hear the tones.

Tom decided to form a quartet of others, including himself, who could not get the tones very well, and sing some of the lessons. He called on those who were having problems and had them sing with him in front of the class. By using the humor, they were able to take themselves less seriously and learn more effectively. Neither Tom nor the other "quartet" members ever mastered tones completely but with Tom's sense of humor and joking to the point where it was totally ridiculous, it broke everybody's tension and they were able to move on.

Tom's passion for meeting learners needs extended even to many not in his classes. Clyde Cook, President of Biola University, was impressed with Tom's graciousness in working with his own daughter:

> What stands out most in my mind was the telephone call I made to Tom, along with my daughter, to get some help that she was need-ing on her Master's thesis. She was doing an M.A. in Education at Biola, and her thesis project was on bilingual education. I thought Tom might be of some help with a particular question with which she was struggling, so I called and we had a good chat. Then the next day he called back after having spent some of his very valuable time doing research, and helped us with a key concept that was crucial to the paper.
>
> We really did not know Tom that well, and yet he took the time to help us—and in such a beautiful and thoughtful way (Cook 1986).

Giving of Himself, to Mona . . .

Tom cared for a lot of people, but he poured himself into three people who needed him. Our sister Martha remembers that he tried to be present any time any of the family members had an "event" in their lives. In particular, Tom gave of himself to his younger sister, his son, and his wife. Mona always remembers Tom's influence on her life with passion and eloquence:

> The significant thing about Tom, the thing that set him apart from any person I had ever known, was his incredible ability to bear someone else's burdens as though they were his own. Tom's taking my burdens on his shoulders was the thing that brought me back to the Lord. Tom was my example of who God really was—uncondi-tional forgiveness, unconditional love. I truly felt that I had been a "prodigal son," but I returned from the pig sty into Tom's waiting arms with never a blink in his eye—to a celebration instead.
>
> In Galatians, Paul says that we are to "bear one another's bur-dens," but very few people know what that means. Few people have the ability to enter into a person's sufferings. Tom had that ability. An example is the first time that I had to [give up the children]. It was the most painful experience I ever had in my life. I came home

from the attorney's office crying and on the verge of hysteria. I called Tom, and all I could say again and again was that it was over. As I wept uncontrollably, I could hear that Tom was sobbing on the other end of the phone. And all he could say as he was crying and sobbing was, "Oh, Mona; my poor, poor Mona." That was all he could say. The fact that he cried was as much comfort as any person could have given me at that point. He walked in my shoes. He wept with me. He carried my burdens. It was his "incarnational ministry" that he was called to do (Tuma 1994).

As a result of Tom's ministry in Mona's life, she developed a very significant ministry of intercession and, as we have seen, often had a supernatural intuition (Spirit given) for his needs and suffering. She wrote of Tom's influence in her ministry of intercession:

The life of an intercessor is not just to be able to pray, but to identify with the suffering of another person. Jesus was our chief identifier. For humanity, the authority and power to intercede comes with the willingness to identify with and lay down your life for another person. Tom spent his whole life identifying with me. Through his life, he taught me the principles of identification. I saw it in everyone he dealt with, but especially in the way he dealt with me. Anybody could sit down and talk with Tom and he would really listen—he would do more than listen. He would identify. He would put himself in your shoes and walk around in them. He was my model for identification, and the inspiration for my intercession (Tuma 1994).

. . . and to Jed . . .

Tom also had a very special relationship with his son Jed. Tom was a very proud father, and he delighted in carrying him on his lap, showing him off to everyone from the moment he was born. As a baby, Jed seemed to have a special understanding that he needed to sit still on Tom's lap or he might fall off, so he never had any problem riding along. In fact, Betty sometimes gave him over to Tom if he was restless on her own lap. As soon as Jed was able to stand, he would crawl up and stand on Tom's foot pedals, and was always comfortable riding around.

Tom loved reading to Jed, and Jed learned to love books. Once before Jed could read, they were walking past a garage sale, and Jed picked up a book. Tom bought it for him for a nickel, and Jed would sit for long periods at a time leafing through it. He must have figured that Mom and Dad did it so he ought to do it too. Not surprisingly, Jed learned to read at an early age. Just after Jed's sixth birthday, Tom wrote about Jed's reading:

> Jed continues to enjoy reading. This week he read *The Lion, the Witch, and the Wardrobe* by C. S. Lewis, and also the *Wizard of OZ* and *Alice in Wonderland*. It is a challenge to keep him in worthwhile books. Part of the dilemma is that although his skill level is quite high, (maybe close to Jr. Hi level), his interest level is only slightly beyond his age level, and we don't want him reading much small print yet until his eyes mature more (1985).

Jed had his first trip out of the country to Guatemala when he was only four weeks old. A very young Jed was a regular at SWM faculty meetings, as well as in Tom and Betty's classes. Tom was strict in his discipline, and Jed learned to occupy himself quietly from a very young age. Betty made him a bag with books, drawing paper, colored pencils, clay and a few toys which kept him quite happy for long periods of time. Occasionally he was called on to serve as an "expert consultant" in language learning activities for the adult learners! Tom wrote to his friend Johan Louw in South Africa about Jed's helpfulness in understanding language learning processes:

> Jed has now past two and a half years (when asked his age, he responds, "Two old"—sometimes we all feel too old!). He continues to be his joyful, loving self. Of course Mommy and Daddy are fascinated by the continual opportunity he gives for us to make observations and hypotheses about the language learning processes (1982b).

One Sunday, when Jed was a three year old, he was playing with some friends and learned that the name Isaac meant "laughter." That struck a chord in Jed and he reported it to Tom and Betty. He said he would like that to be part of his own name. Tom and Betty did not think much about it except that Jed kept bringing it up. It appeared that he was serious about it. Finally Tom asked him if he knew that it cost money and meant going before a judge. Jed did not know that, but was willing to do it any way. Tom said he could if he would save up some money. Tom began giving him $1.00 per week as an allowance, and Jed really did save it up for over a year. So Tom took him to the courthouse in Pasadena.

"Whose idea is this, anyway," the judge asked Tom and Jed.

"It's mine!" Jed assured him.

"Your name is already Thomas Jedidiah Clark Brewster," the judge said. "Do you really want all those initials?"

Jed was confident that he could handle them all, so the judge allowed him to pay his money, and he became officially Thomas Jedidiah *Isaac* Clark Brewster.

(A year or so later, when Jed was with Tom and Betty at Warmbath, in South Africa, an African man noted Jed's sunny disposition, and, following a common African practice, gave Jed the name "Ditshego" which meant "laughing" in his language. The African man did not know that "Isaac" was already part of Jed's name.)

One of Tom's favorite activities with Jed was to go for walks with Jed on his lap. They would stop and Tom would read to him from the Bible, and then they would discuss it and pray together. After Tom's death, Betty said that this was the one thing that Jed consistently mentioned that he missed.

. . . and to Betty Sue

Tom was in love with Betty Sue. And, in spite of being in the wheelchair, he was a hopeless romantic. Tom loved candlelight dinners, buying flowers, and doing other things to let Betty Sue know how much he cared for her. They shared a lovely tradition of celebrating their wedding anniversary every *month*. They called it their "monthiversary," or their "luniversary." In nearly nineteen years of marriage, he never missed the 14th of a month without some kind of celebration, usually fairly small, but sometimes elaborate. In the off months, he would do a poem, love letter, corsage, or a dinner. On their twentieth "luniversary" Tom bought her a corsage and they went out to dinner together. They mentioned to a lady that it was their "20th." "Oh my," she exclaimed to Betty, "You look terribly young to be celebrating your 20th already!"

Betty did a "valentine" to Tom on their 25th wedding anniversary, six years after his death:

> Remember our 50th luniversary? We had an open house in Guadalajara and all our friends (Mexican and American) came to help us celebrate.
>
> Remember our 100th? We were at TIL in Canada and it came, mercifully, on a Saturday so we had time to be together. We went to that restaurant on the 2nd floor of the Pavilion—a fancy, and rather expensive place—and we shared a Caesar salad. It was delicious but even better was our shared joy in celebrating together.
>
> How you delighted in telling me on the 14th of *every* month how many months we had been married and how much you loved me. A wife with that kind of romantic lover-husband couldn't help but be happy and remain very much in love. We've probably share more "anniversary" celebrations in 19 years than most people do who live together to be octogenarians and nonagenarians. Who else do you know who has celebrated 100+? (smile) (1992).

Often Tom made the real anniversaries (on Valentine's Day) even more special. They were new in Pasadena when they celebrated their tenth, and had not yet developed deep roots. Betty wanted to wear her wedding gown and have an open house, but she could not imagine any of their still casual acquaintances actually taking the time to help them celebrate. There was one group though with whom they had already bonded—their students! They decided, "Let's celebrate with them!" The evening before the anniversary they arranged for a potluck right in the classroom at the end of a shortened class. Everyone brought food—even the guys made something. Some students brought their spouses for the celebration.

Then they said their wedding vows with the only ordained minister in the class, Sean Cronin, a Roman Catholic priest "officiating." The next day Betty put on her wedding gown and

Tom dressed up his best suit and they went over to the fine, historic Huntington Hotel, feeling very elegant. To their surprise, the door was inaccessible to Tom's wheelchair. "Remember how we had to go through the kitchen! The kitchen crew all smiled and congratulated us (they thought it was our wedding night!), and we entered the restaurant with the waiters. We chuckled about our 'grand kitchen entrance' for a long time after that" (1992).

> In so many ways you let me know you loved me and were proud of me and enjoyed being with me. What more could a wife ask for? I remember lots of times during those years walking through the halls by myself at Fuller and suddenly realizing I was smiling—just thinking of you, remembering something you had said, a gesture, a smile, a wink.
>
> Yes, those winks! You had my number there (smile). I loved your wink. Maybe that's even one of the things that initially made me fall in love with you (E. Brewster 1992).

Nico Smith, on whom Tom had made such an impression in relating to blacks in apartheid South Africa, also noticed and was moved by Tom's devotion to Betty, and her magnificent response:

> His relationship with his wife and child was so beautiful, and an example of what a family relationship can be. I believe that he influenced many others in their own family relationships. He and Betty Sue's relationship was something so unique. His dependency on Betty Sue's assistance was never a burden to Betty Sue; she assisted Tom in a way as if he was part of her own body. I can never really grasp how Tom and Betty Sue could travel across the world as if there was no burden attached to it. Betty Sue really was a gift from God to Tom. His life would certainly have been much different without her (Smith 1993).

20
IN FAITH LIETH ACCEPTANCE

Pain and suffering are inevitable, but misery is optional (Tim Hansel 1985).

God the miner doesn't waste His time with just any ole' dirt, so there must be some gold in there. So I can't ask God to take away the fire, but to pour it on until I am refined like gold (T. Brewster 1982c).

There's no doubt that God gives special grace to people who, like Tom, suffer severe handicaps or disabilities. Some seem to "waste that grace." But that was never the case for Tom. From the earliest moments after the accident, Tom never doubted or questioned God's will in confining him to a wheelchair, needing special help for most everything he did for the rest of his life. Instead, Tom always *thanked* God for his accident, and was always grateful for the change that it brought into his life. Remarkably, Tom said that the second biggest blessing in his life was the injury and the paralysis over the last years of his life (second after coming to know Christ and pursuing the ministry that God had given them).

Tom recognized that his attitude was unusual.

> I think that sometimes when things happen to us that are out of our control, our attitude is one of bitterness or anger against God. I'm thankful that He spared me from all of that. . . . I realized through this injury that God is the life-giver, and that He chose to give my life back to me a second time. And so my attitude has not been one of questioning God as to why it happened, but rather one of asking why He gave me my life back again. What purpose does He have in my life? What is His plan for my life? I wouldn't have asked these questions were it not for the injury. It has given me an entirely different kind of availability to the Lord than I ever would have had (T. Brewster 1983:14, 15).

Tom did not believe that God caused his accident. He knew that his own foolishness did. Yet he fully believed that God used the accident for much good in his life. A favorite passage of Tom's—one that he lived out each day of his life—was from I Peter:

> In this you greatly rejoice, though now for a little while you may have had to suffer grief in all kinds of trials. These have come so that your faith—of greater worth than gold, which perishes even though refined by fire—may be proved genuine and may result in praise, glory and honor when Jesus Christ is revealed (I Peter 1:6, 7 NIV).

Tom had faith that God could heal him, but he also had faith that God could use him and would have a purpose for him even if He did not heal him. Once a stranger accusingly said to Tom, "If you had faith, you'd be out of that chair." Betty Sue thought, "Tom is a lot more whole and healed on the inside than you could possibly imagine."

Tom often told people that he was not *confined* to a wheelchair, he was *released* by it. It was a tool that he could use. It was an opportunity for him to be vulnerable, to share with others, and to build the kind of relationships that were so important to him.

Tom's Sense of Humor

Obviously, one of the other tools that is so important to handicapped people, or any of us for that matter, in learning to cope, is a sense of humor. Tom's was certainly very well developed. Tom was always joking with people and "pulling their leg." His was a dry sense of humor, which some misinterpreted. He could string people along to an almost embarrassing extent before they realized the ridiculousness of what he was doing and what he was saying.

Tom liked to play on people's sympathies for him and would often good-naturedly "wring" special favors out of officials at games, museums, parks and the like. I remember when the bewildered usher in Yankee stadium let us in through a special gate because of his wheelchair, and because of the odd but important sounding announcement, "My name is Tom. I've got bones in my leg." That puzzled usher at the baseball game in New York was typical of many confused officials who knew they should help, but went beyond the call of duty because of Tom's unselfconscious boldness and sense of humor.

Much of his sense of humor was directed at himself, and he was always able to laugh at his own trials.

Many of those trials revolved around his own limitations and the misfortunes that had befallen him. One time in Mexico before Tom got his electric wheelchair, we were pushing him along a bumpy road toward the fishing hole, with his paralyzed buddy, Buzz. Somehow or other we got going too fast and Tom just bounced out of his chair and landed flat on the ground. A peasant man happened to be walking by and looked at Tom as we were trying to gather him up, and said in Spanish, "Do you always get out of your chair that way?" Tom chuckled about that for years.

Tom's sense of humor helped molehills remain molehills, and made even mountains more manageable. One of the most embarrassing experiences was when they were at the home of Earl Stevik, head of the Foreign Service Institute. They had called on him in Washington, DC to talk about the use of the FSI materials for language institutes that they at that time thought they would be establishing.. When they arrived, they parked at the top of his very steep driveway. Stevik offered to help Tom into the chair, but Betty Sue said, "No, I've done it lots of times." Somehow, though, just as Betty Sue was swinging Tom into the chair, the brakes of the wheelchair let go; the chair went rolling down the driveway, and Tom landed on his backside on the ground. Of course Betty Sue had to ask for Stevik's help to get Tom back into the chair. But they all were able to laugh about this undignified introduction.

Tom's sense of humor and "can do" attitude made most barriers manageable. During his years at TIL, they always took their meals in the dining room with six or eight stairs at the entrance. Thus, three times a day, Tom had to be carried up, wheelchair and all, in order to get to the tables, and then carried back down the steps in order to get back to classes. Tom had a loyal following of students whom he called his "pall bearers" who were always ready to help him out.

His external plumbing occasionally caused embarrassment for Tom, but an embarrassment with which he was always able to deal. As is the case with most quadriplegics, he had a catheter in his lower abdomen, directly into his bladder. The catheter was attached to a rubber bag strapped on his leg. Tom and Betty Sue devised all kinds of discreet ways to "drain the main vein." Airline vomit bags or other makeshift containers worked well for the most part, and they were usually able to "take care of business" without drawing any attention to themselves.

Occasionally, however, the clamps or connections would not work quite right. Tom and I laughed a lot about the time he had a slight leak at the upper connection to the bag. As Tom rested his hands on his lap, his fingers got a bit sticky and Tom, thinking it was something left over from lunch, licked it off. This happened two or three times before Tom realized it was not part of his lunch he was licking off his fingers!

Sense of Dignity

It was frustrating to Tom that everything he did took extra time—getting up, getting dressed, going to classes, getting into the car. For a man in a hurry, this was a constant irritation. Another frustration was the fact that he could help Betty very little with all the extra equipment and supplies he had to take with him everywhere he traveled—plus looking after Jed and his belongings! He would often carry Jed on his lap, and a bag if it could fit, when they were trying to make connections, but otherwise Betty Sue had to do the lifting and carrying. Tom did what he could to lighten her load, frequently recruiting others to help her carry suitcases, and doing the other little things that would ease Betty Sue's load, like lifting the chair, and helping around the house.

While Tom was able to laugh at himself, he would get thoroughly upset when he was treated as less than a person. What really infuriated Tom was being treated as a helpless person—or worse yet, like a patient or even an imbecile.

In his life, Tom made hundreds—perhaps thousands—of airplane flights, and only twice, both in the US, did airlines refuse to board him. In one instance, airline personnel said it was "against the union rules" for them to lift a passenger. On that occasion, an employee of another airline walked by just as they had been refused boarding and said, "My union allows me to lift you." So he boarded them onto another airline's plane.

(After that, Betty Sue went back to the Craig Rehabilitation Center in Denver with Tom and asked what she could do in such situations. They showed her how to do a "standing transfer" where she would stand in front of Tom in his chair, push her knees up against his and then stand up and squat back as fast as she could. At the same time, Tom would lean forward and get his backside up high enough that she could swing him over into an airline seat. She only had to do it a few times, and she never "dumped" him. Most of the time, of course, people were almost too eager to help. Sometimes they would grab him before anyone had a chance to tell them how to hold him, occasionally doing more harm than good.)

In one European airport, Tom had to wait for an ambulance to get him and take him off the plane. The paramedic staff checked "the patient" over, patted him on his knee, and pronounced him fit to enter the country! Another time in London he was taken to an infirmary and forced to lie down during the time between flights. I was not there, but I doubt if he took it "lying down!"

Being treated as a person with no intelligence was even worse for Tom. Occasionally they would go into a restaurant and the waitress would say to Betty Sue, "What does he want?" Tom often replied, also in the third person, "He's of age; ask him!" Others sometimes treated Tom as though his brain was paralyzed, rather than his legs. Occasionally they would go into restaurants and the hosts or hostesses would say that wheelchairs could not sit in certain sections—fire rules or a hindrance to other people, sometimes very legitimately, of course. But Tom knew when they simply planned to find him a corner table back in the dark, dim recesses just because they did not want other people to have to look at a man in a wheelchair while they were eating.

Tom recognized the legitimate concerns that people might have for safety in public places, but had no patience for unnecessary or insensitive rules. Often his wheelchair was not allowed to sit in church aisles, so he had to be transferred to the hard pews. Or, they would put him up in front behind the piano or way back in the back, behind a pillar. Needless to say, Tom and Betty did not go back to those kinds of churches very often.

Perseverance

It is clear that Tom's travels took amazing courage and endurance. Tom always tried to defuse the curiosity and concern that others would have about his physical condition, his use of the wheelchair, and his abilities or lack of ability to do the normal things that people do. But there's no question that his quadriplegia affected every aspect of how he lived. You do not go through life not being able to move more than a few muscles without it affecting everything you do. But it was also true that Tom pushed himself very hard. It was obvious to anyone who watched him:

> I've had the privilege of associating with many outstanding Christian servants over the years, but Tom was unique. I think two things stand out to me, reflecting back on Tom's life. I've never been around anyone who worked so hard! He and Betty Sue were incredible in Cali, Colombia. From early in the morning to late at night, Tom was focused on helping people do better. They were tireless. His handicap just made it all the more amazing. Secondly, Tom had a genuine focus on the glory of God. Daily we would sing one of his favorite choruses about the glory of God. It was contagious, as was his hard work (Cirafesi 1993).

Betty gave me a list of travel supplies required for one twenty-four week trip. It included the following: eight leg bags, sixteen night bags, twelve tubes, four catheters, a hot water bottle, a heating pad, battery charger, folding shower chair, screwdriver, Allen wrenches, chair narrowing strap, an extra cushion and cover, sliding board, and rubber stoppers. In addition to the clothing, they regularly carried a camera and batteries, flash, film and mailers, a clock, flashlight, bungee straps, a transformer and adapter, a tape recorder and microphone, blank tapes, jacks, extension cord, portable chess and backgammon games, small hairdryer, needle and thread, pins, candles, matches, incense, zip lock bags, stationery and envelopes, as well as scotch tape, glue, a stapler, calculator, writing paper, overhead pens, transparencies, and a variety of other items.

Needless to say, their travel clothing was kept to a minimum. The list of clothes for Tom included one suit, two slacks, five shirts, a Safari suit, a couple of ties, some socks, a sweater, vest, three T-shirts, four under shorts, a hat, and a wind breaker. Remarkably, most of these items, plus the above supplies, they were able to stuff into two large suitcases and a couple of carry-on bags. And much of this travel was done while their son Jed was very small, needing his own supplies, and needing to be carried himself!

Randy McGirr, one of the early Campus Crusade for Christ language learners, and later a successful missionary in Austria, wrote me a rather lengthy letter that expresses well the impact of Tom's and Betty's stamina and commitment to helping people:

> In the fall of 1981 I wrote to Tom and Betty Sue Brewster, asking if they would be in Europe anytime in the near future. I wanted to confer with them about the results of a research project I had recently completed. They wrote back and said they were flying to India in a few weeks and they had a layover in Amsterdam for part of a day. They said I could meet them there.
>
> A few weeks later I was seated in a train somewhere between Vienna and Amsterdam. It was the 29th of December. A glance out the window revealed a gray, winter day. I was not enjoying myself. I've never liked to travel. I dislike the shambles it makes of regular hours. Then there's the noise, hassle with baggage, misconnections, and lost sleep. In my estimation, it all adds up to hard work and frustration.
>
> As I sat there feeling sorry for myself, my mind drifted to the Brewsters. As I thought about them, my complaints about traveling began to appear ludicrous. The amount of traveling I have ever done is minimal compared to the "globetrotting" of Tom and Betty Sue Brewster. And I'm a healthy, athletic man in the prime of life, unburdened by the metal cage of a wheelchair. Next to Tom I probably look like a body builder, but when it came to traveling Tom was a man of steel. Not me.

The more I thought about the way they travel, the more it bordered on a miracle. How could a woman like Betty Sue, barely five feet tall, plunge into the fray of international travel—including forays into the difficult third world areas—with a toddler son and a husband tied to a wheelchair. As the additional thought struck me that they usually travel alone, I could only shake my hand.

After arriving in Amsterdam I headed for their hotel. They were asleep when I called their room. They were trying to shake off the jet lag. I said I'd be glad to wait, but Betty Sue invited me up. She said, "We've only got a few hours so let's hit it." We talked for two straight hours. Tom lay in bed the whole time, but that didn't keep him from staying in the middle of the discussion. Jed was sleeping on a comforter on the floor. When our stomachs told us that it was time to get something to eat, I went down to the hotel restaurant to wait for them. It took Betty Sue a good 45 minutes to get her two men ready to move out.

While I was waiting I thought to myself: "How does that small, delicate woman manage to do that day in and day out? It would be difficult enough at home in a controlled situation, but she was doing it in hotels, airplanes, dormitories, conference centers, schools, and even at camps."

Those few hours in Holland were memorable, as was every meeting with the Brewsters. Memorable because of their creativity, their relaxed ability to listen, their maturity, their depth of experience, and their commitment to one another. But also memorable simply because of their tremendous physical performance. Betty Sue is a tiny woman, and Tom was paralyzed—but as far as I'm concerned, their courage and energy easily overshadowed the feats of endowed athletes. . . .

Tom was a man who did not have the strength to pick up his own little son, but with his wife and his faith he had no trouble pushing aside a few mountains in his lifetime. That's the Tom Brewster I knew, and that's the way I'll always remember him (McGirr 1986).

"My Power Is Made Perfect in Weakness"

By necessity, Tom was vulnerable. But he did not view that as something to be ashamed or rid of. Surely one reason why Tom was able to cope as well as he did is that he believed, like the Apostle Paul, that God's power was made perfect in weakness (II Corinthians 12:9 NIV). Tom was always willing to accept his handicap and put others at ease by talking freely about it. He was also willing to accept help. He learned from a blind man who said, "I usually accept help, even if I can go up the stairs on my own. Otherwise, some day I may be in need and want the help, but people will be embarrassed to offer it to me."

Certainly Tom recognized that even he had a normal reluctance to be vulnerable and dependent on others, but he recognized too the fact that we are all vulnerable in one way or another, and can grow if we accept and take advantage of it. Tom viewed vulnerability as a strength. Tom's students and colleagues knew that Tom was willing to be vulnerable. Obviously, he did not have much of a choice, but he did not "waste that grace." One of his students, Adele Fulton, wrote:

> I was always impressed by Tom's commitment to love others, to understand others—regardless of his own physical limitations. He exhibited vulnerability by being in a wheelchair; but more importantly, his character and spirit were teachable and humble. He took advantage of opportunities that presented themselves, and risked a lot to get Christ's message across—regardless of personal discomfort. He crossed language, cultural, and physical barriers that most able-bodied people cannot, or will not, do (Fulton 1993).

Paul Pierson, the Dean of the Fuller School of World Mission for much of the time Tom taught there, talked about Tom's vulnerability, its importance to his ministry and to anyone's ministry:

> Here's a guy who in a sense is totally helpless. He's got to have somebody take care of him day and night. What does that do to you psychologically? It drives you either to bitterness, or it drives you to God. In Tom's case, it did the latter (1987).

In Acceptance (Still) Lieth Peace

Not everyone realizes, as Tom did, that everyone is, in a sense, handicapped. His was only a particular type of handicap, paralysis. Almost everyone has some kind of handicap, many of them much more debilitating than Tom's—because people allow it to be. Betty Sue put it this way, "Angels may look at us and say, 'Poor thing, he would be handsome if he were not lacking in compassion.' Or, 'she would be attractive if she did not have that tumor of bad temper.' 'Too bad her complexion is marred by such immaturity.'"

Perhaps most significant in Tom's ability to make the most of the situation that God had given him was his firmly held, long-standing belief that, "in acceptance *really does* lie peace." For Tom and Betty Sue, acceptance was not a one-time decision, but a daily decision to be content, to rejoice, and to accept from the Father's hands whatever He has to give:

> Acceptance for us, Betty Sue explained, is not the same as fatalism. Fatalism is *"Que será, será*; Whatever will be, will be," and there's nothing we can do about it. Acceptance, however, says, "My heavenly Father can never be unkind. He has a greater purpose for me than I can ever understand." So I will accept this from His hand and rejoice and profit from it (E. Brewster c1987).

Love and joy and contentment are choices. They are acts of the will. They are decisions that people make. Tom realized that one can learn to rejoice, and even find joy in the midst of hardship and handicap. Tom's acceptance of his condition and his confidence that a loving Father could bring good from the circumstance was neither denial (arguing that no problems exist) nor fatalism ("that's life!"). Acceptance, too, is a choice that people make.

Betty Sue—a True Servant

Tom had a remarkable attitude about his injury and resulting physical condition. But one thing that amazed anyone who knew Tom and Betty was the remarkable attitude of Betty Sue no matter what the stress or conditions. Caring for Tom's needs was hard work! He was a perfectionist and could be demanding. And there was just a lot to do. I found that out when I traveled with him as a youngster, when I looked after him one summer at Memphis State, and when I helped out whenever we were together.

Martha also noticed it when she spent several months caring for him. "Sometimes I felt a little negative toward always having to be available to meet his needs. That's why I have always admired Betty Sue so much." That admiration and awe at Betty Sue's faithfulness in meeting Tom's needs with joyfulness and pleasantness was shared by all who knew them. Jonathan McRostie, Minister at Large for Operation Mobilization, who himself used a wheelchair and thus knew of the intensity of the demands, also noticed Betty:

> Tom's being in the wheelchair and facing weakness and illness, yet developing such a strategic and worldwide ministry, challenged me. Since I, too, am in a wheelchair, his example stimulated me even more. Betty Sue's selfless dedication to helping him while teaching also impressed Margit and me. I don't know how she did it. Certainly they both were very creative in living and adapting to their limitations as they did not have a regular helper. They encouraged me at the beginning of my disability (just a year after my accident) to be patient in the adapting process (McRostie 1993).

How did she do it? For one thing, she tried to anticipate his needs so that even if she was busy she could do the things that he needed. It was always obvious that she really did enjoy serving Tom. She had fun doing it. The team work was fun as well as productive. Betty has a unique temperament that enabled her to respond positively to whatever request or demand Tom made of her. She describes the origins of that attractive temperament:

> To a large extent it came naturally. I think because of my upbringing. Go with the flow. Get along with people. I don't remember my mother ever raising her voice. She was very calm. My dad was different. He was more excitable and flappable, but at the same time always easygoing and flexible. Dad occasionally raised his voice but his anger didn't last. I remember one day he was sitting at the typewriter typing and we kids were making a lot of noise. He looked up and he said, "You kids are just . . ."—and then he started making up all sorts of crazy words. Soon we were all laughing as hard as we could. That was his way of blowing off steam. My temper is similar to his. It doesn't go off very often. But when it does, it's very soon over with.
>
> Tom said the only time [!] he ever saw me mad was when I was trying to open a biscuit can. I got so mad that I ended up cutting my finger on it. But as soon as I cut my finger I was over it. But that

was not the only time I was ever mad, that was just the only one that made an impression on him (1994).

Interestingly, Betty says that their major adjustment problems simply had to do with Tom's expectations because of his previous experiences. He expected Betty to respond negatively and to be angry about things, or to have negative attitudes. That she almost never did was one of the beautiful things about her life and their relationship. Betty says

> after all the warnings I had been given, I found it surprisingly easy to adjust to life with Tom. Perhaps because we knew each other very well after having worked so intensely together as co-workers for a number of months, and because we shared the same vision and goals and dreams, other things seemed less important. No, it wasn't totally easy for me to live with my husband in a wheelchair, but Tom was fully worth it (c1987)!

Betty wrote a poem after Tom's death, that speaks of her devotion and outlook:

> The cup was half full
>> I drank eagerly, gratefully, joyfully,
>> slaking my thirst.
>> *The cup was half empty.*
>>> *Why? Why was I not given a full cup?*
>>> *How could anyone be so naive*
>>> *to be happy with a half empty cup?*
>> *Naive*
>>> *In denial*
>>>> *Superficial*
>>>>> *Pollyanna*
>>>>>> *Not a realist*
>>>>>>> *Insensitive*
>>>>>>>> *???*

Perhaps?

Or perhaps . . .

Grateful
  Happy
    Crazily in love (for 19+ years)
      Optimistic
        Fulfilled
          Fulfilling one another
            Drinking fully of life
                ???
Perhaps?

          Or perhaps both.

21
MY TOTAL REASON FOR BEING HERE

My total reason for being here is to glorify God by my life; to grow to be more like Him and to see Him produce remaining fruit (Poland 1977).

For one so handicapped to be so productive must inspire and motivate the rest of us to overcome our own difficulties and handicaps, especially those which are self-created and self-imposed (Crocker 1985).

Our dad never got to fulfill the dream of his life of being involved in missions, but Tom always believed that Dad's "mantle" for missions fell on himself. Tom's belief that his father's unrealized heart for missions had become his responsibility was surely a major influence in Tom's life and commitment. Because of that commitment, the lives of many missionaries and, in turn, many hearers of the Gospel from those missionaries, were profoundly affected by his life and ministry.

Tom sat in a wheelchair for all of his adult life. Everything he did and everywhere he went required the assistance of an complete "other" set of hands, arms and legs—usually those of his loving wife Betty Sue. He had all the attendant problems of all people in that condition. And yet, in reviewing his life, it is not his wheelchair or his disability that is in focus. Rather it is his all-consuming devotion to Christ, and his efforts to equip people with the tools and strategies to reach the lost for Him.

Tom saw that so many of the world's lost are also poor, and his heart ached to reach out to those lost and poor with Christ's liberating Good News. He saw too that most of the unsaved in the world are out of the reach and view of most contemporary missions and missionaries. His burden was to challenge and equip new missionaries with vision and the skills to further God's kingdom among the unreached and hidden peoples of the world. Tom's near total paralysis was, for him, simply a "thorn in his flesh"—a weakness in which he knew God's power was made manifest—and not nearly enough reason to lose the focus on equipping people to fulfill the Great Commission.

Lasting Fruit

What are some of the ultimate contributions of the life of Tom Brewster? Many people have many different opinions about this, but here are a few that seem to be fairly widely shared, in the words of those who benefited.

A Stunning Testimony of Courage, Commitment and Caring

Numerous people have testified of the inspiration that Tom's life was to them personally. Peggy Swartzentruber was one:

> My husband Jim and I met them at the airport upon their arrival in Irian Jaya [February 1984] and took them to our house in Abepura for supper. At the supper table that evening, Tom recounted the swimming accident that paralyzed him, concluding with the statement, "That accident was the best thing that ever happened to me." That statement shocked me and released me from superstition. It shocked me because I had never before heard such a bold statement of Romans 8:28 from one with such obvious physical handicaps. It released me from the superstition because I had subconsciously felt that such a declaration of thanksgiving out of tragedy would undoubtedly bring repeated trials, if not greater ones. That moment brought personal release to me to publicly say that "Even though my first five years in Irian brought near shipwreck into my life, I wouldn't trade those years for anything. My character was built in those years." I've often shared Tom's words in my own personal testimony, and I often see faces registering shock at Tom's bold statement as my own heart did three years ago (Swartzentruber n.d.).

A Commitment to God and to People

Many people felt that Tom's deep commitment to people was the most unique aspect of his personality. Nico Smith, quoted extensively earlier, was among them:

Tom's commitment [to people], I believe, was rooted in his commitment to the Lord, and through this commitment he wanted to make others aware of the love and faithfulness of the Lord. Through his sensitiveness in relationships with others, he not only brought meaning to the life of others, but also found deep meaning for his own life. In this way, Tom was living proof that a human being can only be meaningful in relationship with other human beings. In his life, I have seen a realization of a basic attitude amongst people in Africa which is expressed in their often-used proverb: "A person is a person through another person" (Smith 1993).

Many Practical Tools for Language and Culture Acquisition

The LAMP method and bonding are now assumed throughout the missionary world. They are kind of a starting point for language and culture acquisition, incarnational missionary ministry, and a multitude of examples of successful learners. Wes Collins observes that "the LAMP 'procedure' evolved into a LAMP 'attitude,' and became less of a technique" (1993).

Steven Goode of YWAM and Roger and Susan Scheenstra, missionaries to Ethiopia, wrote about the strategic value of the language learning tools and skills they learned from Tom:

> The Brewsters' impact on our missionary involvement has helped dozens of YWAM missionaries become more effective in their language learning, their bonding to the local people and their culture, and helped us to simply live out the commands of Christ in another cultural situation. Tom's teaching on language learning and the ability of the people to learn that language, particularly people who have failed in the study of another language, I think is invaluable (Goode 1993).

> The language learning techniques (Tom and Betty Sue) taught were so valuable to us. We have been using them since April of 1986 in learning the Orma language. Orma is an unwritten language and there isn't a school setting course to take—even if you wanted to. We feel the methods of LAMP were tailor made for our situation. We would have had no idea how to go about learning an unwritten language without them. But the main blessing is how learning language builds relationships. We were very much

accepted in the Orma culture and they are going about freely telling stories about God and Jesus Christ to this Muslim tribe! (Scheenstra 1987).

Useful Mission Strategies

The missionary strategies of involvement, bonding, incarnation, language-learning, midwifery, and communication as ministry which Tom and Betty championed are also fundamental to missionary orientation and strategizing today. Not every missionary or mission board agrees with these strategies, but few new missionaries or mission boards ignore them. The testimony of many missionaries bears witness to the fruitfulness of Tom's ministry and the influence of his all-consuming commitment to effective communication of the Gospel to hearers around the world. Don Stevens, now the International Director of Mercy Ships, says:

> We often refer to different individuals saying "yes, they were deeply bonded—or, no, they missed something in their bonding process." All of this came to us through Tom and Betty Sue's understanding of identification and compassion with the people they were trying to reach.
>
> I think it shows how deeply bonded we were to Tom. It was not only the excellent material that he so capably prepared, but it was also his sacrificial concentration on serving others in spite of his physical limitations (Stevens 1987).

A Significant Impact on Mission Boards and Mission Strategies

Tom devoted much of his energies to helping individual missionaries, but his influence also changed the strategies of many mission boards. The following are good examples:

Mr. and Mrs. Wally Cirafesi of the Navigators:

> Tom's work, I believe, influenced the Navigators to more aggressively pursue language learning overseas. For example, for some 20 years the Navigators' Middle East work was carried on through English-speaking Arabs. In the late 1970s and early 1980s, that changed as the Navs became more involved with . . . people such as Tom and Betty Sue (Cirafesi 1993).

Tom Hallas with YWAM in Australia:

> [Tom's] approach of total immersion into a culture and his process LAMP for language learning has been proven by YWAMers throughout Asia to be the methodology perfectly designed for YWAM's culture. YWAM's ministry has been deeply affected. We are conscious about appropriate bonding processes for all our new adventures and relationships, particularly new adventures into mission. LAMP has become the preferred method of learning by many. A caring spirit of inquiry, free from prejudice and fear, has become the method of culture learning (Hallas 1993).

Ray Giles with Christian Missionary Fellowship:

> Tom's influence was the most significant factor in changing the direction of our mission in language acquisition. . . . Since that time, all of our missionaries who are learning either Maasai or Turkana have done so with LAMP principles. Concentrating on the heart language of the people rather than Swahili, CMF has been known as the mission who makes an approach within the culture and language of the people. It should not be so, but this is the exception to normal practice (Giles 1986).

Only Paralyzed from the Neck Down

Much can be learned from Tom's life, certainly about courage and endurance in the face of a devastating handicap. Tom knew and demonstrated the fact that even though the body had problems, the mind and spirit can be alive and vibrant—so much so that the handicap, while real, seems far less significant. For Tom, his ability was always much more in focus than his disability.

Tom's defining motto in life was that "In Acceptance Lieth Peace." There were a lot of things in life that Tom did not accept, but his broken neck and the resulting paralysis were not among them. Tom's identity was not defined by his handicap, and he helped others see that the same could be true for them, no matter what the handicap or what the limitation. As Betty says, "Tom's wheelchair was external, it was not a defining part of who he was."

He knew too that for all of us, love covers a multitude of imperfections—not just hiding them, but in that each one's strength compensates for the other's weaknesses, physical or otherwise.

Love and joy and contentment are often a choice, an act of the will, a decision—one *can* learn to rejoice and even find enjoyment in the midst of seeming hardship. Tom chose to rejoice in life and to find God's purpose in sparing his life in the accident. Frankl has said that "it [should] not really matter what we expect from life, but rather what life expect[s] from us. We need to stop asking about the meaning of life, and instead . . . think of ourselves as those who [are]being questioned by life—daily and hourly" (1939:122).

Tom's daily and hourly choice was to create meaning by accepting God's sovereignty about his accident and paralysis. In his mind, neither released him from the Great Commission to go into all the world and preach the Gospel. So that is what he did.

Tom's mind and heart were never paralyzed.

He was only paralyzed from the neck down.

APPENDIX A
DECLARATION OF EXPECTATION AMPLIFICATION— BACKGROUND AND SOME SPECIFICS

[The following is an amplification of the "Declaration of Expectations" that Tom wrote on October 30, 1983 concerning the possibility of God healing him and restoring his failing health.]

1. Many of our intercessors have been moved of God to be praising Him for my complete physical healing.

Some of those who have expressed to me that God has moved them to praise Him and believe that my healing is near include Ramona Brewster Tuma, Cathy Schaller, Jean Barker, Fran Lines, Jewel Nichols, Jennifer Dillaha, Jerry Tuma, Chuck Kraft, Orlando Reyes, and Roger Heim. And still others that God has been using in a mighty way to intercede for my healing include Joy Dawson, John Wimber, Cecil Pomphrey, Rick Love, Perry O'Briant, Louise O'Briant, Bev Kalsbeek, Todd Kunkler, Nancy McRea, and Loren Cunningham—plus members of the 120 Fellowship, our Kinship group, a Church On The Way group, The Cornerstone Church, and our Summer 1983 course.

2. Dreams have been given and confirmed through the Word concerning my walking.

God has given vivid dreams to both Ramona Tuma and Jean Barker of my coming to them to demonstrate my complete healing. While Ramona was sharing her dream with me on the phone, her Bible fell open to Zechariah 10:12, "In His name they will walk,' declares the Lord." Confirmation to Jean came from Ephesians 3:20, "He is able to do immeasurably more than all we ask or imagine, according to His power that is at work within us."

3. Believing faith and expectancy is being built both in me and in praying friends by the Father.

I have marked with a felt marker in my Bible all of the healing events in the Gospel accounts. A large percentage of that part of my Bible is now a vivid, living green. Studies in the lives of Moses, Elijah, Elisha, Peter and Paul have spoken strongly to me. "Faith comes by hearing . . . the Word of God" (Romans 10:17).

The realness of the expectation for my healing has been shown in the words of Cathy, "Lord, I want to be there when it happens!"

4. Words of knowledge and prophetic words regarding my healing have been given by the Spirit through anointed intercessors.

During a service at the Cornerstone Church in Fort Worth three months ago, the Lord spoke through tongues and interpretation, calling me by name and proclaiming that God would raise me up. That very day a lady for whom they had been praying was raised from her wheelchair and she walked up the aisle to the front of the church (accompanied by a thunderous applause and praising of God). A week before that, on August 4, Cecil Pomphrey, praying for me with John Wimber, was given a word of prophesy declaring that within six months I would experience a significant healing.

5. The witness of mighty works of God in healing and miracles has become an increasingly frequent experience for us.

Throughout the world we know (both first and second hand) of many who are seeing God's power through healing, miracles, and authority over Satan. Last spring we had the privilege of staying for a week with Erlo Stegen at Kwa Siza Bantu in South Africa. God has honored their faith and holiness and hundreds of people have been healed there of all kinds of conditions. We spent part of one morning with Lydia, a young woman whom God had wondrously raised from the dead.

God lengthened a short leg of my sister Ramona and healed a scoliosis of her spine.

6. Spiritual warfare has intensified for us and many of our intercessors as Satan seems to be standing against this work of God.

We have had an unprecedented awareness of the fact that we are participants in a cosmic battle between the powers of darkness and the Kingdom of God. "For our struggle is not against flesh and blood, but against the rulers, against the authorities, against the powers of this dark world and against the spiritual forces of evil in heavenly realms" (Ephesians 6:12). Various activities of our ministry have encountered conflict and we have had to take our stand against the devil's schemes and resist him. Ephesians 6:10–20 has been consistently before me.

Like never before, I am aware of the participation in our ministry by those who are fulfilling the crucial role of standing with us in faithful intercession for us and the ministry God has given us.

7. God has convicted me of my unbelief which had been rooted in unbiblical limitations of God from my denominational background. This unbelief resulted in rejection of spiritual gifts and the quenching of His Spirit.

I was nurtured and taught in unbelief. I was once a defender of the perspective that proclaims that sign gifts and supernatural works gradually ceased for the early church and were not needed after the canon was completed. My faith has been based on knowledge and not on power—I had known how Jesus used to be without knowing how He still is. I have reaped the harvest from that perspective, and according to my unbelief it has been unto me (see Matthew 9:29). But Jesus made it clear to the disciples that the new life He wanted to empower them with could not be contained in the wineskins of their old theologies. He is making it clear to me as well.

My habits of unbelief often surface, but God is convicting me: "Do not put out the Spirit's fire; do not treat prophecies with contempt. Test everything. Hold onto the good." (I Thessalonians 5:19–21)

8. God has convinced me that He is preparing me to minister to missionaries in the authority of Jesus and in the power of His Holy Spirit. The timing seems ripe to give Him maximum glory.

Jesus ministered in spiritual authority and He passed that authority on to His followers. Matthew 28:18, 19 says, "All authority in heaven and on earth has been given me. Therefore go." But before they were permitted to go, baptismal fire had to empower them. "You will receive power when the Holy Spirit comes on you." (Acts 1:8)

Through our ministry I have become deeply troubled by the observation that many missionaries demonstrate little spiritual power or authority in their lives. It is ironic (and sometimes tragic) that westerners who do not take the spirit world very seriously are often the very ones bringing a spiritual message to those who experience the spirit world as being indeed quite real. The result has been a spreading of secularism, materialism and generally powerless faith. God has broadly established our ministry, and my healing could now have far-reaching impact for His Kingdom and His glory.

9. Preliminary healings have already begun, and though "small as a man's hand," He seems to be confirming that the "heavy rain is coming."

For years I had been plagued with kidney infections and fevers. Sometimes perspiration left me completely drenched and chilled. On other occasions a severe railing cough has left me unable to breathe or talk. In response to prayer, God has healed each of these. A couple of months ago God healed a pain in my right ear after giving a word of knowledge to Cathy Schaller—"I've been having a pain in my right ear but I knew it wasn't my pain, and I've been praying for you." This past week Betty Sue had a severe pain and weakness in her left knee. She limped to breakfast a couple of blocks away, and afterwards she was dramatically healed when Rick Love and friends in Oxnard prayed for her.

10. He has revealed that persevering, holiness and feeding on the Word are to occupy my attention until the promise has been received.

Over a month ago God strongly impressed these verses on me: "Do not throw away your confidence; it will be richly rewarded. You need to persevere so that when you have done the will of God you will receive what he has promised. . . . My righteous one will live by faith and if he shrinks back I will not be pleased with him" (Hebrews 10:35–38). Smith Wigglesworth, the British evangelist of the early part of this century, feasted on the Word continually. God used him to heal multitudes and raise many from the dead.

It is His will that "we live by faith, not by sight" (II Corinthians 5:7).

> Shout with joy to God, all the earth!
> Sing the glory of His name; make his praise glorious!
> Say to God, "How awesome are your deeds!
> So great is your power that your enemies cringe before you.
> All the earth bows down to you, they sing praise to you, they sing
>   praise to your name."
> Come and see what God has done, how awesome His works in
>   man's behalf! (Psalm 66:1–5 NIV)

APPENDIX B

[The following is a list of the published works of Tom Brewster, mostly co-authored with his wife Betty Sue.]

BOOKS

Language Acquisition Made Practical (LAMP), (Lingua House, 1976), 386 pp.

Language Exploration and Acquisition Resource Notebook! (LEARN!), (Lingua House, 1981, revised 1983), 300 pp. Syllabus and 16 cassette tapes.

EDITED BOOK

Community is My Language Classroom (Lingua House, 1986), 247 pp.

BOOKLETS

Bonding and the Missionary Task (Lingua House, 1981), 28 pp.

Language Learning IS Communication—IS Ministry (Lingua House, 1984), 19 pp. (Originally published in International Bulletin of Missionary Research.) (Published with Bonding in one booklet.)

ARTICLES

"Involvement as a Means of Second Culture Learning." *Practical Anthropology* 19:27–44 (January, 1972).

"I've Never Been So Fulfilled in all My Life (originally published as "What it takes to learn a language and get involved with people"), *Evangelical Missions Quarterly*, April, 1978; pp. 101–105.

"Language Learning Midwifery," *Missiology*, April, 1980; pp. 203–209.

"Jesus' Training Program," *World Christian*, September/October, 1984; pp. 21–22, 27.

"Thinking Missions? Study Abroad!" *HIS*, January, 1985; pp. 21–22.

"As Poor Among Poor," *World Christian*, September/October, 1985; pp. 22–23.

VIDEO SERIES

Language Learning and Mission, (Lingua House), 10–hour seminar (includes an adaptation of the LEARN! syllabus to accompany the videos).

REFERENCES CITED

Aetna Insurance Company. n.d. Workmen's Compensation Case Studies in rehabilitation.

Berkner, Andrew Rev. 1987. Personal letter to author. January 2.

Booth, Nathan. 1993. Personal letter to author. August 11.

Brewster, Elizabeth S. 1967. Betty's Vow to Tom at their marriage on February 14.

_____. 1970. Personal letter to author. November 19.

_____. 1984. "Journal of Mexico City Experience." Unpublished reflections on first Mexico City Servants exposure trip.

_____. 1985. Unpublished diary entry.

_____. c1987. "Thoughts on Living with Handicapped persons." Unpublished notes.

_____. 1991. "Outline of our History." Unpublished notes prepared by Betty Sue.

_____. 1992. "Valentine" to Tom on Tom and Betty's 25th wedding anniversary, six years after his death.

_____. 1993. Based on numerous personal interviews with author. August.

_____. 1994. Based on numerous personal interviews with author. August.

Brewster, E. Thomas (Tom). 1961. Personal letter to Ira (last name unknown).

_____. 1963. "Injury Can't Stop His Soaring Spirit." *Rocky Mountain News*, January 27.

_____. 1966. Personal letter from Tom to supporters. n.d.

_____. c.1968. "Personal notes on Tom's Injury." Unpublished.

_____. c.1969. "Personal Testimony of Tom Brewster." Unpublished.

_____. 1970. "Round Robin" letter From Tom to the Brewster family. November 19.

_____. 1971. "Personality Characteristics of Giving versus Receiving-oriented Individuals." Ph.D. dissertation, Michigan State University.

_____. 1972. Letter to Steve Douglas. April 7.

_____. 1973. "Report on the Translation Conference in Jos [Nigeria]." Report to Dr. Bill Bright. Unpublished.

_____. 1982a. Personal letter to author. October 15.

_____. 1982b. Personal letter to Dr. Johan Louw. March 23.

_____. 1982c. Personal recollection of author.

_____. 1983. *Language Learning & Mission. a LEARN! video seminar* for Youth With a Mission participants. Unpublished transcription. Buchloe, Switzerland.

_____. 1984a. "Learning from a Mosquito." Unpublished notes.

_____. 1984b. "On Listening to Christ." Unpublished notes.

_____. 1984c. "A Dream." Unpublished notes.

_____. 1985a. Unpublished notes. January 30.

_____. 1985b. Personal letter to author. May 19.

_____. c.1985c. "Incarnational Ministry—a Path to Intimacy with Christ." Unpublished notes.

_____. 1985d. "As Poor Among the Poor." *World Christian*, Sept/Oct, pp. 22–23.

_____. 1985e. Personal letter to author. August 4.

_____. 1985f. "Round Robin" letter to Brewster family. August.

_____. 1985g. Personal letter to the author. November 17.

Brewster, E. Thomas, and Brewster, Elizabeth S. 1978. "I've Never Been so Fulfilled in all My Life." *Evangelical Missions Quarterly* 14(2):102.

_____. 1980. "Language Learning Midwifery." *International Review of Missions* 8(2).

_____. 1983. *Language Exploration and Acquisition Resource (LEARN!) Notebook.* Colorado Springs, Colorado: Lingua House.

_____. 1984a. *Bonding and the Missionary Task.* Colorado Springs, Colorado: Lingua House.

_____. 1984b. *Language Learning Is Communication—Is Ministry.* Pasadena, CA: Lingua House Ministries.

_____. 1985. "Thinking Missions? Study Abroad!" *HIS* January.

_____. 1986. *Community is my Language Classroom!* Pasadena, California: Lingua House Ministries.

_____. n.d. "The Story Behind our Language Learning and Mission Course. Unpublished notes.

Brewster, Tom and Grigg, Viv. 1985. *Servants Among the Poor.* Flyer produced for prospective *Servants* missionaries.

Brewster, Roy. n.d. Letter to the editor of the *Gazette Telegraph.* Colorado Springs, CO.

_____. 1953a. Letter to the editor of the Colorado Schools Protective Association News. February 22.

_____. 1953b. Personal letter to Superintendent of Littleton, Colorado High School. April 28.

_____. 1958. "From Colorado: a Message of Gratitude to Muskegon." Letter to the Muskegon Chronicle. c.December.

Cameron, James. 1987. *An Indian Summer.* London: Penguin Books.

Chandler, Marjorie. 1986. "Fuller Seminary Cancels Course on Signs and Wonders." *Christianity Today*, February 21:48–49.

Cirafesi, Wally. 1993. Personal correspondence to author.

Cocking, Carla. n.d. Personal letter to author.

Collins, Wes. 1993. Personal letter to author. December 29.

Cook, Dr. Clyde. 1986. Personal letter to author. October 6.

Crocker, William R. 1985. Personal letter to Betty Sue Brewster. December 23.

Denver Post, The. 1960. "'Tourist'" to Compile Rehabilitation Study." July 22.

Echerd, Stephen M. 1980. "LEAP; Report and Evaluation of the Guatemala Spanish Program March 1980 (condensed)." *Notes on Linguistics*, No. 16, October 1980, p.27. Quoted in E. T. and B. S. Brewster 1984b:15, 16.

Ford, Dan. n.d. Personal letter to Betty Sue Brewster.

Frankl, Victor. 1939. *Man's Search for Meaning.* New York: Pocket Books.

Frederich, John Mark and Emma. 1986. Personal letter to author. October 29.

Fuller School of World Mission Faculty. 1985. Tribute done by faculty for Tom's funeral.

Fulton, Adele Chaney. 1993. Personal correspondence with author.

Gardner, John W. 1963. *Self Renewal*. New York: W. W. Norton & Company. Quoted in "Personality Characteristics of Giving versus Receiving-oriented Individuals." Ph.D. dissertation of T. Brewster. Lansing, Michigan State University, 1971.

Giles, Ray A. 1986. Personal letter to author. October 13.

Gilliland, Dean. 1982. Quoted in "MC 510:Signs, Wonders, and Church Growth." *Christian Life*. (Special Issue) October. p. 46.

_____. 1987. Personal taped interview with author along with other School of World Mission Faculty members.

Glasser, Art. 1985. Funeral tribute to Tom on behalf of the Fuller School of World Mission faculty.

_____. 1987. Personal taped interview with author along with other School of World Mission Faculty members.

Goode, G. Steven. 1993. Personal letter to author. July 13.

Gradin, Dwight L. 1985. Personal letter to Betty Sue Brewster. December 13.

Grigg, Viv. 1984. "Genesis of a Missions Thrust." Unpublished reflections on first *Servants* exposure trip to Mexico City.

_____. 1985. Personal letter to Betty Sue Brewster. December 19.

Grimes, Georgia. 1986. Personal tribute. December.

Guiness, H. Grattan. 1962. *Hudson Taylor Early Years*. Mr. and Mrs. Howard Taylor, eds. London: CIM.

Gunther, Veronica K. 1986. Personal letter to author. November 8.

Hallas, Tom. 1993. Personal correspondence with author.

Hansel, Tim. 1985. *You Gotta Keep Dancing*. Elgin, Ill: David C. Cook.

Hawthorne, Peter. 1988. "White Among Blacks." *Time*, June 27.

Hurnard, Hannah R. n.d. "In Acceptance Lieth Peace." In *The Mountains of Spices*. p. 50. London: Olive Press.

Kalsbeek, Beverly. 1993. Personal correspondence to author.

Klaus, Marshall H., and John H. Kennel. 1976. *Maternal-Infant Bonding*. St. Louis: C.V. Mosby Company.

Kyle, John E. 1986. Personal letter to Betty Sue Brewster. InterVarsity Missions, January 22.

Kraft, Charles H. 1973. *Introductory Hausa*. Berkeley and Los Angeles: University of California Press.

_____. 1979a. *Christianity in Culture*. Maryknoll, New York: Orbis Books.

_____. 1979b. *Communicating the Gospel God's Way*. Pasadena: California. William Carey Library.

_____. 1982a. Quoted in "An Evaluation by Theologians." *Christian Life*. (Special Issue) October. p. 65.

_____. 1982b. Quoted in "MC510:Signs, Wonders, and Church Growth." *Christian Life*. October. p. 46.

_____. 1982c. Quoted in "Fuller Seminary Cancels Course on Signs and Wonders." *Christianity Today*. 30. No. 3:48–49. Feb. 21.

_____. 1994. Personal interview with author. December 12.

Larson, Don. 1985. Personal letter to Tom Brewster. November 20.

_____. 1994. Personal letter to author. October 31.

Leigh, C. W. n.d. Letter to the editor of the *Gazette Telegraph*. Colorado Springs, CO.

Loving, Aretta. 1986. Personal letter to author. November 17.

McCrea, Bruce. 1959. "'Mr. Courage' says Good-by." *Muskegon Chronicle*, c.December.

McGirr, Randall. 1986. Personal letter to author. December 18.

McRostie, Jonathan. 1993. Personal correspondence to author.

Meeks, Stephen. 1983. Personal letter to Betty Sue. April 4.

Montrose Press. 1938. Editorial comments, Montrose Colorado. November 26.

Muskegon Chronicle. 1958. Undated and unsigned piece about Tom. c.October.

Myers, Bryant. 1989. MARC Newsletter. December.

Nerge, Carol. 1987. Personal letter to author. January 31.

O'Malley, Dennis J. 1985. Personal letter to Betty Sue Brewster. December 19.

Overduin, Jacob. 1986. Personal letter to author. October 17.

Perkins, Rev. John. 1986. Personal letter to author. November 26.

Penrose Press. 1939. Wedding announcement. Penrose Colorado, January 20.

Peterson, Paul. 1985. Personal letter to author. n.d.

Peterson, Fern. 1986. Personal letter to author. November 13.

Pierson, Paul. 1982. Quoted in "MC510:Signs, Wonders, and Church Growth." *Christian Life*. (Special Issue) October. p. 46.

_____. 1987. Personal taped interview with author along with other School of World Mission Faculty members.

Poland, Larry W. 1977. Quoted in Brewster, T. (Tom) and Brewster, E. (Betty Sue) *Language Exploration and Acquisition Resource (LEARN!) Notebook*. Colorado Springs, Colorado: Lingua House. p. iv.

Schaller, Cathy. 1994. Personal interview with author. December 30

Scheenstra, Roger and Susan. 1987. Personal letter to author. June 25.

Scott, Waldron. 1986. Personal letter to author.

Service, Robert W. 1987. *The Cremation of Sam McGee*. New York: Greenwillow Books.

Severn, Frank M. 1986. Personal letter to author. October 26.

Severns, Ron. 1986. Personal letter to author. October 20.

Sider, Ron. 1990. *Rich Christians in an Age of Hunger*. Dallas: Word Publishing.

Smith, Nico J. 1993. Personal letters to author. August.

Stevens, Don. 1987. Personal letter to author.

Swartzentruber, Peggy. n.d. Personal letter to author.

Taylor, Ken. 1993. Personal letter to author. July.

Tingsmore, Rona. 1988. Personal letter to Betty Sue Brewster.

Truax, Jim. 1986. Personal letter to author. November 14.

Tuma, Ramona (Mona). 1994. Based on numerous personal interviews with author.

Wagner, C. Peter. 1988. *How to Have a Healing Ministry in Any Church*. Ventura, CA: Regal Books.

Zemdekun, Zedeke. 1986. Personal letter to author. YWAM. Nicosia, Cyprus, October 23.

INDEX

ABOUT THE AUTHOR

Dan Brewster was born in La Junta, Colorado on October 28, 1947. He grew up in Colorado Springs, Colorado, and attended Colorado State University. Though he grew up in a Christian home, he strayed far from the Lord after the death of his father when he was thirteen years of age. He found the Lord again while attending Law School at the University of Colorado. He then went to live with his brother Tom in Guadalajara, Mexico. It was there that he first had the opportunity to learn about and benefit from Tom and Betty Sue's budding ministry.

It was also in Guadalajara that Dan met the woman who would become his wife, the former Alice Brumley. Dan and Alice were married in Portland, Oregon in October of 1971. After obtaining a Masters in Religion at Western Evangelical Seminary in Portland, Dan and Alice went to Africa to work with Daystar Communications, doing consulting with and training of Living Bibles translators. Their son Brian was born in Nairobi, Kenya in 1975.

Dan and his family returned to the States and attended the Fuller School of World Mission from 1976 through 1978, taking a Doctor of Missiology. Their daughter Julisa was born during that time in Pasadena. The family then returned to Africa where Dan worked in Relief and Development for the next 12 years. Dan has been involved in relief programs in Ethiopia, Somalia, and more recently, Rwanda, and has supervised development programs in more than twenty countries in Africa and other countries around the world. Their daughter Kara was born during a stint in what was formerly Salisbury, Rhodesia and is now called Harare, Zimbabwe.

Dan presently lives in Colorado Springs, Colorado working for Compassion International.

DR. SA'EED OF IRAN: Kurdish Physician to Princes and Peasants, Nobles and Nomads, by Jay M. Rasooli and Cady H. Allen, 1983, paperback, 190 pages.
One of the best ways to feel Islam is to read the thrilling but true story of a Kurdish doctor who, after finding Christ, was exiled from his family and native town. This book tells of his struggles and triumphs as a Christian in a country steeped in the Islamic religion.

FREDERICK FRANSON: Model for Worldwide Frontier Evangelism, by Edward P. Torjesen, 1983, paperback, 122 pages.
Franson ranks with Hudson Taylor as one of the few people who embraced missions as a movement to which he mightily contributed rather than seeing it in terms of a personal career. A biographical work with much modern pertinence.

MY PERSIAN PILGRIMAGE (Second Edition) An Autobiography, by
William McElwee Miller, 1995, paperback, 394 pages.
Samuel Moffett writes in his Foreword: "William Miller came from a generation of giants that gave as its legacy to church history what many have called the greatest Christian movement of the last two centuries—the modern missionary movement. His own life span of a hundred years covers fully half of that period, and this book is his moving account of a spiritual pilgrimage in the most resistant field to Christian witness on earth, the Muslim world."

THE REVOLUTIONARY BISHOP WHO SAW GOD AT WORK IN AFRICA: An Autobiography, by Ralph Dodge, 1986, paperback, 211 pages.
Ralph Dodge served in Africa as a Methodist missionary and later was named bishop of the church in Southern Rhodesia. In his ministry he closely identified with the blacks during the years of change before independence and the birth of the new nation of Zimbabwe. This identification resulted in his expulsion from the country in 1964. His life is opened up through a story of the grace and leading of God through trial, tragedy and triumph.

THE SATNAMI STORY: A Thrilling Drama of Religious Change by Donald McGavran, 1990, paperback, 177 pp.
Donald McGavran, researcher, strategist and apologist for Christian world missions, is considered the father of the church growth movement. In *The Satnami Story* we meet McGavran the field missionary. Born in India of missionary parents, he served as an educator, administrator and evangelist for 27 years. The autobiographical content makes this book a delightful narrative which also provides glimpses of missionary life and labor in mid-India in the mid-20th century.